Judaism and Disability

Judaism and Disability

Portrayals in Ancient Texts from the Tanach through the Bavli

Judith Z. Abrams

Gallaudet University Press
Washington, D.C.

Gallaudet University Press
Washington, DC 20002

Library of Congress Cataloging-in-Publication Data
Abrams, Judith Z.
Judaism and disability : portrayals in ancient texts from
the Tanach through the Bavli / Judith Z. Abrams.
p.   cm.
Includes bibliographical references and index.
ISBN 1-56368-068-8 (alk. paper)
1. Handicapped in the Bible.   2. Handicapped in rabbinical literature.
3. Handicapped—Legal status, laws, etc. (Jewish law).   4. Capacity and
disability (Jewish law).   5. Bible. O.T.—Criticism, interpretation, etc.
6. Rabbinical literature—History and criticism.   I. Title.
BS1199.A25A27   1998
296'.087—dc21   98-17641
CIP

For my students . . .
with love and gratitude.

CONTENTS

PREFACE AND ACKNOWLEDGMENTS

THE PAST, they say, is prologue. In the case of attitudes about disabilities and persons with them in ancient Jewish sources, one hopes that this is so, for there is much that has yet to be thought through regarding the topic. The future has yet to be recorded. This book, a historical, literary, and anthropological survey of attitudes toward persons with disabilities in Jewish texts from the Tanach (Jewish Scriptures) through the Bavli (ca. 500 C.E.), offers a view of the prologue. Rather than evaluating ancient works in light of modern mores, it attempts to understand why these works expressed the attitudes they did. Thus viewpoints will be presented that the modern reader may find dismaying—for example, that disabilities are punishments from God, that persons with hearing disabilities have no intelligence, or that birth defects stem from improper sexual practices. These beliefs and attitudes would be deemed harmful and discriminatory today, yet it would be mendacious to present these ancient texts as reflecting modern mores.

A word on methodology is in order. Translations are my own unless otherwise noted. Various versions of the Tanach were used: the Jewish Publication Society commentary on the Torah (various authors and dates of publication), the Jewish Publication Society translation of the Tanach (1917), the Jerusalem Bible (1980), and the Anchor Bible (various authors and dates of publication). Geza Vermes' translations of the Dead Sea Scrolls were used. Other texts used were Albeck's (1952) and Blackman's (1977) Mishnah, Zukermandel's (1970) and Lieberman's (1962) Tosefta, Lauterbach's (1961) and Horovitz's (1970) Mechilta D'Rabbi Ishmael, Finkelstein's Sifre

Deuteronomy (1969), and Mirkin's (1977) Midrash Rabbah, as well as traditional texts of Midrash Rabbah, Sifra Leviticus, Sifri Numbers, and Tanhuma. Passages from the Yerushalmi are cited according to the P'nei Moshe edition and then according to the Venice edition. Traditional Bavli texts were used when the Steinsaltz (1983) version was not available. Italicized passages indicate that a mishnah is being quoted in the source; boldfaced passages indicate that a tosefta is being quoted. This work began as my doctoral dissertation at Baltimore Hebrew University. It has been completely revised for publication. A glossary of terms is provided for those not familiar with some of the ancient Jewish concepts and practices described here.

Terminology regarding both disabilities and theology is in a continual state of flux. "Mental illness" here refers to insanity or conditions such as schizophrenia. "Mental disability" is the term used to describe mental retardation. Ancient sources saw God as male, and the translations in this work reflect that fact.

I thank God for the opportunity to have done this work and I thank the many people who have helped in that process. Professor David Kraemer of the Jewish Theological Seminary has guided me throughout this long process and, indeed, through much of my professional life. I am deeply in his debt. Professor Richard Sarasson of Hebrew Union College–Jewish Institute of Religion in Cincinnati provided many important suggestions for bettering this manuscript and I am most grateful to him. I was helped in the preparation of my dissertation by Professors Robert O. Freedman, Joseph Baumgarten, Barry Gittlen, and George Berlin, all of the Baltimore Hebrew University, as well as by John V. Van Cleve of Gallaudet University, Rabbi Joseph Radinsky of United Orthodox Synagogues in Houston, Professor Jacque Lipetz of Graetz University, and Arnold J. Rudolph, M.D., of blessed memory.

Many people aided me by providing books: David Barish, Ph.D., David Abrams, Rabbi Rosalind Gold, and Gail Labovitz; Dr. Bernard Abrams provided the CD-ROM concordance; and Vanessa Ochs of the National Jewish Center for Learning and Leadership

(CLAL) recommended many important works on medical anthropology for me to read. In addition, I thank the librarians of the Hebrew Union College–Jewish Institute of Religion Library in Cincinnati, especially Bernard Rabenstein; the library of Congregation
Beth Yeshurun, Houston; and the Baylor College of Medicine Library in Houston for graciously providing me with help. Thank you,
too, to Alice Falk for her wonderful editing.

Ivey Pittle Wallace of the Gallaudet University Press has been
wonderful to work with and has been instrumental in bringing this
book to birth. I am deeply indebted to her for her encouragement and
insight. The memory of Cantor Stuart Pittle, Ivey's brother, is a
source of joy Ivey and I shared in the process of creating this book.
His song, his art, and his love of Jewish texts are, I hope, reflected in
the work Ivey and I did together.

Of course, my greatest debt is to my family: Steven, Michael,
Ruth, and Hannah. I thank them for their encouragement and pa-
tience.

All faults in this volume are, naturally, mine.

Judith Z. Abrams
18 August 1997
13 Tammuz 5757
Erev Shabbat Balak

I

Introduction

The River

IF YOU were to stand at Lake Itasca in Minnesota, where the Mississippi River begins, you might doubt that so mighty a river could spring from so small a source. And yet, were you to follow a leaf that fell into the river at its headwater you would soon see how the river grows until it reaches its destination in the sea, some 2,350 miles later.

Studying Judaism's development is something like taking this journey down the Mississippi. The difference between the point where we start and where we leave off is so tremendous that one might doubt that the two have anything in common. Only by beginning at the source and following the development of this faith and culture can one see that traces of the original water are present in the mighty river; here, we will travel that river more than halfway through its journey. The "leaf" we will follow will be the part of Judaism that deals with persons with disabilities. By making this our focus, not only will we learn about our topic but we will be able to follow some of the major constants, and shifts, in the development of Judaism apparent in the Tanach, the Jewish Bible, through the Bavli, the Talmud of the land of Babylonia.

A Map in Time

As a map helps one see the course of a river, a time line may help delineate some major turning points in Jewish history before we start our journey, which begins 2,000 years before the common era (B.C.E., often known as B.C.) and extends into the common era (C.E., often known as A.D.).

2000–1280 B.C.E.	The Patriarchs, slavery in Egypt
ca. 1280 B.C.E.	Exodus from Egypt
1020–1004 B.C.E.	King Saul, first king of Israel
1004–965 B.C.E.	King David
965–928 B.C.E.	King Solomon; First Temple constructed
928 B.C.E.	Divided kingdoms: Judea (South) and Israel (North)
928–722 B.C.E.	Prophecies of Elijah, Amos, Hosea, Isaiah
722 B.C.E.	Israel conquered by Assyria and Israelites deported
627–585 B.C.E.	Prophecies of Jeremiah
621 B.C.E.	King Josiah's reforms begin
586 B.C.E.	Destruction of the First Temple; Jerusalem destroyed; Jews exiled to Babylonia
593–571 B.C.E.	Prophecies of Ezekiel
6th c. B.C.E.	Torah canonized in Babylonian exile
538 B.C.E.	Jews return to Israel
520–515 B.C.E.	Second Temple built
4th c. B.C.E.	Prophets section of Tanach canonized
164 B.C.E.	End of successful revolt against Syrians
70 C.E.	End of revolt against Rome; Second Temple destroyed; Sanhedrin established in Yavneh
132–135 C.E.	Bar Kokhba revolt
135 C.E.	Betar falls, revolt ends
2nd c. C.E.	Writings section of Tanach canonized
200 C.E.	Mishnah redacted
220 C.E.	Tosefta redacted
312 C.E.	Rome becomes a Christian empire
ca. 350 C.E.	Halakhic midrashim redacted
368 C.E.	Julian killed; Judaism loses its favorable standing in the Roman Empire

| ca. 400 C.E. | Yerushalmi and aggadic midrash collections redacted |
| ca. 500 C.E. | Bavli redacted |

Part of a fuller understanding of Jewish history rests in simply appreciating how the location of the land of Israel, on a bridge between Africa and Asia, shaped the fate of the Jewish people. The "superpowers" of the periods with which we are concerned were Egypt, to Israel's southwest; Assyria and Babylonia, to Israel's northeast; and, later, Rome and Greece, to the northwest. As the great powers battled each other through the centuries, they necessarily had to traverse the land bridge on which Israel was located. Thus, the history of the land of Israel is something like that of the Baltic states, caught between Germany and Russia. As the balance of power would swing between those superpowers, conquering armies would march through the countries separating them, sometimes forcing local residents to adopt the culture of the conqueror. Likewise, Jewish history is a story of great powers, wars, invasions, revolts, and exiles.

Survey of Jewish History and Its Documents

Judaism began in the Patriarchal era, when Mesopotamia (modern Iraq) was the dominant power. Avraham, the Torah tells us, the founder of Judaism, came from Mesopotamia to the land of Israel. From there, the Hebrews migrated to Egypt, became enslaved, were liberated, and returned to Israel. Israel was eventually settled and came to be ruled by one king: first Saul, then David, and finally Solomon. The First Temple was constructed under Solomon's rule. The priesthood, comprising descendants of Aaron, Moses' brother, officiated in that cult while other members of the tribe of Levi helped in the Temple service and provided musical accompaniment to it. It was during this period that the earliest component of the Torah, the first five books of the Jewish Bible, was produced. After the kingdom of Israel—Judea in the south and Israel in the north—split into two, more parts of the Torah were created.

The Tanach, the Hebrew acronym for the Jewish Bible—*Torah*, *N'vi'im* (Prophets), *Ketuvim* (Writings)—can be studied in many ways (for an overview of approaches, see S. McKenzie and Haynes 1993). Traditionally, it is believed that God authored the Torah and Moses wrote it down, in its entirety, on Mount Sinai. One of the most widely used methods for studying Scripture, which sees the document we now possess as a composite of several component works, is called source criticism. The oldest source, called J because the name it uses for God (Jahweh or Yahweh) starts with the letter *yud*, stems from the time of David and Solomon (10th c. B.C.E.), while the source that refers to God by the name Elohim, and is thus known as E, came from the northern kingdom after the division of Israel (during the 9th c. B.C.E). These sources are combined in the Torah to form the narrative of Judaism's genesis. Another source, found primarily but not exclusively in the Book of Deuteronomy (e.g., see 2 Kings), expresses the viewpoint of King Josiah, whose sweeping reforms threw off the cultural and religious domination of then-superpower Assyria in 621 B.C.E. and fostered a renaissance of Israelite nationalism. King Josiah cleansed the cult of foreign influences, closed down regional sacrificial altars, and consolidated worship in Jerusalem's Temple. This source is called D, for the Deuteronomist. ("Deuteronomy" means "the second telling"—here of the Torah, since this book recapitulates and amplifies much of the Torah's first four books.) Finally, the latest sources in the Torah are P, the priestly code, and HS, the holiness school. Most of P is found in Leviticus 1–16; most of HS, in Leviticus 17–27. P and HS were produced before the exile to Babylonia in 586 B.C.E., and HS probably edited P and, hence, the whole Torah (see Morgan 1990). While P focuses on priestly rites and procedures, HS extends priestly concepts and rituals to the entire land and people of Israel. These documents were redacted—that is, edited and put together—to form the Torah, the first five books of the Bible. This work was canonized, or closed to further official augmentation and accepted as a holy work, during the Babylonian exile and so was probably composed before that time—perhaps before and during the Deuteronomic revolution by priests whose local altars had been closed by King Josiah.

The section of the Tanach called Prophets begins with the history of the conquest of Israel by Joshua; it extends through the periods of the kings and the divided monarchy as well as including the prophecies generated in that era by Isaiah, Jeremiah, and others. The Book of Isaiah, as we have it today, combines the words of three prophets who lived in three different eras (J. McKenzie 1968, i). The prophets provided the counterpoint to the worldly viewpoints of the kings, speaking in God's words to the rulers of those days.

The Writings include a diverse set of works: Psalms, Proverbs, short novellas (e.g., the Books of Ruth and Esther), and sustained poems (e.g., Job and the Song of Songs), as well as a retelling of the story of Israel during the monarchy (Chronicles) and how the Temple was rebuilt (Ezra and Nehemiah).

In defining, in the broadest terms, what the different parts of the Tanach were about, we might say that the Torah is the template for Israel's place in the universe and for how it could become a monotheistic faith in a world of idolatry. The Prophets are concerned with how to make the theory presented in the Torah into a living reality and with the struggle to adhere to the ideal faith that the Israelites developed in their years in the wilderness, which is described in the Torah. The Writings present diverse views on life, suffering, sin, repentance, prayer, and history. Ideas are expressed in Writings that conflict with basic motifs of the Torah (e.g., Deuteronomy's vision of God working through history vs. Job's inscrutable Deity), yet all these works were included in the canon.[1] This ability of Judaism to contain within itself diverse views will also be seen in rabbinic literature.

To understand the Judaism of the biblical and rabbinic eras we must comprehend the idolatry against which those Judaisms were rebelling. Idolatry is not, as is commonly believed, the worship of mute, lifeless statues. The statues merely provided a focal point for meditation and devotion. Idolaters related to their gods in terms of three major religious metaphors:

1. As élan vital, the spiritual cores in phenomena, indwelling wills and powers for them to be and thrive in their characteristic forms

and manners. The phenomena are mostly natural phenomena of primary economic importance.

2. As rulers.
3. As parents, caring about the individual worshiper and his conduct as parents do about children.

Of these three different ways of viewing and presenting the gods, the first would appear to be the oldest and most original; for it is the one that is never absent. . . . The second metaphor, that of the ruler appears to be later. . . . [Then] the major gods became national gods, identified with narrow national political aspirations. (Jacobsen 1976, 20–21)

Idolatry was a developing, changing entity. Idolaters related to the gods in ways that changed as their societies developed.

So, if idolaters were aware that the gods they worshiped were not contained in statues, nor even in the heavenly bodies with which the gods were associated, how did they see their deities in relationship to these physical symbols? There are three possibilities:

1. The god is the star.
2. The god [can be seen] as an institution and the star as the building in which the institution is housed. The institution's building is often a convenient way of identifying the institution, but obviously the institution's identity will be preserved even if it is moved to another building.
3. An alternative model for the relation between a god and its associated star is the relation between the mind and the body, where the god is the mind and the star is the body. The god dwells in the star as the mind dwells in the body. . . . When a god is described as being fixed to a star, the fixed relationship is generally a punishment for rebellion, which transforms the god into an entity lacking freedom and limited in the realization of its desires. (Halbertal and Margalit 1992, 142–43)

Jews and non-Jews differed in the ways they conceived of idolatrous relationships, according to Halbertal and Margalit, "roughly" as follows: "the view that the god of the sun is identical with the sun is the view that the monotheist attributes to the idolater. The view of institutional identity between them is the attribution of the neutral observer. But it is the mind-body relation as the model for relation between the god of the sun and the sun that is apparently closest to the view of the sun worshiper himself" (143–44). Judaism characterizes idolatry as foolish and unsophisticated, a childish worship of what one sees rather than a recognition of the single essence at the heart of all creation that is true faith.

Why was Judaism born at all? Why were Jews dissatisfied with idolatry as a paradigm? What, specifically, was lacking in Mesopotamian idolatry? (Avraham, the founder of Judaism, had Mesopotamian roots.) The answer is order and reason, dependability and mutuality. As Nahum Sarna puts it,

> The pagan worshiper had no reason to believe that the decrees of his god must necessarily be just, any more than he could be convinced that society rested upon a universal order of justice. According to the pagan world-view the fate of man was not determined by human behavior. The gods were innately capricious, so that any absolute authority was impossible. . . . Man always found himself confronted by the tremendous forces of nature, and nature, especially in Mesopotamia, showed itself to be cruel, indiscriminate, unpredictable. Since the gods were immanent in nature, they too shared these same harsh attributes. To aggravate the situation still further, there was always that inscrutable, primordial power beyond the realm of the gods to which man and gods were both subject. Evil, then, was a permanent necessity and there was nothing essentially good in the pagan universe. In such circumstances there could be no correlation between right conduct and individual or national well-being. The universe was purposeless and the deities could offer their votaries no guarantee that life had meaning and direction, no assurance that the end of human strivings was anything but vanity. (1966, 17)

Judaism formulated the Jew's relationship to God to address this problem created by Mesopotamian theology. The Jewish God is as closely bound by the covenant as is the human Jew. Thus, the Jewish God, though omnipotent, allows divine power to be limited by the agreement the Deity entered into with the Jewish people.

Idolatry was, of course, practiced in other cultures besides Mesopotamia. Roman and Greek gods were served in solemn, yet joyful, rituals. Sacrificial animals were offered up and the smoke went to the gods while the celebrants and others ate the animal's flesh. "Scraps from the meal were left on the altar and beggars spirited them away. When sacrifice was made not on a household altar but at a temple, the custom was to pay for the priests' services by leaving them a set portion of the sacrificial animal; temples earned money by selling this meat to butchers" (Veyne 1987, 196). Indeed, Judaism adapted idolatrous rites in the Temple service to God. Priests in the Temple cult were given an allotment of the sacrificial meat and worshipers came to the Temple with sacrifices in joyful gratitude as well as to atone for sins. The sacrificial animal's blood could, in an atonement sacrifice, metaphorically take the place of the sinner's. The symbols of the sacrificial cult—the offered animal, the incense, the physically perfect priest of unblemished lineage in his special garb, and the dangerous sense of holiness and the concomitant restricted access to the inner precincts of the Temple—formed a coherent system of meaning. Life in its purest form, symbolized by (1) an absence of the taint of death (i.e., ritual impurity), (2) the embodiment of perfect human life (the blemishless priest), (3) perfect animal life (the likewise blemishless sacrificial animal), and (4) senses fully stimulated by incense, bells, loaves, and so forth, was at the heart of the Temple's ritual system (Haran 1985, 216). It was believed that a congregation of angels gathered in a heavenly Temple during the earthly sacrificial rites. As pure a reflection as possible of the heavenly spheres was needed in the corporeal world to ensure that the sacrifices were acceptable above (Nickelsburg 1981, 123). These requirements of perfection applied to the Temple cult and the people who performed its rites, but not to the general population.

For the priesthood, particularly in the Temple, ritual purity, or *taharah*, was a necessity; *tum'ah* (impurity) was forbidden in the holy domain. These words have nothing to do with cleanliness and everything to do with the boundaries between life and death and the assurance that (despite their ambiguities) those boundaries are clearly distinguished. Only whole, complete items—not incomplete or broken items—can become impure. So, for example, a piece of pottery could become ritually impure but the shards of a broken piece of pottery could not. As we encounter these terms in our sources, it may be most productive to think about them as ways of considering embodiment, the soul, and wholeness rather than as pertaining to dirt or defilement.

In the Second Temple period (516 B.C.E.–70 C.E.), great changes enveloped the Jews in the land of Israel. Alexander the Great conquered the Persians in Israel in 332 B.C.E. and Jewish culture thereafter fell under Greek, and later, Roman, rule and cultural influence. Under Seleucid rule, Jews came to be more and more oppressed, until finally they rebelled against Antiochus IV Epiphanes and liberated Jerusalem in 164 B.C.E. Members of the Hasmonean dynasty, who led the revolution, ruled Jewish life until 63 B.C.E. Independent Hasmonean rule ended when Judea came under the rule of Rome. A turbulent political period followed, culminating in the revolt against Rome that began in 66 C.E. and ended with the destruction of the Temple in 70. When a decision was made to establish a Roman colony on Jerusalem's ruins, the Bar Kokhba revolt ensued in 132. By 135 C.E., when the revolt ended, the Jewish population in the land of Israel had been decimated through death, enslavement, and emigration.

The literature produced during the Second Temple period was vast and varied. The texts from this era that have survived consist of testaments, apocalyptic literature, biblical exegesis by Philo (ca. 20 B.C.E.–50 C.E.), and the Dead Sea scrolls. Though some Jews had lived in Babylonia since the First Temple's destruction in 586 B.C.E., with their presence continuing throughout the whole Second Temple period, diaspora communities became more populous, prosperous, and important after the Second Temple's fall.

When the Temple was destroyed in 70 C.E. by the Romans, a new form of Judaism gradually came into being, based on continuing interpretation of the Tanach. While the synagogue already had existed in some form during the Second Temple period, it became more important after the Temple's destruction. In time, a culture of study, text development, and worship services within the synagogue came to replace the Temple. The replacements, though, were generally considered to be second best, and a lingering nostalgia for the Temple permeates Jewish texts and worship to the present day. The sages who promulgated the "Oral Torah"—that is, interpretations of the "Written Torah," as the Tanach came to be called—engaged in persuasive creativity to convince Jews to follow their vision of a Judaism without a Temple. Eventually this vision was accepted, but the sages who composed this rabbinic literature never operated from a base of easy authority and universally accepted symbolism as did the priests in the Temple. The texts that we will examine will reflect the development of rabbinic culture and its glacial pace of ascendance over the priestly culture that preceded it.

The document serving as the foundation of rabbinic literature is the Mishnah. Its component parts, called *mishnayot*, were composed after the destruction of the Temple in 70 c.e.[2] These mishnayot, or oral teachings, were promulgated in many schools and were finally culled, organized, and codified by Rabbi Yehudah HaNasi around 200 c.e. Instead of being organized according to the structure of the Torah, as were the halakhic midrash collections (see next page), the Mishnah is organized according to six overarching areas: Seeds, Seasons, Civil Law, Women, Holy Things, and Purities. In each of these sections, known as "orders," the format of the Mishnah remains constant. Its language is formulated for easy memorization, since the transmission of its materials was in large part oral.[3] These individual teachings, which became the Mishnah, may have been collected to provide a binding code of law or to be a textbook of laws that were not necessarily binding. At this point, we can probably never know, conclusively, which sort of document the redactors of the Mishnah intended to produce. Indeed, as Strack and Stemberger (1991, 154) point out, the very question of whether to think of it as "a collection, a teaching manual or a law code . . . probably arises only for modern readers; what is more, it fails to account sufficiently for the utopianism of M[ishnah], its idealized order of the perfect harmony of heaven and earth, and the underlying philosophy. For in principle the ancient tradition is of course regarded as law which must be transmitted in teaching—and thus the three concepts almost coincide."

The Mishnah, which outlines how the sages wanted the world to be, conveys very little of how the world actually was. In some cases, its teachings are completely theoretical—exercises in logic rather than laws meant to be applied to everyday life. Embedded in this picture of the world the sages painted are fundamental concepts of what is important, and most praiseworthy, in the Deity and in humanity. A paradigmatic existence is outlined in the Mishnah, based on village life, a pastoral economy, and holiness centered around the Temple cult. Tractate Avot, also known as Pirkei Avot, is presented as part of the Mishnah but was redacted later. Nonetheless, it stems from the same circles of sages who produced the Mishnah.

As its name would imply, Tosefta, meaning "additions" to the Mishnah, contains different and additional viewpoints and commentary on subjects found in the Mishnah. Tosefta is approximately four times larger than the Mishnah (Herr 1972b, 1283; Goldberg 1987, 283). It is generally agreed that its composition took place in the Land of Israel one generation after the redaction of the Mishnah, that is, 220–230 C.E. (Goldberg 1987, 284; Neusner 1986b, 4). Tosefta provides commentary to all six orders of the Mishnah, though the relation between the two works and indeed the intention of the creators of Tosefta remains unclear.[4]

The next group of texts to be redacted were the halakhic midrashim, also called tannaitic midrashim, on the Books of Exodus, Leviticus, Numbers, and Deuteronomy. These works relate rabbinic law to Torah texts, according to the order of those texts, unlike the Mishnah, which organized its teachings thematically. These works, Mechilta d'Rabbi Yishmael (on Exodus), Sifra (on Leviticus), and Sifre (Numbers and Deuteronomy) were probably redacted around 300 C.E. (see Kraemer 1995, 80; Strack and Stemberger 1991, 273; Neusner 1990, 32; Herr 1971a, 1269). Mechilta d'Rabbi Ishmael (hereafter, "Mechilta") contains some of the oldest material found in the midrash collections, though its complicated redactional history makes an accurate dating of the whole quite difficult. Sifre to Deuteronomy (Sifre D.) is most often thought to be a tannaitic midrash compilation, but it is not a homogeneous work, and different component sections of this work originated in different periods and circles (Fraade 1991, 298). Sifra to Leviticus and Sifre to Numbers (Sifre N.), like the other tannaitic midrashim, probably date from the second half of the third century and underwent further development (Strack and Stemberger 1991, 287, 292).

The aggadic midrashim of the period under study—Genesis Rabbah, Leviticus Rabbah, Lamentations Rabbah, Pesikta d'Rav Kahana, and Tanhuma—approach Scripture differently than do the halakhic midrashim. Genesis Rabbah, the exposition of the first book of the Torah, was brought to its final form in Israel in the fifth century, probably in its first half (Strack and Stemberger 1991, 304). This was a period of crisis in Jewish history. With Constantine's conversion in 312 C.E., Rome had accepted Christianity. At that stage, Judaism was a protected religion; Jews could not be forced to violate Shabbat. Then, in 360 C.E., Julian (whom Christians call "the apostate") reaffirmed paganism and threw off Christianity. As part of his program to embarrass the Christians, in 368 he gave the Jews permission to rebuild the Temple, thereby disproving Jesus' prediction (Matthew 24:2) that no stone on another of the Temple would remain. However, Julian died within the year, and the Jews' hopes for the reinstitution of the Temple cult were dashed. Now Judaism became a persecuted religion; Israel's rights to security and freedom were limited. Synagogues were destroyed, and Jews lost the right to convert slaves they had purchased. In contrast, Jews who became Christians enjoyed the protection of the state. By around 410, Jews' institution of self-government in the land of Israel, the rule of their patriarch, came to an end. In short, it was a very difficult time. Neusner (1990, 141–70) sees the sages' reinterpretation of the Book of Genesis in Genesis Rabbah as their attempt to understand Israel's relationship with Rome.[5] Leviticus Rabbah, the contents of which were finalized closure around 400–500 C.E., comprises a set of thirty-seven topical essays (Neusner 1986a, 57, 59–72). Lamentations Rabbah is an early midrash, originating in the land of Israel and probably composed in the first half of the fifth century (Strack and Stemberger 1991, 310). Pesikta de-Rav Kahana is a homiletic midrash for the festivals and special sabbaths. Its origin was in the land of Israel and it was composed in the fifth century, "approximately contemporaneous with Leviticus Rabbah" (Strack and Stemberger 1991, 321). Tanhuma is a homiletic midrash on the entire Torah that combines halakhic and aggadic midrashim. It was composed in the land of Israel and probably existed in substantially its present form around 400 (Strack and Stemberger 1991, 332).

The Talmud of the land of Israel, called the Yerushalmi, appears to have been redacted in the early fifth century. One of the Yerushalmi's most distinctive features is its paucity of midrashic material, that is, stories and biblical exegesis, when compared with the Babylonian Talmud (the Bavli), even though the bulk of midrashim we possess originated in the land of Israel. Approximately one-sixth of the Yerushalmi is aggadah (stories), while in the Bavli the proportion is approximately one-third (Goldberg 1987, 306). This is almost certainly because much of the midrashic material of the schools that produced the Yerushalmi were compiled in independent collections. Another feature that distinguishes the Yerushalmi from the Bavli is the relatively less rigorous and elaborate editing process it has undergone.

Up to this point, all the rabbinic materials mentioned were generated in the land of Israel. The commentary to the Mishnah—that is, the Gemara of the Babylonian Talmud, also known as the Bavli— may have been completed as early as 427–520, according to one scholar (Halivni 1986, 76), or as late as the mid–seventh century, as proposed by another (Kraemer 1988, 288). As its name suggests, it is a product of the land of Babylonia. The Bavli has a character all its own, reflecting its genesis in a decentralized Jewish community characterized more by pluralism than by strong rabbinic leadership (Kraemer 1990, 199). Like the Yerushalmi, it is a commentary to the Mishnah. It uses all the sources previously composed by the sages in its commentary: Tosefta, tannaitic teachings not included in the Mishnah (*baraitot*), and passages from the Yerushalmi and the midrash collections. The Bavli also adds its own materials to the mix: stories and sayings of the sages, as well as detailed analyses of earlier materials, often characterized by "argumentation": that is, the purposeful presentation of multiple points of view in the late, anonymous layer of the Bavli's composition that is the product of *stamma* (the compositor[s]) and is called *stammaitic* material (Kraemer 1990, 89–90). A concept or ruling may be justified by appeals to logic, Scripture, or actual experience. Often all three sorts of justifications are used.

The roots of the Bavli's emphasis on argumentation are political, literary, and philosophical in nature. Kraemer (1990, 43) and others

TABLE 1. Primary Sources

Document	Date of Composition	Abbreviation
Torah		
Jahwist	10th c. B.C.E.	J
Elohist	9th c. B.C.E.	E
Deuteronomist	621 B.C.E.	D
Priestly school	586 B.C.E.	P
Holiness school	586 B.C.E.	H or HS
Prophets	4th c. B.C.E.	
Writings	2nd c. C.E.	
Pseudepigrapha	586 B.C.E.–70 C.E.	
Mishnah	200 C.E.	M. + tractate name
Tosefta	220 C.E.	T. + tractate name
Halakhic midrashim	ca. 300 C.E.	
Mechilta d'Rabbi Yishmael		Mechilta
Sifra		Sifre
Sifre Numbers		Sifre N.
Sifre Deuteronomy		Sifre D.
Aggadic midrashim	ca. 400 C.E.	
Genesis Rabbah		
Leviticus Rabbah		
Peskta d'Rav Kahana		
Lamentations Rabbah		
Tanhuma		
Talmud Yerushalmi	ca. 400 C.E.	Y. + tractate name
Talmud Bavli	427–650 C.E.	B. + tractate name

(e.g., Cohen 1990, 149) suggest that the sages were trying to impose their will on the resistant ancient Jewish community of Babylonia and therefore had to compose a document that "sold" more than it "told" its point of view. This, in turn, changed the form of their literary creation, making argumentation more desirable.[6] The medium and the message become one, in the Bavli: the study of Torah, in its broadest sense, convinces one to study more and to perform its dictates as interpreted by the sages.

Table 1 summarizes the names, dates, and abbreviations of the documents we will study.

A Preview

In this study of persons with disabilities in Jewish sources from the Tanach through the Bavli, we will focus on five main areas of inquiry: (1) the way disabilities affected priests and their functioning in the Temple and the way the priestly concept of physical perfection was adapted to the sages' system of observance once the Second Temple was destroyed, (2) how persons with disabilities were used as symbols of collective Israel, (3) how the life stories of individuals with disabilities often became literally object lessons in theology and God's justice, (4) the comparisons of how persons with disabilities were seen in Judaism and the cultures that surrounded it, and (5) the way persons with disabilities were grouped into categories and the significance of those designations. In general, to be able to act fully in the sages' system, a person must (1) have *da'at* ("cognition" or "consciousness"), (2) have the ability to act on that *da'at*, and (3) be entitled to put his or her *da'at* into action in the society the sages constructed.

In our study of these documents, we must remember whose vision of society and faith we are reading. The sages, intent on their vision of society and its members, were not concerned with an inclusive account of everyone's experiences. The actual lives of persons with disabilities remain largely hidden from us, as they were not generally described in the sources.

2

Priestly Perfection

"THE FEW, the Proud, the Marines" is a phrase we associate today with exceptionally fit men and women who, because of their physical condition and training, are able to survive the most dangerous aspects of combat. The phrase implies that there is another group, "the many, the weak, the humble and forlorn"—that is, those who would surely perish in battle's perilous theater. The priests who officiated in the Temple cult were an exceptional elite of the spirit. Like marines, the priests operated in a dangerous environment: the Temple was filled with a holiness that could be lethal to those lacking the right protective qualifications. These qualifications—correct blood in a blemishless, perfectly life-filled body—allowed the priests to enter the realm between heaven and earth and mediate between God, and God's heavenly retinue, and Israel.

The Symmetry of Heaven and Earth

To understand the role of the priest—and the need for a priest to be blemishless in his physicality and lineage—we must understand the symmetry between heaven and earth and how crucial the priest was in mediating between the upper and lower realms. The world is full of death, disorder, and imperfection. The Temple, by contrast, allowed average Israelites to have access to the upper world of everlasting life, utter order, and complete perfection through the cult and through the person of the priest. The priest, then, had to stand in

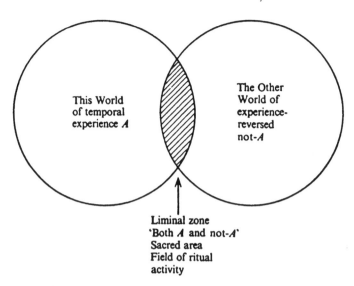

FIGURE 1. Schematic of the liminal zone. Reprinted by permission, from Leach, *Culture and Communication*, fig. 8, 82.

two worlds at once (Levine 1995, 43–44). He had to be worthy of the heavenly beings whose company he shared.

The Temple, its rites, and those who officiated at them were the link between heaven and earth. They were therefore liminal, that is, on the threshold, in the most literal sense, as depicted in figures 1 and 2. The Temple is the place where the best representatives of humanity meet with God. This is the theology of the Temple and its cult recorded in our earliest texts up to our latest ones. Thus, it provides the reason explicitly given for constructing the Tabernacle, the predecessor of the Temple: "Let them make me a sanctuary and I will dwell among them" (Exodus 25:8; 29:45).

The Tabernacle, and later the Temple, is where Israel meets God.[1] The promise of God in the Temple meeting with His people is the climactic finale for Ezekiel's vision of the risen bones:

And my servant David will rule them and they shall all have one shepherd. And they shall walk in my laws and keep my statutes and do them. And they shall dwell on the land which I have given to my servant, Jacob, [the land in] which your fathers dwelt, and they shall dwell on it, they and their children and their children's children forever, and David my servant shall be their ruler eternally. And I shall make a covenant of peace, an eternal covenant with them, and I will give it to them and I will multiply them and I will put my sanctuary among them forever. And my dwelling place (*mishkani*) shall be over them and I will be their God and they will be my people. And the nations shall know that I am the Lord who sanctifies Israel while I am in my sanctuary, among them, forever. (Ezekiel 37:24–28)

When Israel is in its proper abode, the Land, God will be in His proper abode, the Temple. Proper earthly rule, the Davidic dynasty, is complemented by proper heavenly rule.

Not only does God have an earthly dwelling place, corresponding to His heavenly abode, but the Israelites have a symbolic, exalted place in the heavenly spheres. Indeed, the heavenly beings have to wait until human beings praise God before they can do so:

And from whence [do we learn that] the ministering angels do not mention the name of the Holy One, blessed be He, on high until Israel mention it below? [From where] it is said, "Hear O Israel, the Lord our God the Lord is One" (Deuteronomy 6:4), and [where] it says, "When the morning stars sang together, and all the sons of God shouted for joy" (Job 38:7)—"the morning stars"—these are Israel, who are compared to the stars, as it is said, "I will multiply your seed

```
Sacred—————————————————Profane

    God   Priesthood        People    Gentiles

Temple              Camp              Wilderness

    Life                              Death

    Being   Transient      Existence   Nothingness

    Order————————RITUAL————————Chaos
```

FIGURE 2. The liminality of the priesthood. Reprinted from Davies, in *Anthropological Approaches to the Old Testament* by Bernhard Lange, 156, copyright © 1985 Fortress Press and SPCK. Used by permission of Augsburg Fortress.

as the stars of the heaven" (Genesis 22:17); "and all the sons of God shouted for joy," these are the ministering angels, and thus it says, "The sons of God came to present themselves before the Lord" (Job 1:6). (Sifre D., Piska 306)

That the "sons of God" are celestial creatures can be seen from the full verse of Job 1:6: "Now there was a day when the sons of God (*b'nei HaElohim*) came to present themselves before the Lord and the adversary (*hasatan*) came also among them." We have here an image of angels and human beings praying in tandem, with human prayer necessarily preceding angelic praise.

The correspondence of heaven and earth is extended beyond the Temple and moments of prayer. God is depicted as participating in other rituals:

R. Yoshiya opened [his discourse with the text], "Happy is the people that know the sound of the blast; they walk, O Lord, in the light of Your countenance (*Adonai b'or panecha y'haleichun*)" (Psalm 89:16). R. Abbahu interpreted the verse [as referring to] the five elders who enter [into session] to prolong the year. What does the Holy One, blessed be He, do? He leaves His senators on high and contracts His Presence to be among them, below. The Ministering Angels say: This Mighty One, this Mighty One! This God, this God! [He] of whom it is written, "A God dreaded in the great council of the holy ones" (Psalm 89:8) leaves His senators and contracts His Presence to be among those below. Why all this? So that if they err in a matter of law the Holy One Blessed be He enlightens their countenance (*Hu mei'ir p'neihem*). Thus is it written, "In the light of Your face they walk." (Leviticus Rabbah Emor 29:4)

Not only, as we will see in subsequent sources, is there a Temple above the earthly one, but there is also a heavenly deliberative body that corresponds to the sages' decision-making assemblies. Indeed, God, according to this passage, would rather participate in sages' debates and their process of intercalating the calendar than in those of the angels. (During the sages' era the calendar was determined by observation of the moon.) The shofar was blown on the new moons (e.g., Psalm 81:4) and the light of God's presence was made manifest, according to this interpretation, through the judgments of the sages. According to M. Sanhedrin 1:2, Rabban Gamliel states that these deliberations start with three sages, are debated by five sages, and are concluded with seven. These numbers correspond to the priestly benediction, whose lines contain three, five, and seven words respectively:

> God bless-you and-keep-you.
> (*Y'varech'cha Adonai v'yishm'recha*)
> God will-shine His-countenance upon-you and-grace-you.
> (*Ya'eir Adonai panav eleicha vi'huneka*)
> God will-raise His-countenance upon-you and-give to-you peace.
> (*Yisa Adonai panav elecha v'yaseim l'cha shalom*) (Numbers 6:24–26)

The five words of Numbers 6:25 refer to God's light and the verse from Psalm 89:16 also refers to God's light. Thus, the light of the new moon, the light of God's presence evoked by the priestly benediction, and God's light transmitted through the sages and their decisions are all connected. In this way, the equivalence is made not just between the heavenly and the earthly Jerusalem but also between the heavenly and the earthly Jewish court. Though one avenue of bridging the gap between heaven and earth was closed off when the Temple and Jerusalem were destroyed, nevertheless another was opened via the sages' deliberations.

In addition to a spiritual correspondence between the earthly and heavenly Temples, the two were thought to be physically linked. The heavenly Temple is located directly above the earthly one.

> "*Let him direct his thoughts to the chamber of the Holy of Holies*" (*M. Berachot 4:5*). To which chamber of the Holy of Holies? R. Hiyya the great [said], "Toward the [chamber of the] Holy of Holies above [in heaven]." Rabbi Shimon ben Halafta said, "Toward the chamber of the Holy of Holies below [in the Temple]." Said R. Pinchas, "They do not dispute one another. For the chamber of the Holy of Holies down below is opposite the chamber of the Holy of Holies up above [as implied in the verse], "The place (*makhon, mem chaf vav nun*); O Lord, which you have made for your abode [i.e., the Temple]" (Exodus

15:17). [Read the verse rather as follows:] "Situated opposite (*m'kha-ven, mem chaf vav vav nun*) your abode [i.e., the Temple]." [What is situated opposite it? It is, "The sanctuary, O Lord, which Your hands have established" (Exodus 15:17).] (Y. Berachot 4:5, 8c)

Starting with the premise that there are two Holy of Holies, this passage from the Yerushalmi makes a pun on the words *machon* and *m'khaven*, which differ by only one letter (adding one letter is not an uncommon practice in Hebrew), to demonstrate that the two are located opposite each other. The larger point being made is that one should direct one's heart to the Holy of Holies when praying. The conclusion reached is that directing the heart toward one is like directing it toward them both, since they are linked spatially and spiritually.

In this heavenly Temple are an altar and a high priest, just as there are in the earthly one: "*Zevul* is that [level of heaven] in which [the heavenly] Jerusalem and the Temple and the Altar are built, and Michael, the great Prince, stands and offers on it an offering" (B. Hagigah 12b; B. Menachot 110a). So, when the high priest officiated at the cult, below, he was a reflection of the cult above and corresponded to Michael, Israel's "national" angel (each of the seventy nations has a representative angel, and Michael defends and represents Israel before God; B. Yoma 77a). In the parallel text, we find a link between the cult and the sages: "'This is an ordinance for ever to Israel' (2 Chronicles 2:3), R. Giddal said in the name of Rav. This [refers to] the altar built [in heaven], and [upon which] Michael the great Prince stands and offers on it an offering. And Rabbi Yohanan said, These [words refer to] students of sages who are occupied with the laws of [the Temple] service. Scripture accounts it to them as if the Temple were built in their days" (B. Menachot 110a).

The verse from Chronicles here expounded should be read in its entirety: "Behold, I am about to build a house for the name of the Lord my God, to dedicate it to Him and to burn before Him incense of sweet spices, and for the continual showbread, and for the burnt offerings morning and evening and on the sabbaths and on the new moons and on the appointed seasons of the Lord our God; this is an ordinance for ever to Israel" (2 Chronicles 2:4). How were the sages to understand this verse? More specifically, if it were an eternal ordinance, and the Temple was destroyed, how could the verse be fulfilled? They concluded that it could either be fulfilled at the heavenly altar or it could be fulfilled below by sages piously studying the laws of the sacrifices, thus in a sense keeping the flame burning on earth.

Mishaps and misfortunes in the earthly Jerusalem, and its worship, could delay the process of heavenly worship and function:

> Rav Nahman said to Rabbi Yitshak: What [is the meaning of what] is written [in Scripture], "The Holy One is in your midst and I will not come into the city" (Hosea 11:9). [Surely it cannot be that] because the Holy One is in the midst of you I shall not come into the city! He said to him: Thus said Rabbi Yohanan: The Holy One, blessed be He, said, "I will not enter Jerusalem above until I can enter the Jerusalem below." Is there then a Jerusalem above? Yes, for it is written, "Jerusalem, you are built as a city that is compact together" (Psalm 122:3). (B. Taanit 5a)

While Israel is in exile, and the earthly Jerusalem destroyed, God voluntarily goes into exile as well, waiting for Jerusalem to be rebuilt and for the cult to be reinstituted. The verse from Psalms can be taken to mean that the earthly Jerusalem has a companion Jerusalem in the heavens, with the exposition in the Bavli seeming to depend on the words *shechubrah la yachdav*, which could loosely be translated to mean "together with its companion."

In these texts we see that the idea of a connection between heaven and earth that found its corporeal link in the Temple was remarkably long-lived, as it is given expression in our earliest and latest sources.[2] The sages, with their study, filled the breach created by the Temple's destruction. Both priests and sages did their work cognizant not only of the audience before them but also of the audience above them. It is in this context of the connection between heaven and earth that the priest's physical perfection, and the sages' understanding of it, must be examined.

The Priest's Perfection in the Temple

An examination of the priest's physical perfection should begin with the Torah. The priest, as we have already seen, mediates between heaven and earth, between holy and profane. To survive in such a dangerous position, the priest had to be fit for the company of angels: blemishless, pure of lineage, and untouched by the taint of death (i.e., ritually pure).

> And the Lord spoke to Moses, saying: Speak to Aaron, saying, A man of your lineage, for [all] their generations, who has a blemish shall not come near to offer the bread of his God. For any man who has a blemish shall not come near: [whether he] is a blind man or a lame man or [has] a flat nose or any extra [limb or growth] or a man who has a broken leg or a broken hand or a crooked back or [is] a dwarf or has obscured sight in [even one] eye or has scurvy or scabs or has crushed testicles. Any man of Aaron's lineage who has a blemish shall not draw nigh to offer the fire [offerings] of God. He has a blemish and he may not approach to offer his God's bread. He shall eat the bread of his God, [both] of the most holy, and of the holy. But he may not go [in]to the veil [before the ark], nor come near to the altar, because he has a blemish. Let him not profane My holy [places]: for I the Lord [Myself] sanctify [these places]. And Moses spoke [these words] to Aaron and to his sons and to all the children of Israel. (Leviticus 21:16–24)

Deafness, mental illness, and mental disability are not mentioned in this passage, perhaps because they were not considered readily visible defects. As we will see shortly, this stands in sharp contrast to the rabbinic system, where these very disabilities, though not visible, are perceptible and considered most salient (indeed, Sifra on this passage will make these exclusions explicit concerning priests). In the most perfect of places—that is, the Temple—in the presence of the most perfect entity—that is, God—only the most perfect of persons, someone of unblemished priestly lineage and perfect physical form, may offer up sacrifices (which must also be unblemished).

The list of blemishes that disqualify sacrificial animals, like that for the priest, numbers twelve items:

And a man who offers a peace offering to God, to fulfill a vow or whosoever brings a sacrifice of peace offerings unto the Lord in fulfillment of a vow or for a freewill offering, of the herd or of the flock, it [must] be perfect to be accepted; it may have no blemish. Blind or broken[-limbed], or maimed or having a wen or scabbed or scurvy; do not sacrifice [such as] these to God nor make a fire [offering] to God of them on the altar for God. Either a bullock or a lamb that has any thing too long or too short, that may offer for a freewill offering; but for a vow it shall not be accepted. That which has its testicles bruised, or crushed, or torn, or cut you must not offer to God, nor may you perform [castrations] in your land. (Leviticus 22:21–24)

Milgrom (1991, 722) shows the equivalence of these two sets of criteria for acceptability of man and animal in the cult in figures 3 and 4. A third diagram, figure 5, might fill out this picture. The areas of greatest holiness are the inner circles, where the priest and the sacrificial animal come into contact with God in the Temple. Spreading out in the next circle, in diminished holiness, all Israel is bound by the commandments in a holy relationship with God that is, in the Torah, intrinsically linked to the land and to restrictions on which animals may be consumed through the laws of *kashrut* (Leviticus 11:1–47), although these laws are less restrictive than those applying to animals offered in the cult. (To be sure, no nonkosher animals were offered there!) Finally, the rest of the world may eat any animal it wants in any place that it wants.[3]

The verses preceding those under discussion outline how the priest must avoid the taint of death (ritual impurity, Leviticus 21:1–6) and how he must preserve the lineage of the priesthood by marrying appropriately and ensuring that his daughters behave appropriately (21:7–9). The even stricter rules that apply to the high priest regarding ritual impurity (21:10–12) and marriage (21:13–15) come just before the mandate regarding his blemishlessness. The intervening verses between the two passages under discussion (22:1–16) prescribe those special offerings that only a priest, and a priest's family, may eat. These offerings may only be consumed by members of priestly families who are in a state of ritual purity. However, a priest who has a blemish that bars him from officiating in the cult may still eat these offerings (21:22). This whole section of the Torah, then, deals with (1) how one maintains priestly status through ritual purity and lineage, (2) how one maintains high priestly status through their even more rigorous maintenance, (3) physical qualifications for officiating in the cult, (4) emoluments for maintenance of priestly status, and (5) what sort of animals may be part of the

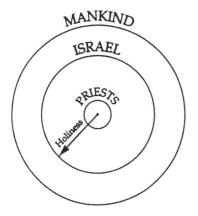

FIGURE 3. Holiness of persons. Reprinted by permission, from Milgrom, *Leviticus 1–16*, *The Anchor Bible*, fig. 13, 722.

FIGURE 4. Holiness of animals. Reprinted by permission, from Milgrom, *Leviticus 1–16*, *The Anchor Bible*, fig. 13, 722.

FIGURE 5. Holiness of places.

system of sacrifice and priestly emoluments. In essence, the priest and the priest's family may not eat any animal that has characteristics which, if the priest had them, would disqualify him from the cult. Here the usual phrase, "You are what you eat," seems to have been recast as "Don't eat what you don't want to become." The priest is linked to the perfect sacrificial animal as Israel is kosher animals.

As the section of the Torah we are considering makes clear, although disabilities disqualify a priest from officiating in the cult, he is still considered a priest in all other respects. More serious problems for a priest would be a defect in lineage, which would utterly disqualify him not only from officiating at the cult but from receiving priestly emoluments, or a state of ritual impurity, which would deprive him of these same benefits. Thus a priest in a state of ritual impurity is more disabled than a priest who is blind: while a blind priest may still consume the food set aside for him, a priest who is ritually impure cannot. Nothing with the taint of death may be associated with the place of life in its purest form on earth: the Temple. In addition, those substances that would be carriers of life—primarily, blood and semen—are, when flowing in an uncontrolled way (e.g., menstrual blood or any seminal emission), those items that contaminate with ritual impurity. Since a corpse is the very embodiment of death, it is the most defiling item in the ritual purity system and cannot be allowed to come into contact with the priest. The taint of death (i.e., blood that does not carry life) disqualifies him from consuming his priest's due and from officiating in the cult until he has undergone a purification ritual and the state of impurity has passed. The priest must embody the best blood (i.e., not tainted by ritual impurity and of the best lineage) in a perfect vessel (i.e., a blemishless body) to withstand the lethal aura that surrounds the innermost parts of the Temple. Access to the Sanctuary of the Temple was severely limited precisely because of the danger liable to befall those who approached this holy area improperly. Even if one's motives and intentions were of the most pious sort, the danger was still present. One need only think of a physician handling contaminated body fluids to understand this immediately: no amount of good intention will make up for a careless needle stick or protect the practitioner from a hole in his or her protective gear. Holiness is "blindly" lethal in this sense: intention, which will become so important to the sages, is relatively meaningless when it comes to issues of ritual purity and priestly status.[4] Nothing impure could enter the sacred realm. Something can be ritually pure and in the common realm, and certainly an item can be common, that is, not sanctified, and impure; but nothing within the sacred realm of the Temple could be ritually impure.

Ritual impurity defiles different parts of the cult in different ways. And different sorts of sin are seen as more related to death, and more injurious to the cult, than others. The more heinous the sin, the deeper into the sacred parts of the cult the impurity penetrates (see figure 6). Only the rituals of the Day of Atonement can take away this impurity. And only the finest human specimens, as defined by the source and state of their blood and the "vessel" containing it (i.e., the priest's body) can withstand this caustic environment.

The Mishnah elaborates on the Torah's descriptions of blemishes that would disqualify priests from officiating in the cult: "These blemishes [which disqualify animals as sacrifices], whether permanent or temporary, [also] disqualify a person [i.e., a priest from Temple service].[5] There are more [disqualifications] for a person [than

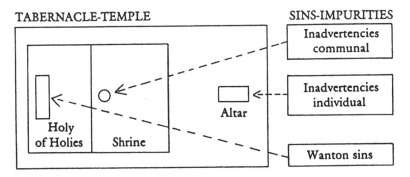

FIGURE 6. Depth of penetration of ritual impurity. Reprinted by permission, from Milgrom, *The JPS Torah Commentary, Numbers*, 466.

these, namely] a wedge-shaped head or a turnip-shaped head or a mallet-shaped head or a sunken head or [the head] flat behind,[6] or a hunchback. Rabbi Yehudah declares [the humpbacked priest] qualified, but the sages disqualify [him]" (M. Bekorot 7:1). The Mishnah explicitly recognizes the link between the sacrificial animals and the priests, and the role blemishes play in their disqualification from the cult. The Mishnah, here, seems to hew to the Torah's line about priests: almost any blemish disqualifies him from participating in the cult. (Of course, such great stringency applied in theory only, since the cult did not operate during the era of the Mishnah; as we will see below, a priest offering a blessing in the synagogue is treated much more leniently.)[7]

It may seem surprising that the Mishnah was able to extrapolate the expanded list of blemishes from the relatively compact Torah text, but the tannaitic midrash on Leviticus, Sifra, shows how this may have occurred:

I have nothing [here in Leviticus 21:16–24] but these [blemishes] alone. From whence [do we know] to augment [and include] other blemishes? Scripture says, "blemish" (21:17) [and it says in the next verse] "blemish" (21:18). From whence [do we know that] the negro and the lame [person] and the one with white spots on his face and the hunchback and the dwarf and the deaf-mute and the mentally ill and the drunkard and [those with] ritually pure plagues [cannot officiate in the cult]? Scripture says, "a man" (21:17) [and] "a man" (21:18) to augment [the meaning]. (Sifra Emor 3b:1 p. 114)

Commenting on Leviticus 21:16–24, Sifra notes some apparent redundancies in the text. In general, the sages held that no word of Scripture was superfluous. So why, wonders the midrash, does Torah use the words "blemish" and "man" in two consecutive verses? This must be, the conclusion is reached, to multiply the meanings of the words. Thus, to the list of blemishes that disqualify priests, Sifra adds several additional visible blemishes and three "nonvisible" ones: persons with speaking and hearing disabilities, persons with mental disabilities, and persons who are intoxicated.

The inclusion of the drunkard here gives us the clue as to why such persons are disqualified from service in the cult. An intoxicated person does not think clearly, cannot control his behavior, and may inadvertently pollute the cult with ritual impurity. Hence, because such a person poses a danger to the cult and to himself, he may not officiate there. We may surmise that persons with speaking and hearing disabilities and persons with mental disabilities were seen as similar to the intoxicated priest in this respect. Reliable communication with, and ordered action from, such persons were deemed impossible and they were therefore barred from officiating. This prohibition was in no way a function of their intentions; as we have seen, the priest's intention was irrelevant in the confines of the Temple. Rather, they posed a danger to the cult of polluting it with ritual impurity (being unable, perhaps, to determine whether or not they were ritually impure or being unable to communicate their status properly) or of behaving in an uncontrolled or untutored manner in the Temple's dangerous environment.

Interestingly, the minor is also disqualified from officiating in the cult, even though he may be blemishless, have the correct bloodlines, and be in a state of ritual purity:

> "And God spoke to Moses saying, 'A man of your seed for their generations who will have a blemish shall not draw nigh to offer the bread of his God.'" Said Rabbi Akiba in [the name of] Rabbi Yosi: How [do we know that] a child is unfit [to offer sacrifices in the Temple] even though he is [in some senses] fitting? From what time is his service acceptable? From the time when he produces two [pubic] hairs but his fellow priests do not induct him into his [active] service until he is twenty years old. (Sifra Emor 3a:1, p. 112)

Even a minor who has shown clear signs of reaching puberty is not permitted to officiate in the cult until he is twenty years old. We may surmise that by the time he reaches his twentieth year, he will be full-grown and, in most cases, produce a full beard—conditions that would not be achieved by a boy in the beginning of puberty. So even a person who has the correct blood in a blemishless body must also appear fully, maturely male to officiate in the cult.

One late source confirms the lethal nature of God's presence residing in a synagogue made of stones from the First Temple's ruins. It involves one of the most prominent sages of Babylonia, Rav Sheshet (290–320), who was blind. In this case, his disability actually protects him from God's lethal presence, from which other sages must flee: "Rav Sheshet was [once] sitting in the synagogue which 'moved and settled' in Nehardea,[8] when the *Shekhinah* [God's presence] came. He did not go out [of the synagogue as did other sages when the *Shekhinah* approached]. The ministering angels came and [tried to] scare him [away]. He [Rav Sheshet] said to Him [God]: 'Master of the Universe, if one is afflicted and one is not afflicted,[9] who gives way to whom?' God [then] said to them [the angels]: 'Leave him'" (B. Megillah 29a). The assumption behind this story is clear: God's presence is awful in every sense of that word and human beings must flee from it. Rav Sheshet, who may not have been able to flee, asked for and was granted mercy. Perhaps the greatest part of God's holiness was conveyed through sight (which leads to blinding insight). Yet Rav Sheshet clearly has great insight and is enlightened, though physically blind.

The Priest's Perfection outside the Temple

When the Temple was destroyed in 70 C.E., the locus of the priests' functioning was gone. Only in limited circumstances could they continue to serve as priests. One such occasion was the priestly benediction offered during worship services in the synagogue. To this day, priests from the congregation come forward, shed their shoes, have their hands washed with the help of those who have descended from the Levites, and ascend the platform (*bimah*) to bless the congregations with the words of Numbers 6:24–26. As part of this ritual, the priests raise their hands over the congregation. God's presence is thought to descend while this blessing is being offered; hence, congregants are not supposed to look at the priests while the blessing is being recited lest the glance prove fatal. We see, then, that in this ritual moment, the atmosphere of lethal holiness that always obtained in the Temple is recreated in the synagogue.

We might expect, by logical extension, that the priests who offer this blessing must be blemishless, but this is true only to a limited extent. Sifre N., Piska 39, on Numbers 6:23, which demonstrates that the priestly blessing must be offered while standing and with raised hands, makes no mention of blemishes on the priests' hands. The Mishnah focuses on the priests' hands and their defects: "A priest whose hands have blemishes may not raise his hands [in the priestly blessing]. Rabbi Yehudah says, 'Moreover one whose hands are stained with woad [blue dye] or madder [red dye] may not lift his hands because the people would gaze at him'" (M. Megillah 4:7). Thus, the Mishnah holds that the priest's hands must be blemishless when he lifts them in blessing the congregation during synagogue worship. Not only that, even perfectly formed hands are not in themselves satisfactory: they must also have the correct color.[10] The concern here is that the congregation would stare at the priests' discolored or deformed hands during the blessing and in so doing put themselves in harm's way.

Tosefta, commenting on this mishnah, expands on it and, simultaneously, mitigates its severity where it can without exposing the congregation to the lethal holiness that surrounds the priestly blessing: "*A priest who has a blemish on his* face, *hands*, or feet, *lo this one should not raise his hands [in the priestly blessing], because the people will stare at him (M. Megillah 4:7).* But if he was an associate of the town [and therefore well-known,] lo, this is permitted" (T. Megillah 3:29). Tosefta first expands the teaching of the Mishnah: not only blemished hands but blemished feet or face should disqualify a priest from coming forward to recite the priestly benediction. The priests' feet would be visible to the congregation since their shoes are removed prior to giving the blessing, and their faces, too, could have been visible to the congregation at this ritual moment. Therefore, blemishes in any of these areas might cause congregants to stare at the priest, and this could not be allowed. However, if, for example,

many of the people worked in dyes so that the sight of someone with
bright blue or red hands would not cause staring, or if the priest and
his deformities were well-known to everyone and would likewise
not draw attention, then this priest represents no danger to the congregation and he may offer up the benediction.

The Yerushalmi builds on the Mishnah and Tosefta and, further,
brings reports of cases where these rules were applied selectively:

A priest who has blemishes on his hands should not raise his hands in the
priestly benediction. . . . (M. Megillah 4:7)
Gemara: It has been taught: [If the priest has blemishes also] on his
face [he should not raise his hands in the priestly benediction.] It has
been taught: **But if he was well-known in his town, he is permit-**
ted [to do so] (T. Megillah 3:29).

Rabbi Naftali had crooked fingers. He came and asked Rabbi Mana
[if he might offer the priestly blessing]. He [Rabbi Mana] said to him,
"Since you are well-known in your town it is permitted."

Rav Huna would take away [someone with] a thin beard (*zald'kan*)
[from saying the priestly benediction]. But it was taught, **If he was**
well-known in his city he is permitted [to recite the priestly
blessing] (T. Megillah 3:29). Said Rav Muna, His [i.e., the man
with only a few hairs in his beard] legs were small [and so he was not
allowed to give the priestly blessing], so that [the congregation]
shouldn't say, "We saw a *katan* (a minor) raise his hands [in the
priestly blessing]."

Said R. Yose, "That indicates that it is forbidden to look at the
priests when they are blessing Israel."

Said R. Haggai, "Did they not say that they do not look at the
priests because of thereby distracting oneself (hisi'a da'at) [from receiving the blessing]? By Moses! I can look at the priests and not be
distracted!" (Y. Megillah 4:8, 75b–c; Y. Taanit 4:1, 67b)

The standard definition of a person who is no longer a *katan* is one
who has two pubic hairs and who has reached the age of twelve (for
girls) or thirteen (for boys). Someone with only a few hairs in his
beard is disqualified, in this passage, from giving the priestly blessing whereas a priest with deformed fingers is not, if he is well-known
in his town and his hands' appearance will not cause people to gaze

at him. The difference is that in the former case the priest's childlike appearance might cause the congregation to stare. Therefore, fulfilling the rabbinic standard of maturity—producing two pubic hairs—is not enough: only a man who also appears to be a full-grown male may offer this blessing. This priest's disqualification is based solely on his outer appearance and has nothing to do with his *da'at*, his cognitive ability to say the blessing with intention, or even with his being a man, as opposed to a minor. It is his *appearance* of being a minor that disqualifies him.

The Yerushalmi supplies Rabbi Haggai's view as to why staring at the priests while they are offering the benediction is forbidden: staring might distract one from fully receiving the blessing. However, if one is able to look and concentrate at the same time, then looking at the priests while they bless the congregation is permitted.[11] Does this represent an attenuation of the concept of the "lethal holiness" that surrounded the priests in the Temple and that may have faded over the centuries since the Temple's destruction? Does it perhaps reflect Rabbi Haggai's principled objection that such holiness obtains only in the Temple itself? Or do we see here a subtle shift in emphasis from appearance and seeing to inward states, such as cognition? The Hebrew here—*hisi'a da'at*, literally "removal of cognition"—may hint that the latter is the case, but all these motivations may be in play.

The Bavli to this mishnah brings in tannaitic sources (*baraitot*) to support various additional restrictions on which priests may raise their hands in the priestly blessing while continuing to uphold Tosefta's stance that as long as a priest's blemish is familiar to the congregants and, we may infer, does not cause them to stare, then he is permitted to offer up the blessing.

> A tanna stated: *The blemishes which [the sages] said [disqualify a priest] are on his [the priest's]* **face,** *his hands* **and his feet** (*M. Megillah* 4:7 and **T. Megillah 3:29).**
> Rabbi Yehoshua ben Levi said: [If] his hands are spotted he should not lift up his hands [in the priestly blessing]. It has been taught similarly: If his hands are spotted, he should not lift up his hands. If they

are curved inward or bent sideways, he should not lift up his hands [in the priestly blessing].[12]

Rav Assi said: [A priest from] Haifa or Beit Sh'an should not lift up his hands [in the priestly blessing]. It has been taught similarly: Men from Beit Sh'an or from Haifa or from Tib'onim may not go down before the ark [to lead the congregation in prayer] because they pronounce *alef* as *ayin* and *ayin* as *alef*. Said Rabbi Hiyya to Rabbi Shimon bar Rabbi: If you had been a Levite, you would have been disqualified from chanting [songs in the Temple] because your voice is coarse. He [Rabbi Shimon bar Rabbi] went and told his father [about this insult]. [His father] said to him: Go and say to him [R. Hiyya], When you come to the verse, "And I will wait [*ve-chikiti*] for the Lord" (Isaiah 8:17), will you not be a blasphemer and a reviler?[13]

Rav Huna said: A man whose eyes run should not lift up his hands [in the priestly blessing]. But was there not one [such priest] in Rav Huna's neighborhood who used to spread forth his hands? [This was permitted because] he [was a resident] of the town [and his neighbors] were used to his appearance. It has been taught similarly: "A man whose eyes run should not lift up his hands [in the priestly blessing], but if he [was a resident] of the town [and his neighbors] were used to his appearance [and would not stare when he offered the blessing] he is permitted [to offer the blessing]."

Rabbi Yochanan said: A [priest] blind in one eye should not lift up his hands [to offer the blessing]. But was not there one in Rabbi Yohanan's neighborhood who used to spread forth his hands? He [was a resident] of the town [and his neighbors] were used to his appearance. It was taught similarly: "A man blind in one eye should not lift up his hands, but if the townspeople are accustomed to him, he is permitted [to do so]."

"*Rabbi Yehudah says: A man whose hands are discolored should not lift up his hands.*" (M. Megillah 4:7) A tanna [said]: If most of the men of the town [work in] the same occupation it is permitted [since the off-color hands will not cause the congregation to stare]. (B. Megillah 24b)[14]

The Bavli continues the process, already seen in the Tosefta and Yerushalmi, of further specifying the restrictions on what sorts of blemishes disqualify priests from offering the priestly benediction. The main additions here are that priests whose speech is inaccurate and those whose vision is impaired are disqualified. The former disqualification is quite logical: to offer the blessing one must be able to pronounce it correctly (Hauptman 1988, 128). If one were to make an *aleph* into an *ayin* while reciting the benediction, some problematic utterances might result. For example, the word *ya'eir* (*yud-aleph-reish*), "to cause to shine," might be confused with a word from the root *ayin-reish-heh* that signifies stirring up, intermixing, and even sexual excitement—a most inappropriate meaning in the context of the priestly blessing. The insults that follow relate to speech impediments but have nothing to do with the priestly benediction. A Levite, whose main role was to sing, obviously needed to have a sweet voice; but since the Temple wasn't standing at the time, the insult seemed a bit gratuitous and was responded to in kind.

The preoccupation with eye blemishes is a bit more problematic. Even if a man's eyes run or if he is blind in one eye, he is still sighted. Hence, the concern of the Gemara here cannot be that he might stumble on his way up to the platform, thereby casting doubt on his fitness to bless the congregation and disrupting the service (see B. Sotah 37b–40b, particularly the bottom of 40a). This may have to do with the very issue of gazing, which is forbidden to priests and congregants alike. A priest with these eye blemishes might attract the gaze of the congregation and such staring, as we know, is forbidden.

This concern with the undisrupted decorum of the service, and the blind man's possible interference with it, is brought out in another mishnah:

> A *katan* may read the Torah and translate [its text for the congregation], but he may not spread [a cloak over his head and recite the prayers preceding and following the] Shema, nor go before the ark, nor lift his hands [in the priestly blessing].
>
> One who has holes in his clothes [may spread a cloak over his head and recite the prayers preceding and following the] Shema and translate [the text of Torah for the congregation] but he may neither read the Torah nor go before the ark nor lift his hands [in the priestly blessing].
>
> A blind person may spread [a cloak over his head and recite the prayers preceding and following the] Shema and translate [the text of the Torah for the congregation but he may not read from Torah, since

he cannot see]. Rabbi Yehudah says, "Anyone who has never in his lifetime seen light may not spread [a cloak over his head and recite the prayers preceding and following the] Shema." (M. Megillah 4:6)

This mishnah concerns the participation of persons in synagogue functions whose age, dress, or demeanor might disrupt the dignity of the service; its rulings are summarized in table 2.

Someone inappropriately dressed, or one who other members of the congregation feel is unqualified to recite a prayer, must be dealt with in a way that preserves decorum in the congregation. Presumably, one could lead the Shema and translate Scripture from one's seat; hence the blind man and the man in rags are permitted to perform these functions, which do not require that these persons move from their places, revealing either a shocking piece of anatomy (the man in rags) or difficulty in moving (the blind man), either of which might be disruptive.

The honor of the congregation and the solemnity of the service must not be impaired. However, if blind or inappropriately dressed persons can participate without offending the community's sensibilities, then they are permitted to do so. They are linked by the common possibility that they might embarrass themselves before the congregation and disrupt the service (the naked and the blind man are also paired, because of their vulnerabilities, in M. Baba Kamma 8:1). Rabbi Yehudah excludes one blind from birth, who has never seen light and who, to his thinking, is therefore unable to genuinely thank God for light, as is done in the first blessing before the Shema.

TABLE 2. Restrictions on Priests (M. Megillah 4:6)

Who	May Read Torah	Translate	Lead Shema	Priestly Blessing
Katan	yes	yes	no	no
In rags	no	yes	yes	no
Blind	no	yes	yes	no*

*Added in the parallel text in Tanhuma (Warsaw) Toldot 7.

Torah, however, could not be read from one's seat, nor could the priestly blessing be offered except from the *bimah;* hence the person in rags and the blind person are not allowed to participate in these rituals. The *katan* of this mishnah is certainly competent in many ways: he can read and could lead prayers, but permission is not granted to him to lead the Shema since he is not yet subject to this commandment. We have already seen how the priestly blessing (offered in the Temple by those a minimum of twenty years old) retained some of its priestly aura in the synagogue. Not surprisingly, none of the categories of people listed in our mishnah may offer the priestly benediction, because it might disrupt the service: the child would appear scandalously young, the man in rags might show too much of his body, and the blind man is considered blemished and unfit to offer the blessing.

Thus, the role of the priest in this ritual moment that evoked the Temple, and the emphasis on his physical blemishlessness, is preserved in our sources. The assumption that a dangerous aura of holiness surrounds the priest and congregation during the blessing also remains. So only if members of a congregation are not tempted to stare at the priest, and in doing so either expose themselves to God's dangerous presence or lose their concentration and be unable to fully accept the blessing, will he be permitted to offer the blessing. Even 400 years after the destruction of the Temple, the need for priestly blemishlessness continued to hold sway, mitigated in only minor ways.

We have seen the relative strictness with which priests' blemishes were treated. But such imperfections do not bar participation in priestly rewards. We have a few texts that show some tendency to be lenient with regard to priests' ability to eat holy foods when they have blemishes:

> "The priests, the Levites, even all the Tribe of Levi, shall have no (portion nor inheritance with Israel)" (Deuteronomy 18:1): These are included, [because of the verse in] which is said, "Then he shall minister in the name of the Lord his God" (Deuteronomy 18:7). [This verse would include] only able-bodied individuals [since only

blemishless priests may "minister"]; whence [do we learn that this applies also] to blemished ones? From the phrase, "*all* the Tribe of Levi." (Sifre D., Piska 163; see also Sifre D., Piska 208)

Deuteronomy 18:1–8 outlines the emoluments that the priests may consume. The passage ends: "And when a Levite comes from any of your gates out of all Israel, where he sojourns, and he comes in all eagerness to the place which the Lord shall choose; then he shall minister in the name of the Lord his God as all his brothers the Levites do, who stand there before God. They shall have equal portions to eat" (6–8). In context, these verses demonstrate that priestly identity is not specific to place: it is valid in all cities and priests may serve and receive emoluments wherever they go. Because "ministering in God's name" is mentioned here, and because it is assumed that priests with blemishes may consume emoluments, we may conclude that just as a blemished priest may consume holy foods, so might a blemished priest minister in God's name. We might further conclude that such a priest may offer the priestly benediction, since that is the most visible form of ministering in God's name. We should note, however, that the parallel text, Sifre D., Piska 208, explicitly refutes this deduction.

In the Bavli, we find one passage that shows a similar tendency to include priests in the benediction who have blemishes: "Just as one who serves [in the Temple must] not have a blemish, so a priest blessing [the congregation with the priestly blessing] should not have a blemish. Surely he [this priest] was compared with a Nazirite. And why did you compare them for leniency? Compare them [in order to make the law] stringent! These [biblical verses cited here are] supports (*asmachta*) [for laws derived by the] sages [and in such cases we rule] leniently" (B. Taanit 27a). The section in the Torah outlining the priestly benediction (Numbers 6:22–27) immediately follows the section concerning the Nazirite (6:1–21), a person who voluntarily took on extra religious obligations, such as abstaining from haircuts. In the Bavli, this connection is used to draw the conclusion that just as a Nazirite may not be intoxicated, neither may a priest offering the benediction be intoxicated. Then the Gemara submits that just as a Nazirite may be blemished, so too could a priest offering the benediction be blemished. Because the laws concerning blemishes in priests offering the benediction in synagogue are only decrees of the sages and not Toraitic law, one may interpret them leniently. These lines in the Gemara are in Aramaic and do not cite named sources. We may surmise that they are of the Gemara's later, *stammaitic* layer. It is possible that they reflect a subsequent development in thought regarding blemished priests offering the blessing, perhaps demonstrating a more lenient tendency, though the evidence for such an assertion is, obviously, quite sketchy.

The Extension of the Ethos of Priestly Blemishlessness: The Holiness School and Its Interpreters

As we noted earlier, there are five major theological strands in Torah literature: Jahwist (J), Elohist (E), priestly (P), holiness school (HS or simply H), and Deuteronomistic (D). While the priestly stratum concerns the priest and cult, the holiness school is "priestly-popular" (Knohl 1987, 67). The distinction between them is important, for the way HS treats P forms the template for much of rabbinic literature's treatment of the priestly ideal. So, for instance, HS prohibits all labor on Shabbat and the Day of Atonement, thus involving all Israel in their observance, rather than making the commemoration of these days only a Temple matter (Knohl 1987, 104, 74). Milgrom summarizes the differences between P and HS as follows:

> The most important ideological distinction between P and H rests in their contrasting concepts of holiness. For P, spatial holiness is limited to the sanctuary; for H, it is coextensive with the promised land. Holiness of persons is restricted in P to priests and Nazirites; H extends it to all Israel. This expansion follows logically from H's doctrine of spatial holiness: as the land is holy, all who reside in it are to keep it that way. . . . P's doctrine of holiness is static; H's is dynamic.

On the one hand, P constricts holiness to the sanctuary and its priests. P assiduously avoids the term *kadosh* "holy" even in describing the Levites.[15] . . . H, on the other hand, though it concedes that only priests are innately holy (Leviticus 21:7), repeatedly calls on Israel to strive for holiness. (1991, 48)

Given these marked contrasts, we might expect to see differences in the way P and HS regard physical perfection and imperfection.

Obviously, physical perfection was important to P. HS brought that concept into the popular realm by requiring Israelites to respect and treasure all human bodies.[16] Gratuitously inflicting bodily harm would incur severe penalties:

And you shall speak to the children of Israel, saying: Whoever curses his God shall bear his sin. And he that blasphemes the name of the Lord shall surely be put to death; all the congregation shall certainly stone him, likewise the stranger and the homeborn [shall stone him]; when he blasphemes the Name shall he be put to death. And whoever [fatally] smites any person shall surely be put to death. And whoever [fatally] smites a beast shall make it good: life for life. And whoever blemishes his neighbor, as he has done, so shall it be done to him: a break [in a limb] for a break [in a limb], an eye for an eye, a tooth for a tooth: as he has blemished a man, so shall he be blemished. And whoever kills an animal shall make it good and whoever kills a man shall be put to death. You shall have one law, [just] as for the stranger, [so] as for the homeborn for I am the Lord your God. (Leviticus 24:15–22; see also Exodus 21:22–27)

There are many similarities between the priestly attitude toward physical blemishes and H's. First of all, the same word, *mum*, is used here as it was used in Leviticus 21:17 and 22:20 to describe blemishes in priests and sacrificial animals. Here, too, animals and humans are paired, and the death of one is likened to the death of the other. The maiming of a person is paired, in this passage, with the cursing of God. The implication is clear: human bodies are not to be harmed, just as God is not to be defied. Either transgression will yield some separation from the community, up to and including execution. The emphasis on symmetry here is like the priestly emphasis on the symmetry between heaven and earth as they overlap in the cult. Blaspheming God, denying God's existence and singularity, is the equivalent of killing God and it merits death. It is as great a crime as murder in the earthly realm and forms the basis for linking the two. Symmetry is maintained throughout this passage whether what is mirrored is God and human being, human being and animal, Israelite and resident alien. Wounds in animals or humans, or their deaths, then, are like wounds and death to God. The symmetry of heaven and earth applies, according to this passage, to all Israel and to all who partake in its life—Israelites and resident aliens alike—not just to the Temple and the priests.

The link between harming human beings and harming God is brought out in the following midrash:

> How were the Ten Commandments given? Five [commandments] on one tablet and five [commandments] on the other. On one tablet was written: "I am the Lord your God." And opposite it was written, "Do not murder." Scripture tells [by this] that anyone who spills [human] blood it is accounted unto him as if he diminished [the divine] image. [It is like the] parable of a king of flesh and blood who entered a province and [the populace] set up for him portraits and made images of him and struck coins for his [honor]. After a time, they upset his portraits, broke his images, and invalidated his coins and diminished the image of the king. Just so, anyone who sheds blood is counted as one who diminished [the divine] image as it is said, "Who so sheds man's blood by man [shall his blood be shed;] for in the image of God made He man" (Genesis 9:6). (Mechilta Bachodesh 8 on Exodus 20:2)

This midrash echoes quite precisely the principal passage under discussion (Leviticus 24:15–22). It begins by linking the diminution of the divine image and murder and then expands on this theme by showing that harming the divine image in human form by extension harms God. Indeed, this midrash continues in this way, linking sins against humanity to sins against God (e.g., relating idolatry and adultery).

This relationship of humanity and divinity is spelled out by using the example of persons with disabilities. Even though, we may surmise, persons with diminished hearing and seeing were among the most identifiably vulnerable members of society, one is prohibited from taking advantage of their vulnerabilities because such behavior is abhorrent to God: "You shall not curse the deaf nor put a stumbling block before the blind, but you shall fear your God; I am the Lord" (Leviticus 19:14). As maiming or killing a person was equated with cursing God, so righteous treatment of persons with disabilities is equated with the respect of God. The theology of HS is clear: persons and their bodies, that is, life, is to be preserved, protected, and honored throughout the Israelite community. Though absolute perfection may be required only of priests, each person's body, regardless of its state of perfection or imperfection, is to be honored and protected. Even if persons with hearing disabilities would never know you cursed them, and even if persons with seeing disabilities, presumably stumbling anyway, would not recognize that you were the source of yet another stumbling block, *God* knows—and such actions are an offense before the Deity. This is even true when a person is characterized as barely alive, as is the case for a person with hearing disabilities:

"Do not curse a deaf person." I have here nothing but a deaf person. From whence [do I know] to augment [the verse to refer to] every person? Scripture says, "[Judges you shall not curse (*t'kaleil*)] nor a prince of your people shall you revile" (Exodus 22:27). If so, why is it said, "a deaf person"? A deaf person is distinctive in [that he is] alive. This [phrasing of the Torah verse] excludes the dead person who is not alive [and there is no prohibition against insulting the dead].

"And before a blind person do not place a stumbling block." Blind in a thing [i.e., a blind spot]. [If] a man came and said to you, "The daughter of so-and-so, how is she [with regards to eligibility to marry into] the priesthood?" Do not say to him, "She is fit," and she is unfit. If he would take advice from you, do not give advice to him that is not fit for him. . . . This matter [of giving honest advice] is transmitted to the heart [i.e., only known to the heart], as it is said, "And you shall fear the Lord your God, I am the Lord" (Leviticus 19:14). [Because only God knows whether you were sincere or not.] (Sifra, Kedoshim 3:13–14; see also B. Temurah 4a; B. Shevuot 36a)

The distinction between our sources' views of a person with hearing disabilities and of one with visual disabilities is made dramatically in this midrashic exposition. A person with hearing disabilities is invoked to demonstrate that no living person should be cursed precisely because he or she is the lowest form of humanity. Persons with hearing and speaking disabilities are living, but otherwise they are so far outside the realm of everyday communal, or even private, life that they are closer to death than to life. But persons with visual disabilities are not even considered literally. The idea of a stumbling block before the blind is immediately taken as a metaphor for a vulnerability of any sort that impairs a person in a specific way (e.g., lack of good judgment, desire for a specific woman), demonstrating the metaphorical extension of sight to sexuality. Persons with visual disabilities symbolize anyone who functions with some impairment but who nevertheless is a functioning member of society.

We should not think that Sifra's designation of the *cheresh*, the person with hearing and speaking disabilities, is idiosyncratic. Mechilta also considers such a person as little better than a corpse: "But Scripture says: 'You shall not curse the *cheresh*' (Leviticus 19:14). Here Scripture speaks of the most unfortunate people (*b'umlalim sheb'adam*). . . . The common feature of all three of them is that they are 'of your people' and, therefore, you are warned against cursing them" (Mechilta, Tractate Nezikin 5, on Exodus 21:17 and 22:27; see also B. Sanhedrin 66a). We need a knowledge of three scriptural verses for this passage to make sense. Exodus 21:17 mandates against cursing one's parents; Exodus 22:27 states, "You shall not revile the judges, nor curse the ruler of your people"; Leviticus 19:14 prohibits cursing persons with hearing disabilities. The exposition seeks to find the common ground that links these groups, each singled out by the Torah for protection against curses. Mechilta suggests that persons with hearing disabilities are the most unfortunate in the world. Mechilta therefore concludes that the feature they all share is their membership in "your people." While princes and judges may be taken as constituting the top echelons of

Jewish society, the person with hearing and speaking disabilities is unquestionably at the bottom. Hence, in demonstrating the ban on cursing anyone, the exposition of this verse also shows the *cheresh*'s place in society: again at the outermost edges, little better off than a corpse.

The person with visual disabilities, by contrast, is consistently interpreted in the Bavli metaphorically, as a person who could in some sense be tripped up because of a blind spot:

> Rabbi Natan said: From whence [do we know] that a person should not hold out a cup of wine to a Nazirite [who has vowed not to drink wine] nor a limb [taken] from a living animal to [one who has undertaken to observe the] Noachide [commandments, which forbid eating food taken from a living animal]? Scripture says, "You shall not put a stumbling block before the blind" (Leviticus 19:14). (B. Avodah Zarah 6a–6b)

> Rav Yehudah said in Rav['s name]: Anyone who has money and lends it without witnesses transgresses [the precept], "and you shall not put a stumbling block before the blind" (Leviticus 19:14). (B. Baba Metsia 75b)

> Rav Huna tore up silk in the presence of his son Rabbah, saying, "I will go and see whether or not he becomes angry enough [to transgress the precept of honoring his father]." But perhaps he will become angry and then he [Rav Huna] would have violated [the precept], "You shall not put a stumbling block before the blind" (Leviticus 19:14). (B. Kiddushin 32a)

It is immoral to tempt people to commit transgressions; particularly those transgressions which they are prone to commit in the first place. Thus, one may not offer wine to a Nazirite, who has obligated himself to abstain from alcohol. Nor may one offer the limb torn from an animal to one who follows the Noachide commandments, which forbid such food. One should not lend money without witnesses, for this tempts the borrower to forgo repayment. And one should not destroy a valuable object in the presence of others who are short-tempered, just to see if they can control their ire. Note that each of these examples plays on the metaphorical linkage of sight with appetite (usually expressed as sexual appetite, as in the Sifra passage, but here also the appetite for forbidden drink and meat, ill-gotten gain, and flamboyant emotional expression).

When the biblical text is interpreted, persons with visual disabilities are immediately taken out of their literal reference and are used figuratively; persons with hearing disabilities, who appear as frequently, are not. The explanation for this may lie in the relationship of sight and insight, which provides so obvious a metaphor. It may reflect the difference between the perspective of the sages on persons with hearing and speaking disabilities and HS's perspective. This differentiation is logical: if HS is extending P's vision of the body, then all blemishes such as blindness and deafness are equal. The sages, however, promulgating a later culture in which hearing and speaking were crucial, reinterpreted HS's text, marginalizing the person with hearing and speaking disabilities but treating the one with visual disabilities sympathetically, making problems with eyesight a metaphor for ethical or emotional blindness.

Qumran: The Extension of the Ethos of Priestly Blemishlessness

In priestly thought, heaven and earth were linked—navel/Temple to placenta/heaven. According to P, this connection was formed only in the Temple and only the priests needed to be unblemished as they alone ventured into this dangerously holy environment.

Sources from the late Second Commonwealth period (150 B.C.E.–70 C.E.), found in the caves of Khirbet Qumran, show that the priestly view of holiness and of the importance of blemishlessness spread in a different, and more comprehensive, way to the Qumran community. This group upheld the superiority of the priestly class, envisioning an ideal community in which the priesthood reigned (Cohen 1990, 108). The priestly aristocracy would also provide authoritative interpretations of the Torah (Baumgarten 1977, chap. 2).

In the end of days, the Priest-Messiah would reign, even over the King-Messiah (IQSa 2:1ff.; cf. Ezekiel 44:3ff.). Thus, the superiority of the priesthood would be utterly complete, embodying the three "crowns" of Judaism: the priesthood, the kingship, and the sages' society.

It is not surprising that a community so connected to the priestly model would adapt priestly ideals about the body to its local practices. The Qumran community took the core priestly concepts—the symmetry of heaven and earth, and the congregation of angels that corresponds to the earthly congregation—and applied them *outside* the Temple to *everyone* in the community, not just to those of priestly stock. The Qumranites may have instituted this innovation because they rejected the priestly establishment of the Hasmoneans, who they felt defiled the Temple. Thus, in their community itself they met God, as if in the Temple, so that ideas of physical perfection applied to all persons. For them, even a blemishless body was not considered fit enough, as any corporeality, through which one might be contaminated by impurity or sin, represented a state of separation from God. David Flusser (1989, 54–55), in his examination of the Thanksgiving Hymns of Qumran, notes that these works express a kind of disgust with the body in general, a belief "that the entire man, body and soul, existed within the sphere of revulsion, from which one should recoil. . . . The flesh was, then, unredeemed man, and the spirit given to the elect alone was what brought them out of impurity and sin." The Qumranites augmented the priestly concept of blemishlessness to include not only outward physical appearance but also mental and physical ability as criteria for full membership in the community.

We can establish the continuity between priestly attitudes toward persons with blemishes or disabilities and those found in the scrolls by looking at the War Rule (IQM, 4QM). This work, dated sometime between 160 B.C.E and the beginning of the first century C.E., echoes quite closely priestly requirements for participation in the cult and Toraitic injunctions about who ought to go to battle in the final war against Darkness (Vermes 1987, 104).

No boy or woman shall enter their camps, from the time they leave Jerusalem and march out to war until they return. No man who is lame, or blind, or crippled, or afflicted with a lasting bodily blemish, or smitten with a bodily impurity, none of these shall march out to war with them. They shall all be freely enlisted for war, perfect in spirit and body and prepared for the Day of Vengeance. And no man shall go down with them on the day of battle who is impure because of his "fount," for the holy angels shall be with their hosts. (War Rule IQM, 4QM, VII)

The war camp, in this passage, is likened to the biblical camp, which itself had certain similarities to the Temple. The camp was certainly no place for those who did not have the authority to act decisively on their own (women and children). The condition that everyone in the camp be ritually pure and blemishless is reminiscent of rules regarding the camp and the Temple, respectively. The camp is to have no ritually impure persons in it because God dwells in it (Numbers 5:1–4). The requirement of a "perfect spirit" is a corollary to mandates (Deuteronomy 20:1–9) that soldiers have good motivations when entering the army. This passage seems to conform closely to priestly precedent demanding blemishlessness in participants.

Other texts from Qumran, however, expand on the priestly ideas of the Torah. For example, within the whole community, not just in the priestly caste, persons with disabilities may play only a limited role. The Damascus Document, which contains commandments for the life of the community, excludes persons with disabilities (Nickelsburg 1981, 123): "No madman, or lunatic, or simpleton, or fool, no blind man, or maimed, or lame, or deaf man, and no minor, shall enter into the Community, for the Angels of Holiness are with them [the congregation]" (Damascus Rule 15). We see here an enlargement of the priestly ideal expressed in P. There, neither mental disabilities nor disabilities of hearing were considered. Here, mental and hearing disabilities are given equal weight with physical disabilities. And these restrictions now apply to all community members. Everyone must be basically blemishless: fully functional and sensate.

In our next passage, priestly ideas are extended in a different direction than they are in HS, where a reverence for all life is expressed. Here, we find an emphasis on competence. This document of the mid–first century B.C.E. outlines the community's rules in the last days and during the messianic war that was expected to come at the end of time. The eschatological legislation covers two areas: the duties of every citizen in the future congregation of all Israel and the formal assembly of the leading elite in the messianic age.

> When a man is advanced in years, he shall be given a duty in the [ser]-vice of the congregation in proportion to his strength.
> No simpleton shall be chosen to hold office in the congregation of Israel with regard to lawsuits or judgment, nor carry any responsibility in the congregation. Nor shall he hold any office in the war destined to vanquish the nations; his family shall merely inscribe him in the army register and he shall do his service in task-work in proportion to his capacity. (Messianic Rule IQSa I)

This passage expresses an openness to accepting persons in accordance with their abilities. The ban on a simpleton holding office or adjudicating cases is common sense: one needs a person of discernment to try cases and shoulder other responsibilities. And while excluded from bearing arms, persons with mental disabilities could provide other services to the community and army.

The assembly that will rule over the congregation at the end of time is subject to priestly concepts of blemishlessness, now broadened to include general mental and sensory competence:

> And no man smitten with any human uncleanness shall enter the assembly of God; no man smitten with any of them shall be confirmed in his office in the congregation. No man smitten in his flesh, or paralyzed in his feet or hands, or lame, or blind, or deaf, or mute, or smitten in his flesh with a visible blemish; no old and tottery man unable to stay still in the midst of the congregation of the men of renown, for the Angels of Holiness are [with] their [congregation]. Should [one] of them have something to say in to the Council of Holiness, let [him] be questioned privately; but let him not enter among [the congregation] for he is smitten. (Messianic Rule IQSa, II)

Though persons with any blemish are ineligible to enter this assembly, their words can still be heard. It is only their flawed appearance or, perhaps, irregular demeanor that defiles or offends the angels who are present, just as was the case with the priests in the Temple. A far later text may serve to demonstrate what attributes of human beings might be unlike, and hence offensive or defiling, to angels: "[With regard to] three [things], they are like the ministering angels: they have understanding (*da'at*) like the ministering angels; and they walk erect like the ministering angels; and they can talk in the holy tongue [Hebrew] like the ministering angels. [With regard to] three [things], they are like animals: they eat and drink like animals, they propagate like animals, and they relieve themselves like animals" (B. Hagigah 16a). Naturally, an angel would be blemishless in intellect (*da'at*) and body. So this description of angels corresponds well with the list of exclusions in our present text.

From these examples, we see how priestly ideas about blemishes and disabilities were extended to include everyone in the Qumran community, regardless of their lineage. For the Qumranites, blood lines became less important as priestly rules and concepts were applied to all persons, regardless of their pedigree. This gradual progression in the extension of P's vision might also buttress Eilberg-Schwartz's (1990, 211) contention that the Essene community was balanced between priestly and rabbinic modes of thought in its treatment of the role intention played in classifying things ritually pure or impure.

Hagigah: The Extension of the Priestly Outlook into Rabbinic Literature

Unlike the Qumran community, which did not recognize the priestly establishment, the sages clearly legitimated a distinctive role for priests, even after the Temple's destruction. But the sages' culture also manifests an extension of the priestly ideal that encompassed lay Jews. Three times a year, Israelites were to come to the Temple and appear: "Three times a year shall all your males appear (*yeira'eih*) before the Lord your God in the place which He shall choose [i.e., the Temple]; in the feast of unleavened bread, and in the feast of weeks, and in the feast of booths" (Deuteronomy 16:16; see also Exodus 23:14–17). Though women, slaves, and minors (and presumably others) came to Jerusalem during the festivals (Deuteronomy 16:11, 14), only the males were required to appear with an offering. This commandment to appear thrice yearly at the Temple is called *r'ayon*. It is in the context of this mitzvah (commandment) that we find the priestly concept of physical perfection extended to the entire Israelite community.

The list of those exempt from performing this commandment is extraordinary in its completeness. It effectively eliminates anyone who is not a blemishless, full-grown male.

> All are obligated to appear [at the Temple on the festivals] except a *cheresh, shoteh v'katan*, a hermaphrodite or an androgyne or women and slaves who have not been freed or the lame [man] or the blind [man] or the sick [man] or the old [man], or the one who cannot go up [to the Temple Mount] on his feet. Who is [considered] a *katan*? Anyone who cannot ride upon his father's shoulders and go up from Jerusalem to the Temple Mount. This is the opinion of the School of Shammai. But the School of Hillel says, "Anyone who is unable to hold his father's hand and go up from Jerusalem to the Temple Mount, as it is written, 'Three pilgrimages'"[17] (Exodus 23:14). (M. Hagigah 1:1)

The makeup of the congregation at these moments surely had symbolic significance, as it does in other cultures:

> Calendrical rites . . . almost always refer to large groups and quite often embrace whole societies. Often, too, they are performed at well-delineated points in the annual productive cycle, and attest to the passage from scarcity to plenty (as at first fruits or harvest festivals) or from plenty to scarcity (as when the hardships of winter are anticipated and magically warded against). To these also one should add all *rites de passage*, which accompany any change of a collective sort from one state to another, as when a whole tribe goes to war, or a large local community performs a ritual to reverse the effects of famine, drought, or plague. Life-crisis rites and rituals of induction into

office are almost always rites of status elevation; calendrical rites and rites of group crisis may sometimes be rites of status reversal. At such a moment, when the entire community goes through a liminal, i.e., intrastructural, phase, apparently only the best representatives of the group participate in the ritual which reinforces the society's structure. (Turner 1969, 168)

The festivals of Pesach, Shavuot, and Sukkot are intimately linked to the agricultural cycle of harvesting and planting. It is on these holidays that the Israelites described in M. Hagigah 1:1 must appear in the Temple with an offering. If, at these moments, God is inspecting the troops, as it were, and determining if they were worthy of further support and agricultural bounty, and if the priests were considered the finest representatives of the Jewish people, then it is logical that at such a moment of transition, all Israelites who appeared at the Temple for God's inspection would be required to be as close to the priestly ideal as possible.[18]

Sifre D. brings out God's close connection with, and scrutiny of, the Jewish people at these three times of the year: "[Three times a year shall all your males appear] before [*et p'nei*] the Lord your God [in the place which he will choose] (Deuteronomy 16:16). If you do all that is said about [this] matter [of the appearance offering] I will turn (*poneh*) from all my affairs [of business] and I will occupy Myself only with you" (Sifre D. 143). The wording of the biblical verse is somewhat strange. Normally, one would expect it to say *lifnei*, "before God." Sifre D. interprets the anomalous words, *et p'nei*, to mean something special. God will actually turn (the words *p'nei*, "face," and *poneh*, "turn," are related) to the people of Israel at these moments and forsake all other matters to do so. God's intense scrutiny suggested by this interpretation would certainly justify the exclusion of all but "the best representatives of the group."

The Tosefta to Hagigah 1:1 adds another category of persons to the Mishnah's list of persons exempt from this mitzvah as well as further explaining its categories:

> 1. The unclean [person] is exempt from [the requirement of making] an appearance, as it is said, "And you will come there and you will

bring there" (Deuteronomy 12:6). [The requirement applies] to one who is suitable to come into the [Temple] courtyard, [which] excludes an unclean person, who is not suitable to come into the [Temple] courtyard.

2. Yohanan ben Rahavai said in the name of R. Yehudah, "Also the blind person [is exempt from the requirement of making an appearance], as it is said, 'will see' (Exodus 23:17), excluding a blind person." Rabbi [Yehudah HaNasi] retorted to the opinion of Yohanan ben Rahavai [reading, "will appear," not "will see"]. [The] sages inclined toward favoring the opinion of R. Yehudah [i.e., favoring the reading, "will see"].[19]

3. "And Hannah did not go up" (1 Samuel 1:22). (T. Hagigah 1:1)

Section 1 adds to the exemptions provided in M. Hagigah 1:1 by releasing a person in a state of ritual impurity from the obligation to appear at the Temple on the festivals. It brings scriptural support from Deuteronomy 12:6, which follows a description of how all the local altars are to be closed and mandates that all offerings are to be brought to the Temple in Jerusalem (12:1–5). This is a completely logical extension of priestly categories of fitness. A priest cannot officiate, nor can a lay Israelite offer a sacrifice, while tainted with ritual impurity.

Section 2 discusses a blind person's obligation to make an appearance at the Temple based on differing readings of this verse: "Three times in the year all your males shall be seen (*yeira'eh*) [or "see," *yir'eh*] before the Lord God" (Exodus 23:17). The word *yud-reish-aleph-hey* can be vocalized *yireh*, "will see," or *yeira'eh*, "will be seen." If it is taken to be the former, those who do not see need not appear. If the word is given the latter meaning, then one's vision has no bearing on the question. The reading found in the Torah obligates a blind person to appear.

Finally, section 3 simply cites the verse from 1 Samuel 1:22, which follows the birth of Samuel: "And the man Elkanah, and all his house, went up to offer unto the Lord the yearly sacrifice, and his vow. But Hannah went not up; for she said unto her husband: 'Until the child be weaned, when I will bring him, that he may appear (*v'nir'ah*) before the Lord, and there abide forever'" (1 Samuel 1:21–

22). From this passage, it would appear that a child who was not yet weaned was not old enough to bring along to an altar when one was offering sacrifices. Obviously, the sacrifice referred to here cannot be at the Temple in Jerusalem, for the First Temple was built by Solomon, son of David, and David is anointed by Samuel. However, Shiloh was a precursor of the Temple and had the ark. Lieberman (1992, ad loc.) notes that this sentence about Hannah more precisely defines the *katan* in the School of Hillel's ruling in Mishnah 1:1. The School of Hillel, he says, brings proof from this scriptural passage that Samuel did not go up to Jerusalem even though he could have ridden on his father's shoulders, and according to the School of Shammai, such a child is obligated to appear.

In its discussion of the obligation to appear at the Temple on the festivals, *r'ayon*, the Yerushalmi provides a rationale for the various exclusions:

> The lame: Since it is written, "pilgrim-festival [*r'galim*, 'feet,' and they cannot walk on theirs]."
> The sick: Since it is written, "And you will rejoice" (Deuteronomy 16:14).
> The old: Since it is written, "*r'galim*" [and the aged cannot come by foot].
> Said R. Yose, "The intent of both exclusions is to impose a lenient ruling (*tarteihon l'kula*). If one can rejoice [being in good health] but he cannot walk, I cite in his regard the reference of Scripture to 'pilgrim festivals.' If he can walk but cannot rejoice [being sick] I cite concerning him the reference of Scripture to 'rejoicing.'" [Both then need not make the trip.] (Y. Hagigah 1:1, 76a)

This is an innovation. Until now, our sources have excluded groups of persons from the obligation to perform this mitzvah without giving a clear reason. Here, the Yerushalmi explicitly labels its motivation as leniency: the journey is arduous and those who are lame, sick, or old need not make it. While the Yerushalmi adds this new dimension, the ruling still serves to uphold the priestly standard of perfection extended to lay Israelites at these three moments of the year.

Another way that the Yerushalmi connects priestly values to the appearance of lay Israelites at the thrice-yearly appearance at the Temple is by emphasizing visible blemishes that disqualify potential participants. A discussion of whether a person with polyps or blisters may be part of the "appearance" of all Israel concludes: "Persons afflicted with blisters or polyps, even though [such] are not fit to come with all Israel, they are fit to come by themselves [by way of contrast]. A person in a state of ritual impurity is fit neither to come by himself [to the Temple] nor [to come] with all Israel" (Y. Hagigah 1:1, 76a). This judgment nicely summarizes the role that temporary blemishes play in disqualifying a person from the obligation to appear. No person in a state of ritual impurity was ever qualified to enter the Temple, whether as part of a group or as an individual making an offering. A person with temporary skin problems might come and offer a private sacrifice but was *not* fit to participate in the group representing all Israel. This ruling indicates that the criteria applied to *r'ayon* were closer to priestly rules about the body and the perfection required of it than to what was normally required of lay Israelites in the Temple environment.

The Yerushalmi's definition of the *shoteh*, who is grouped with the *cheresh* and *katan*, is remarkably brief and does nothing to mitigate the *shoteh*'s stigmatized position with regard to the obligation to appear at the Temple for festivals three times a year (or to do any mitzvot, for that matter): "A *shoteh*: Said R. Elazar, 'It was clearly demonstrated to you (*hareita lada'at*)' (Deuteronomy 4:35) [thus excluding those to whom knowledge (*da'at*) is inaccessible]" (Y. Hagigah 1:1, 76a). When the Yerushalmi has no argument with the Mishnah, it may simply supply scriptural proof for the Mishnah's ruling. Thus the term *shoteh* here is merely linked to a verse from the Torah, which precedes a passage detailing the wonders that were displayed in Egypt and at Sinai: "To you it was shown, that you might know that the Lord, He is God; there is none else beside Him" (Deuteronomy 4:35). Since the *shoteh* is deemed incapable of knowing, he is not considered part of the adjuration that finishes the passage: "And you shall keep His statutes and His commandments, which I command you this day, that it may go well with you, and with your children after you, and that you may prolong your days upon the land, which the Lord your God gives you forever" (4:40). The Yerushalmi links text and category with no attempt to explore the category *shoteh* or delve into the practical limitations a *shoteh* might face on a trip to Jerusalem. The *shoteh* is stigmatized, discredited; because the Yerushalmi accepts this designation, there is no need for further discussion of the matter.

In its long commentary to this mishnah, the Bavli examines the following issues:

liminal individuals: half slaves, those blind in one eye
the *cheresh*
the lame
the merit of congregating for the purpose of Torah study
the *shoteh*
the hermaphrodite and the androgyne
women and slaves
the lame, blind, sick, aged, uncircumcised, and impure
Torah verses that make sages weep
what makes God unhappy and the great lengths to which the
    sages would go to study Torah
the *katan*
comparison of various sacrificial offerings

For those appearing at the Temple, physical perfection was required. The sages also mandated an inner commandment associated with the festivals—the obligation to rejoice, which does not require physical perfection but only *da'at*, cognition: "Likewise it is also taught: All are obligated to appear [at the Temple] and to rejoice except a *cheresh* who can speak but not hear, [or] hear but not speak, who is exempt from appearing. But even though he is exempt from appearing (3a) he is obligated to rejoice. But [a *cheresh*] who can neither hear nor speak and the *shoteh v'katan* are exempt even from [the obligation of] rejoicing, since they are exempt from all the precepts stated in the Torah" (B. Hagigah 2b–3a). The Bavli here divides the act of *r'ayon* into two parts: (1) Appearing, which requires physical perfection; any disability, even merely being unable to speak or hear, which normally does not constitute a problem (M. Terumot 1:2), causes one to be exempt from this precept. (2) Rejoicing, which only requires *da'at* (cognition). These components are summarized in table 3.

This short passage demonstrates both the different emphases of the priests' and sages' cultures and how the sages dealt with priestly constructs. The priests' culture requires physical perfection while the sages' culture requires *da'at*. Moreover, the sages do not overrule the priestly structure; indeed, they preserve it. However, they encompass it with a layer of their own worldview. The priestly views form the core around which the sages' system is built and grows.

The Bavli examines the categories that the Mishnah lays out, drawing on T. Hagigah and halakhic midrashim and displaying many similarities to the Yerushalmi. But sections 4, 9, and 10—that is, aggadic material thematically related to the halakhic discussion—have no parallels in Tosefta's and the Yerushalmi's considerations of M. Hagigah 1:1. These aggadic sections of the Bavli's commentary point to an association between the duty to appear at the Temple (with the arduous journey and high standards required of participants) and the enterprise of Torah study. The linkage is far from accidental: both involve a difficult process whereby one eventually appears before God. In addition, in Babylonia, lay people met in periodic study sessions called *kallot*, to which they would journey, much as pilgrims periodically went to the Temple. Furthermore, the Bavli was redacted at a certain remove, in time and space, from the

TABLE 3. The Bavli's Analysis of *R'ayon*

	Obligation to Appear	Obligation to Rejoice
Deaf only	o	+
Mute only	o	+
Cheresh, shoteh, katan	o	o

o = no obligation; + = obligation exists

Temple; it seems natural that the vacuum left by its physical destruction would come to be filled with the "Temple" of Torah study.

One story in this long passage well illustrates in what ways Torah study and *r'ayon* are similar and different. *R'ayon* demands that only the fittest representatives be present, and the Bavli certainly upholds these stringent priestly requirements. For instance, it exempts even the person who is deaf only in one ear from appearing, whereas the Yerushalmi obligates such a person to appear (B. Hagigah 3a; Y. Hagigah 1:1, 76a). And the sages in their assemblies of study are portrayed as like the priests, deciding issues of ritual impurity just as the priests declared who was leprous and who was not: "'Masters of assemblies' (Ecclesiastes 12:11). These are the students of the wise who sit in assembly [after] assembly and occupy themselves with the Torah, these declaring [an item] ritually impure and these declaring [an item] ritually pure, these prohibiting and these permitting, some disqualifying and others declaring fit" (B. Hagigah 3b). What is remarkable in this passage is the carte blanche given to the sages to disagree with each other and the assurance given to the student, directly following this description of the sages, that this multiplicity of opinions is good and should be relished. Torah study sessions are similar to the pilgrimage festivals in that an elite group of experts decides who among those gathered is fit and who is not. However, unlike the considerable uniformity that the priestly criteria would have yielded—blemishless, male, free, full-grown—here we see the sages legitimately disagreeing about all sorts of issues of Jewish law.

This contrast between uniform blemishlessness in the Temple and variety in the study sessions is seen in yet another commentary from the Bavli on this mishnah:

> Behold there were two mute men in Rabbi [Yehudah HaNasi's] neighborhood, sons of the daughter of Rabbi Yohanan ben Gudgada (and [some] say, [they were] sons of the sister of Rabbi Yohanan ben Gudgada), who would go in to the House of Study whenever Rabbi [Yehudah HaNasi] entered [there] and they would sit before him [and the other sages] and they would nod their heads and move their lips.

And Rabbi [Yehudah HaNasi] prayed for them and they were healed, and it turned out that they knew Halakhah (i.e., Mishnah), Sifra, Sifre, and the whole Talmud! (B. Hagigah 3a)[20]

Ordinarily, a person who is mute would be ineligible to study the sages' wisdom, just as a blemished priest would be unfit for the Temple service. The sages' method of pedagogy was, to a great degree, oral; hence the abilities to speak and hear were crucial prerequisites for taking part in study sessions. Yet, in this story, we find that these men were allowed to participate in study sessions, even though they were unable to speak. This is where the parallel with priestly concepts stops: a priest in a state of ritual impurity or with a physical defect would never be allowed to officiate in the cult. But here, we find that two persons who are truly "disabled" (from the sages' point of view) are allowed to study and turn out to be competent to do so.

While the priests adhered to a relatively inflexible ethic of blemishlessness, the sages, according to this legend, had a place in their system of thought for the severely disabled. The Bavli maintains the rigid priestly standards, when applicable, but surrounds them with a more inclusive ethic regarding Torah study. And Torah study becomes the sages' new locus in which to meet God after the Temple is destroyed.

Valuation of Persons

Another way that lay Israelites might interact with the cult and be subject in part to the priests' ethic of "blemishlessness" was through their monetary value, were it vowed to the cult. In earliest times, one could pledge one's life to the cult, as Hannah (1 Samuel 1) promised that her son would serve at Shilo. Later, one could pledge the value of one's life to the cult, thereby maintaining a connection with the ancient ethos of personal sacrifice and dedication and also helping to maintain the cult financially. Leviticus 27:1–7 outlines the value of any individual, the worth of whose life has been dedicated to the sanctuary, as declared by God to Moses. It is determined according to gender and age, regardless of the person's physical condition, as follows:

SHEKELS	PERSON
50	male, 20–60
30	woman, 20–60
20	male, 5–20
15	male, over 60
10	female, 5–20
10	female, over 60
5	male, one month–5 years
3	female, one month–5 years

This valuation is fixed. However, if a person has vowed to pay the (slave) market value of a person to the sanctuary, he must pay the going rate, in which case physical and mental condition would obviously affect the price, which would vary accordingly.

The *cheresh, shoteh v'katan* cannot participate actively in this system of valuation and vowing because it requires *da'at:* in this case, the separation of money for a certain purpose.

> All [persons] are fit to evaluate or to be made the subjects of valuation, are fit to vow [another's worth] or have their worth vowed: priests and Levites and [lay] Israelites, women and slaves. A hermaphrodite or an androgyne are fit to vow [another's worth], or to have their worth vowed, and are fit to evaluate, but they are not to be made the subjects of valuation, for the subject of valuation may be only a person definitely male or definitely female. The *cheresh, shoteh v'katan* are fit to have their worth vowed or be made the subject of valuation, but they are not fit to make either a vow [of another's worth] or to evaluate, because they have no *da'at*. (M. Arakhin 1:1; see also Sifra Behukotai 8: Parshata 3)

Men, women, and slaves may participate fully in this system, both vowing another's worth and being the object of a vow. A hermaphrodite, one with characteristics of both genders, and an androgyne, one with characteristics of neither gender, are not allowed to be the object of such a vow since the whole Torah system of valuations requires clear gender distinctions. The *cheresh, shoteh v'katan* may be the object of a vow but cannot make one, since making a vow requires *da'at*. Table 4 summarizes who may perform what function or be the object of a given function.

It is easy to see that the *cheresh, shoteh v'katan* may function in this system only in a passive way. Their worth may be evaluated or vowed (as an animal's value might be vowed; see Leviticus 27:9–13), but they may neither vow nor evaluate. We also see that clear gender is as crucial as functioning *da'at* for participation in this aspect of the cult's operation. Both blemishlessness, in terms of gender, and *da'at* are necessary for full participation in the Torah's system. No moderation of that ethic is offered.

Revelation, Resurrection, and the Extension of Priestly Perfection

Until now, we have witnessed the need for a priest to be blemishless and noted how this ethic was extended to include lay Israelites. In

TABLE 4. Participation in Valuation and Vows

	Valuation (Leviticus system)		Vow (market value)	
	Active Role	Passive Role	Active Role	Passive Role
Priests	+	+	+	+
Levites	+	+	+	+
Israelites	+	+	+	+
Women	+	+	+	+
Slaves	+	+	+	+
Hermaphrodites	+	o	+	+
Androgynes	+	o	+	+
Cheresh	o	+	o	+
Shoteh	o	+	o	+
Katan	o	+	o	+

+ = may participate; o = may not participate

the midrash collections, we can see how this principle was made to apply to the most potent meeting between God and Israel: the revelation at Sinai. Unlike in the Tabernacle in the wilderness, or the Temple in Jerusalem, at Sinai the entire people witnessed God's presence and holiness.

The Torah text itself gives evidence of the extension of the priestly notion of perfection to all Israel at that moment. Just before preparations are made to receive the covenant at Sinai, God transmits the following message to the Israelites: "Now, if you will truly obey My voice and keep My covenant you will be My treasured possession from among all the peoples. For all the earth is Mine, and [yet] you shall be kingdom of priests (*mamlekhet kohanim*) and a holy nation" (Exodus 19:5–6). Here, it is clear: entering into this covenant with God makes Israelites, in some sense, priests.

The compositors of the midrash collections expound on this concept in detail, assuming that at such a moment all Israel, like the priests, must have been blemishless, else they never would have survived the contact with God:

> Another interpretation: ["And all the people saw the thunder and the lightening and the sound of the shofar" (Exodus 20:15).] This is to [let you] know the praiseworthiness of Israel, for when they all stood before Mount Sinai to receive the Torah, [Scripture] says there were no blind ones among them. For it is said: "And *all* the people *saw*." It [also] tells that there were no mute ones among them, as it is said: "And *all* the people *answered* together" (Exodus 19:8). And it [also] teaches that there were no deaf ones among them, as it is said: "All that the Lord has spoken will we do and *listen to*" (Exodus 24:7). And it [also] teaches that there were no lame ones among them, as it is said: "And they *stood* at the nether part of the mount" (Exodus 19:17) And it also teaches that there were no ignorant ones (*tipshim*) among them. For it is said: "You have been shown to *understand* (*lada'at*)" (Deuteronomy 4:35). (Mechilta, Tractate Bachodesh 9, on Exodus 20:15; see also Mechilta, Tractate Bachodesh 3, on Exodus 19:11)[21]

Through the close reading of the biblical verse, the midrash shows how well the Israelites conformed to the priestly, and rabbinic, ideals of perfection. Not only were the Israelites blemishless in ways that were important in the priestly model, that is, neither blind nor lame, but they were also blemishless in ways that were particularly important to the sages, that is, able to understand, hear, and speak. This viewpoint is expressed not only in a halakhic midrash collection (Mechilta) but also in an aggadic one: "In the moment when Israel stood on Mount Sinai and said, 'All that the Lord has spoken we will do and obey' (Exodus 24:7), in that moment there were among them neither persons with issue nor lepers [i.e., ritually impure persons], neither lame nor blind, neither mute nor deaf nor mentally disabled persons (*shotim*). About that moment [Scripture] says, 'You are all fair my beloved and there is no defect (*mum*) in you' (Song of Songs 4:7)" (Leviticus Rabbah Metsora 18:4; see also Midrash Song of Songs Rabbah 4:7 ¶1). Here, the priestly criteria are laid out even more explicitly: the concern with ritual impurity has no explicit Toraitic basis in the verse under discussion, yet these categories are included as ones that would, naturally, disqualify anyone from participation in a "priestly" activity.

Similarly, God's ultimate redemption and the resurrection of the dead will involve the healing of Israel's physical wounds, just as her political and religious wounds will be healed as she is restored to wholeness. This restoration is envisioned as the healing of individual Israelites from their disabilities at the moment of redemption in numerous prophetic visions: "Is it not yet a very little while, and Lebanon shall be turned into a fruitful field, and the fruitful field shall be considered a forest? And on that day shall the deaf hear the words of a book, and out of obscurity and darkness the eyes of the blind shall see. The meek also shall increase their joy in the Lord and the poorest among men shall rejoice in the Holy One of Israel" (Isaiah 29:17–19; see also Isaiah 35:3–6; Jeremiah 31:7–9; Micah 4:6–8; Zephaniah 3:19–20). Here individual Israelites become a metaphor for Israel as a whole, and their individual healing is a symptom, or an outcome, of the generalized redemption at hand. As John McKenzie (1968, 11) suggests, healing is a "deliverance from guilt" and from the judgment of which their ills were a sign. They will, then, appear blemishless as priests.

The midrash elaborates on how this healing will take place and what it will mean:

> "And he sent Yehudah before him unto Joseph" (Genesis 46:28). It is written, "the wolf and the lamb shall feed together and the lion shall eat straw like the ox [and dust shall be the serpent's food. They shall not hurt nor destroy in all my holy mountain, says the Lord]" (Isaiah 65:25). Come and see how all whom the Holy One, blessed be He, has smitten in this world He will heal in the future that is to come. The blind will be healed, as it says, "Then the eyes of the blind shall be opened" (Isaiah 35:5); the lame shall be healed: "Then shall the lame man leap as a hart" (Isaiah 35:6); the mute shall be healed: "And the tongue of the mute shall sing" (Isaiah 35:6). And just as a person goes [out from this world] so shall he enter [into the next]: If he goes [out] blind, he will come back blind. If he goes [out] deaf, he will return deaf. If he goes [out] mute, he will return mute; if he goes [out] lame, he will return lame. . . .
>
> Why does a person return as he went? So that [people] should not say: After they died God healed them and then brought them back! Apparently these are not the same [people who died,] but others. The Holy One blessed be He said, "If so, let them rise as they went [to the grave] and after [the resurrection] I will heal them. Why so? [That you may know that . . .] before Me there was no God formed, neither shall any be after Me" (Isaiah 43:10). And I shall heal them.
>
> And even the animals will be healed, as it is said, "the wolf and the lamb shall feed together." (Genesis Rabbah, Vayigash 95:1; see also Exodus Rabbah, Shmot 5:5; Kohelet Rabbah on Ecclesiastes 1:4 ¶2)

Near the end of his narrative, Joseph is reunited with his father; Jacob sends Yehudah before him to Joseph. Yehudah was the brother who had suggested selling Joseph into slavery (Genesis 37:26–27), so for him and Joseph to get along amicably, as Genesis 46:28 suggests, is as remarkable as peace between a lamb and a wolf. This leads the exposition to the topic of God's ultimate act of redemption. At that time, disabled persons will be resurrected with their disabilities, in order to prove God's ability to resurrect those who died, and will then be miraculously cured. Just as in the Temple, through their connection with God, both human beings and animals in the end will be perfectly blemishless, as befits creatures in the presence of the Deity.

From Priest to Judge to Witness

One last example of the way the priestly ideal was extended to the sages' model of Judaism may show how pervasive this paradigm was. Priests functioned outside the cult as well as inside it. One of their main duties was to diagnose leprosy, which necessarily called for good eyesight in the priest. This requirement was confirmed by the Mishnah: "A priest blind in one of his eyes or whose sight is dim may not inspect [for] leprosy [symptoms], as it is said, 'as far as appears to the priest' (Leviticus 13:12). Windows in a dark house may not be opened up to inspect its leprosy [symptoms]" (M. Negaim 2:3). The correct determination of sources of uncleanness, an issue of great concern to the priestly class, was too important to allow for the possibility of any mistakes in its assessment. The emphasis on seeing and appearance in these passages is quite remarkable. Not only must the priest have a blemishless appearance, but the way things appear to him is crucial. The relationship between the two is underscored here: a priest is the one who is most disadvantaged if he becomes ritually impure; thus, he has the most at stake when diagnosing impurities and will do it most reliably. Even so, this mishnah is rather stringent; a person with one eye is, after all, sighted. This ruling probably derives from the wording of the verse in Leviticus 13:12, translated word for word: "for all the appearance in the *eyes* of the priest." The use of the plural makes it logical to interpret the verse as meaning that the (singular) priest must have two eyes (this reading is born out in Sifra Tazria 4:4).

The Qumran scrolls followed the Torah's mandate (Leviticus 13:1–14:57) that the diagnosis of leprosy must be done by a person of priestly lineage, going so far as to hold to the requirement even if that priest seems mentally incapable of performing the task adequately: "But should there be a case of applying the law of leprosy to a man, then the Priest shall come and shall stand in the camp and the Guardian shall instruct him in the exact interpretation of the Law. Even if the Priest is a simpleton, it is he who shall lock up (the leper); for theirs is the judgment" (Damascus Rule 13; see also Sifra Parshat Tazria, Parshat Nega'im 1:9). Thus even a priest who does not possess sufficient cognitive ability is still the one to proclaim the judgment of leprosy. The scroll allows a "guardian" to instruct the priest and the halakhic midrash on Leviticus, Sifra, reiterates this rule, stating that if the priest is a *shoteh*—that is, mentally ill or disabled— a sage (*hakham sheb'Yisrael*) makes the diagnosis and then has the priest declare it. Perhaps both the Qumran community and the sages felt that a priest's mental insufficiency, a nonvisible defect, could be remedied by the guidance of another appropriate authority because the Torah is silent on the subject, thus granting them space for their own solutions.

Tosefta extends the priestly requirement for sightedness to a wide variety of situations that necessitate judgment:

> A person who was blinded in one of his eyes is not permitted to judge, as it is said, "with the entire vision of the eyes of the Priest" (Leviticus 13:12). And [Scripture] says, "And by their word every dispute and every plague shall be [decided]" (Deuteronomy 21:5). [Scripture] links disputes to plagues. Just as plagues [are decided in accord with] the entire vision of the priest, so too disputes [are settled in accord with] the entire vision of the eyes of the priests. (T. Negaim 1:7; see also Sifra Parshat Tazria, Parshat Nega'im 1:9)

Here, the priest is given jurisdiction over all sorts of disputes, not just questions of ritual impurity. Diagnosing leprosy and examining witnesses in a court case require some of the same qualities: participants' trust in the adjudicator, a search for the truth, and a careful consideration of the evidence. In whatever context priests are active, it is reasonable to expect that their blemishlessness will be valued, as it was important in their primary venue of operation, the Temple.

This valuation of blemishlessness in the courts is seen in the criteria for witnesses in certain kinds of legal cases. This scenario begins with a biblical text of notable harshness:

> If a man have a stubborn and rebellious son who does not listen to his father's voice or to his mother's voice, and they shall chasten him and he [still] will not listen to them. [Then] his father and his mother will lay hold of him and take him out to the elders of his city and to the gate of his place. And they shall say to the elders of his city, "This, our son, is stubborn and rebellious and will not listen to our voice. He is a glutton and a drunkard." And all the people of his city shall stone him with stones and he shall die. And you shall put out evil from among you and all Israel shall hear [of it] and fear. (Deuteronomy 21:18–21)

The sages, with their reluctance to apply the death penalty, interpret this passage in a way that restricts the parents' ability to bear witness against their son.[22]

> If one of them [the parents of a stubborn, rebellious son] had a maimed hand, or was lame, or was blind, or was mute or was deaf, he [their son] cannot be made a stubborn and rebellious son. For it is said, "And his father and his mother shall lay hold of him" (Deuteronomy 21:19) and [those] with maimed hands cannot [do so]. "And bring him out" (21:19) and [those who are] lame cannot [do so]. "And they shall say" (21:20) and [those who are] mute cannot [do so]. "This, our son" (21:20) and [those who are] blind cannot [do so because the phrase implies they are pointing to the son]. "He does not hearken to our voice" (21:20) and [those who are] deaf cannot [hear whether their son has listened to them or not]. (M. Sanhredin 8:4; see also Sifre D. Piska 219)

The sages make the requirements for testimony in this case almost as stringent as the qualifications for officiating in the priesthood. We may wish to reach for the most obvious explanation—that the Mishnah wishes to minimize the infliction of this punishment as far as possible. But another factor may be at work, as well. Perhaps the moment of truth, literally, in a trial, particularly in a capital case, invokes God's presence in many of the same ways as the Temple rite did. It is a matter of life and death. Those officiating and those witnessing must be in the most perfectly functioning state possible so that the rite is performed correctly.

The Yerushalmi applies this same method of interpretation in considering the elders of the court who perform the rite of the heifer executed to purify a community from the guilt and impurity of a slain man found in their community. The biblical passage mandates that when a corpse is found in a field and no one knows how the man came to be killed, a heifer will be sacrificed to atone for that blood. At the conclusion of the rite, the elders do as follows: "They shall answer and say, 'Our hands have not spilt this blood and our eyes have not seen. Forgive your people Israel, whom you redeemed, Lord, and lay not innocent blood among your people Israel.' And the blood shall be forgiven them. And you shall put away the innocent blood from among you and do what is right in the sight of God" (Deuteronomy 21:7–10). This passage about absolving the community of guilt regarding the found corpse is juxtaposed, in the Torah, with the one about the stubborn, rebellious son. In fact, they are mirror images of each other. In one, a guilty party is taken outside the city and killed; in the other, an innocent person is discovered, slain, outside the city. In one, the person is accused by parents, who are certainly authority figures; in the other, the collective "parents" of the town, the elders, communally proclaim their innocence of this blood. The Yerushalmi explicitly draws the parallel between the two cases:

> Just as you expound about his father and about his mother, so you should expound about the elders of the court, as it is said,
>   "And they shall go out"—to exclude the lame.
>   "And they shall say"—to exclude the mute.
>   "Our hands have not spilled"—to exclude those with maimed hands.
>   "And our eyes have not seen"—to exclude the blind.

The Scripture tells [us] that just as the elders of the court must be whole in righteousness thus they must be whole in their limbs. (Y. Sanhedrin 8:5, 26b)

What do the two kinds of wholeness have to do with one another? There is no obvious reason that a person who has a maimed hand could not be wholly righteous and function quite well as an elder.

Two explanations for such restrictions immediately come to mind. One draws on the phenomenon we have been exploring in this chapter: the extension of the priestly ideal to other situations. God is addressed directly by the elders; heaven and earth meet in this ritual through blood (human and animal) and words. At a meeting of heaven and earth, particularly one that involves blood, it appears that the priestly requirements of blemishlessness remain at least partially in place. The other explanation rests on a metaphorical extension; as being physically whole is metaphorically equivalent to being wholly righteous, so physical imperfection is equated with imperfect righteousness. Thus, as the state of one's body serves as a metaphor for one's *inner* state, any blemish or disability may attest to a person's inner blemish. That this equation may as a matter of fact be in error—that is, a beautiful, blemishless person may be utterly evil and a person with disabilities may be completely righteous—is obvious. Nonetheless, these metaphorical extensions clearly take place and are validated by readings such as this passage from the Yerushalmi.

While we will examine the case of the suspected, adulterous wife whose status was elucidated through the ritual of bitter waters (*sotah*) in greater detail in chapter 4, the requirements of husband and wife for blemishlessness while testifying during that ritual, which took place in the Temple, are quite similar to those of the parents and the elders in our present discussion. The husband must be sighted (Sifre N., Piska 7, on Numbers 5:13; see also Y. Sotah 2:5) and neither husband nor wife may lack a leg or arm; nor may the wife be mute (B. Sotah 27a–b). A *sotah* case is similar to the ones already examined, especially since the trial took place within the precincts of the Temple. Disabilities disqualify participants in this ritual because they need sight, speech, arms, and legs to adequately perform the ceremony. What is different in this case is the way disabilities relate to the participants' moral states.

Disabilities are again linked here with vulnerability to moral shortcomings. A husband with disabilities, in this scenario, cannot avail himself of the aid this ritual would give him in restoring marital harmony. Nor would a woman with disabilities have the chance to prove her innocence. However, the woman with disabilities, or the woman whose husband had disabilities, did not have to fear being unjustly put to the arduous test of the bitter waters. Here, disabilities are linked with a somewhat undefined moral state; the metaphorical equivalence is not clear. Because persons with disabilities were unable to participate in the ritual, doubt remained about the woman's innocence. The disabilities are not caused by her sin; but their existence, in herself or in her husband, could exacerbate an already-tense situation. Depending on the participants, the disqualification of persons with disabilities from this ritual could be a blessing or a curse.

The Effect of an Ideal

Just as the ideal of a model marine—strong in body and spirit—tells us about the requirements of the marines *and* the ideals of our society in general regarding physical fitness and bravery, so the ideal of the priest and the way that ideal was adapted in venues where God's holiness was present tells us about the way Judaism developed over time. As demonstrated by the nostalgia for the sacrificial cult, which is expressed in Jewish liturgy to this day, there was no institution as efficacious as the Temple for creating and sustaining a connection to God. Nonetheless, God could be met in other places and on other occasions: when Torah was delivered (at Sinai and subsequently during intense study),[23] during moments of trial and judgment (e.g., leprosy inspections and trials of justice), and at the moment of resurrection. And at these times, the ideal of priestly perfection is extended to all Israelites.

These ideals may be unattainable without divine intervention (as at resurrection), and hence everyone may be considered in some respects disabled, or even stigmatized, in comparison. Erving Goffman notes the importance of the ideal to understanding the notion of what he calls "spoiled identity":

> Further, while some of these norms, such as sightedness and literacy, may be commonly sustained with complete adequacy by most persons in the society, there are other norms, such as those associated with physical comeliness, which take the form of ideals and constitute standards against which almost everyone falls short at some stage in his life. And even where widely attained norms are involved, their multiplicity has the effect of disqualifying many persons. For example, in an important sense there is only one complete unblushing male in America: a young, married, white, urban, northern, heterosexual Protestant father of college education, fully employed, of good complexion, weight and height, and a recent record in sports. (Goffman 1963, 128)

Just as this represents (the 1960s) ideal of American masculinity, the sources we have examined have outlined the ancient Jewish ideal of personhood and set forth the times when it was most necessary for community members to conform as closely as possible to it. Did this represent an attempt to raise the sanctity of lay Israelites nearer to the level of the priests? Or was it an attempt to exclude as many persons as possible from certain important moments in Jewish life? The answer may depend on the situation. For trials that incurred heavy punishments (e.g., the suspected adulterous wife and the stubborn, rebellious son) the latter motive was probably operant. For ritual and spiritual moments such as Torah study or appearing at the Temple, the former may have been in play. In either case, the unblushing Jew who could best meet every test, human or divine, was the blemishless, full-grown, free man of priestly lineage: a group whose members were few and proud.

3

Persons with Disabilities, Symbolism, and Collective Israel

IF THE Statue of Liberty's light were to go out one day, we would expect that great pains would be taken to fix it, as, indeed, great trouble and expense were lavished on the statue's refurbishing some years ago. In many movies, the downfall of America is represented by the toppling of this statue, which symbolically embodies the country's best ideals. Human bodies frequently are made to bear such symbolic weight.

The Temple and its environs were well-guarded and subject to well-defined restrictive policies that kept out those who were deemed unfit to approach: persons suffering from ritual impurity, those without proper lineage, and priests who, despite having the required lineage, suffered either from ritual impurity or from a physical blemish. However, it was impossible to ban persons with disabilities from the rest of society. The Temple was a special environment, though one occasionally recreated in lesser, miniature, and temporary forms, as we saw in the previous chapter. What, then, was the role of persons with disabilities the rest of the time, in all the other situations of normal human interaction? We have already begun to see that such persons' conditions were interpreted symbolically to say something about these individuals and about their society.

The Body and Metaphor

It is axiomatic that we understand a great deal of our environment and the people in it through our bodies and the metaphors we create from the experience of our bodies' interactions with the environment. Anthropologists George Lakoff and Mark Johnson (1980, 132), in their study of metaphors, refer to the "me-first orientation"; that is, "up," "front," "active," "good," "here," and "now" are all viewed positively and are also deemed the norm. "Down," "backward," "passive," "bad," "there," and "then" are all oriented away from the "canonical person," which forms a "conceptual reference point" within our culture. We develop metaphors through our physical selves:

> Understanding emerges from interaction, from constant negotiation with the environment and other people. It emerges in the following way: the nature of our bodies and our physical and cultural environment imposes a structure on our experience, in terms of natural dimensions of the sort we have discussed. Recurrent experience leads to the formation of categories, which are experiential gestalts with those natural dimensions. Such gestalts define coherence in our experience. We understand our experience directly when we see it as being structured coherently in terms of gestalts that have emerged directly from interaction with and in our environment. *We understand experience metaphorically when we use a gestalt from one domain of experience to structure experience in another domain.* (Lakoff and Johnson 1980, 230; emphasis added)

Such basic metaphors are important for our study because they may actually create social realities. As Lakoff and Johnson observe, "Since much of our social reality is understood in metaphorical terms, and since our conception of the physical world is partly metaphorical, metaphor plays a very significant role in determining what is real for us" (146). We saw one such an extension as the gestalt from one domain (the Temple and the priesthood) was applied to other rituals, including trials involving capital offenses. The larger meta-

phorical basis underlying those extensions was the equivalence between a whole body and a whole soul.

The human body often serves as an explicit, or implicit, metaphor
for society and its values and beliefs. Sometimes it is directly linked
with the divine. Indeed, the internal processes of the Deity are con-
ceptualized in the form of a body in later, Jewish mystical, thought
(e.g., see Tishby 1989, 1:273–74). Human beings are metaphorically
linked to the processes within the "body" of God, that is, the *sefirot*.
That Victor Turner (1967, 107) makes a similar point while describing Ndembu rites of passage shows how widespread this notion is:
"Whatever the mode of representation, the body is regarded as a
sort of symbolic template for the communication of gnosis, mystical
knowledge about the nature of things and how they came to be what
they are. . . . Whatever the precise mode of explaining reality by the
body's attributes, *sacra* which illustrate this are always regarded as
absolutely sacrosanct, as ultimate mysteries." More broadly, Mary
Douglas (1966, 116) argues that "The body is a model which can
stand for any bounded system. Its boundaries can represent any
boundaries which are threatened and precarious. The body is a complex structure. The functions of its different parts and their relation
afford a source of symbols for other complex structures. . . . [We
must be] prepared to see in the body a symbol of society, and to see
the powers and dangers credited to social structure reproduced in
small on the human body." A working body can be a metaphor for a
working soul or a working society. For example, Paul (1 Corinthians
12:12–31) describes the church in terms of a functioning body; and
in India, society is conceived of as a body, with the different castes
as organs of that body (Lakoff 1987, 274). We might compare this
attitude with that of the sages who considered their "caste" to be the
eyes of the world.

If each group of persons is to be a working "organ" in the entity
that is society, how do persons with disabilities, who might not fit
into this standard metaphorical scheme, become incorporated, or
fail to become incorporated, into that society? The different answers such a question elicits are precisely what interest us here, for

they are highly revealing. As Gelya Frank (1986, 216) observes in an American context, "Physically variant members of the culture, simply as a consequence of their appearance, serve as metaphors for fundamental issues of human consciousness and evoke powerful feelings. . . . Our presumably able-bodied reactions can reveal much about our culture's formulation of embodiment. . . . Conversely, understanding the culture's formulation of embodiment makes us more cognizant of what physically variant individuals must accomplish in order to live fully in society at a given time." "Embodiment" is defined by Frank as identifying and describing "the essential forms of human experience, beginning with the body as a locus for sensation, perception and interaction" (189).[1] The ways in which one views different attributes of the human body—particularly in "the formation of an ideal body image"—reveal much about one's culture, and one's role in and identification with that culture (Fallon 1990, 96).

Such metaphors are so embedded in a culture and language that they may be almost invisible. It is only when we examine them and literalize their messages that we begin to understand how they express deeply embedded concepts and evaluations of different senses and disabilities. In different subcultures, disabilities may be metaphorically constructed and valued differently.[2] It is through examining such metaphors—for example, the common equation of the body as a container, expressed in the Bavli as "All human bodies are carriers; happy are they who are worthy of being receptacles of the Torah" (B. Sanhedrin 99b)—that we uncover basic attitudes toward the body and its abilities.

Judges and Scholars As the Eyes of Israel

If all Israel can metaphorically be seen as a body, then we may ask how different groups function as its organs. Sight, insight, and judges' ability to administer justice are all metaphorically linked in the Torah. Two parallel verses demonstrate this nexus of meaning:

"You should take no bribes, for bribes blind them *that have sight* (*pik-chim*)" (Exodus 23:8); and "You shall take no bribes, for bribes blind *the wise* (*hakhamim*)" (Deuteronomy 16:19). Obviously, bribes do not literally blind a judge. One gestalt is used to explain another: sight is standing in for insight, which is clouded by immorality—that is, taking bribes. *Pikeach* here means not sighted but rather insightful; it will have this meaning later, in rabbinic literature, as well. The verse from Deuteronomy extends the metaphor of sight to insight, then to wisdom, and ultimately to wise men (see Weinfeld 1991, 64).

We see a continuation of this metaphor in a much later text, the Bavli, in a passage that is part of a longer discussion concerning Herod and his wickedness. Herod reportedly killed all the sages except Baba ben Buta, whose eyes he had put out (B. Baba Batra 4a–b). In reproaching Herod for having killed the sages, Baba ben Buta describes the sages and the Temple as the sources of insight and light for the Jewish world.

> As you [Herod] have extinguished the light of the world [i.e., the sages], as it is written, "For the commandment is a light and the Torah a lamp" (Proverbs 6:23), go now and engage the light of the world [which is the Temple, of which] it is written, "And all the nations become enlightened by it" (Isaiah 2:2).[3] Some say [Baba b. Buta] said to him: As you have blinded the eye of the world [i.e., the sages], as it is written, "If it be done unwittingly by the eyes of the congregation" (Numbers 15:24),[4] go now and engage the eye of the world [which is the Temple], as it is written, "I will profane my sanctuary, the pride of your power, the delight of your eyes" (Ezekiel 24:21). (B. Baba Batra 4a)

The sages and the Temple are likened both to light and eyes, without either one of which sight is impossible. These metaphors imply that the world, not just Israel, is a body, of which the sages and the Temple are not only the eyes but the light, as well.[5] We have here the equation of many things: Torah = light = sages = Temple *and* eyes of congregation = eyes of world = sages = Temple. The sages liken themselves to the Torah and to the Temple (but not to the priesthood, to which they had no claim). The Temple was where God dwelt and so the sages become God's address on earth.

Disabilities As Metaphors for Sinful Israel

Israel is sometimes characterized metaphorically as a person with a disability. Here, the use of one gestalt to explain another is obvious: moral disability is equated with physical disability. Israel is conceived of as a body, a person; and her immorality is symbolized by various physical disabilities.[6]

Isaiah, the prophet, characterizes Israel as willfully disabling herself: "Hear, deaf ones and look [in order] to see, blind ones! Who is blind but my servant? or deaf, as my messenger whom I sent? Who is blind as the one I send, and blind as God's servant? Seeing much but observing nothing; [having] hearing hears but not attending" (Isaiah 42:18–20). Israel's deafness and blindness are not due to any lack of properly functioning organs, for the opposite is clearly stated: God's servants have eyes and ears that presumably operate, but they are too stubborn and willful to use them to see and understand the truth of God's message. When they stop being recalcitrant and stop "blinding themselves" to the reality of God's presence, they will themselves become the "light of the world": "I, God, have called you in righteousness, and will hold your hand, and will keep you, and place you [as] a covenant people, [as] a light for the nations; to open the blind eyes, to bring out the prisoners from the prison, and them that sit in darkness out of the prison house" (Isaiah 42:6–7). In this passage, the "blind eye" is clearly meant as a metaphor for bringing knowledge of God to those who lack it. Sight, once more, stands for insight.

In the powerful prophetic image of Isaiah's suffering servant we find an explicit linking of sin, disabilities, suffering, and atonement. The suffering servant is clearly disabled and wounded. His wounds, like the sacrifices in the Temple, make an expiation for sin:

Behold, my servant shall prosper, he shall be exalted and extolled, and be very high. As many were astonished at you, saying, Surely his visage is too marred to be human, and his form, to be from humanity['s mold]: so shall he startle many nations; kings shall shut their mouths: for that which they had not been told them shall they see; and that which they had not heard they shall comprehend. Who [would have] believed our report, and to whom is God's arm revealed? For he grew up before him as a tender plant, and as a root out of a dry ground: he had no form nor comeliness, that we should look at him, and no countenance, that we should desire him. He was [the most] despised and rejected of men; a man of pains, and knowing sickness: and we hid (as it were) our faces from him; he was despised, and we considered him not. But he has borne our sicknesses and endured our pains; yet we considered him stricken, smitten of God, and afflicted. But he was wounded because of our transgressions, bruised because of our iniquities: his sufferings were that we might have peace, and by his injury we are healed. (Isaiah 52:13–53:5)

The suffering servant appears in Deutero-Isaiah; that is, he was created by the author of Isaiah chapters 40–55, who lived in Babylonia during the exile and wrote during the sixth century B.C.E. Theories as to his identity and the meaning of this passage abound. Yehezkel Kaufmann (1977, 124–25) suggests that Deutero-Isaiah lived in an environment composed of three basic classes: the completely faithful and humble mourners for Zion, the faithless who assimilated, and the masses who remained faithful, but without much intensity. According to Kaufmann, the suffering servant embodies the first group. John McKenzie (1968, lii) suggests that the suffering servant embodies "all the religious gifts and the religious mission of Israel." In either case—whether the servant is "not historical Israel, neither the whole of Israel, nor its faithful core, but Israel idealized" (J. McKenzie 1968, xliv) or he symbolizes the faithful mourners of Zion— then Israel is idealized, either in whole or in part, as a person with disabilities.

The servant's strengths come from his intellectual and spiritual qualities, not from his physical, ascribed attainments. He is the literary creation of a stateless teacher, trying to define Judaism in exile.

He has no role in politics, war, or the cult (J. MacKenzie 1968, lii). Rather, it is through his devotion in the face of suffering that he attains his purpose. This description could also fit the situation of the sages after 70 c.e., and significantly, they are the ones who will later emphasize the concept he so vividly illustrates—that suffering may replace the atonement previously found in the cult. We should also note that the suffering servant is not described as blind, deaf, or mentally disabled. In other words, his ability to learn and teach are unimpaired by his disabilities; he is not debilitated intellectually or spiritually, but only physically. These disabilities, and indeed this image as a whole, could naturally be seen as political metaphors, not only moral ones, by Jewish readers of later eras. The servant suffers as the faithful of Israel suffer. He is downcast as the exiles are downcast. To be stripped of one's country and cult is to be disabled.

Another character who symbolizes Israel and suffers a disability is Tobit, a blind man whose story is presented in a source not canonized into Hebrew Scriptures. The Book of Tobit, whose date and provenance are uncertain (see Nickelsburg 1981, 35), addresses the issue of a righteous person's suffering. Tobit's message differs from Job's, in that it deals not only with the fate of individuals but the fate of the nation (Nickelsburg 1981, 33). Indeed, as George Nickelsburg (1984, 43b) puts it, "For the author of Tobit, God's dealings with the suffering righteous person are paradigmatic of His dealings with Israel." In this, then, Tobit bears a resemblance to the suffering servant.

Tobit is an Israelite among the exiles in Assyria. The land of Israel was, at that time, divided into two kingdoms: Judea in the south and Israel in the north. Israel was conquered in 723 b.c.e. and its population deported to Assyria. Tobit is persecuted for burying the bodies of fugitive Jews executed by the king (1:3–18). Although he becomes blind and suffers from it, he is healed by the angel Raphael through his son Tobias. Tobit ends by praising God. Nickelsburg (1981, 34) points out that Tobit is representative of the nation collectively and individually: "The author is addressing the Tobits of his own time, assuring them of God's gracious presence and activity and calling them to doxology and to repentance and the pious life." Tobit's tale of disability, and its cure, offered a paradigm of suffering and redemption to its exiled listeners, suggesting they would be healed from their exile when they returned to Israel. Significantly, his tale is set in a time when the (First) Temple was not available to effect atonement and redemption. Like the suffering servant, Tobit represents Israel, is disabled, and looks forward to redemption and healing.

In rabbinic literature, this metaphor continues to operate. Israel, metaphorically represented as a person with disabilities, is the object of God's love and God's regret that such misfortunes come to Israel through her (or her leaders') own sins. For example, in Numbers 20:2–13, Moses sinned by striking the rock to make water appear from it, rather than simply speaking to it, as he was commanded to do. The waters that came from this rock are called the Waters of Merivah, which is a pun on the word meaning "rebellious struggling" (*ravu*, Numbers 20:13). The phrase is repeated three times in Scripture and is related not only to the ban on Moses' entering the land but to his death and the deaths of his siblings, inspiring the following expositions:

> Rabbi Shimon said: This may be compared to a king who was traveling with his son in his carriage. They came to a narrow spot [and] his carriage turned over onto his son. His eye was blinded, his hand was cut off, his leg was broken. When the king came to the same place, he [would] say: "Here my son was wounded. Here his eye was blinded. Here his hand was cut off. Here his leg was broken." Just so does God mention three times, "the Waters of Merivah" (Numbers 20:13), "the Waters of Merivah" (Numbers 27:14), "the Waters of Merivah" (Deuteronomy 32:51), [as if] to say, "Here I killed Miriam, here I killed Aaron, here I killed Moses." And thus [Scripture] states, "Their judges are brought down on account of a rock" (Psalm 141:6). (Sifre D., Piska 26; see also Leviticus Rabbah Emor 31:4 on Leviticus 24:2)

This midrash purports to explain why the Waters of Merivah are mentioned three times in Scripture (in fact, they are mentioned twice more; see Numbers 10:24 and Deuteronomy 33:8). In each case, God is mourning the death of a great leader who was associated with these very waters.[7] In the exposition, three inflictions of disabilities are likened to Miriam's, Aaron's, and Moses' deaths.

Thus, the Jewish people is likened to progeny (the king's son) whose body (like the son's) becomes disabled. What is perhaps most surprising are the disabilities with which the different leaders are associated:

> an eye blinded = Miriam's death
> a hand amputated = Aaron's death
> a leg amputated = Moses' death

This could be merely logical: a person blind in one eye can still journey, even after the loss of a hand. However, a person missing leg, hand, and eye is disabled, indeed. Thus the Israelites could still wander after Miriam's and Aaron's deaths; but Moses' passing was the final blow. In addition, Miriam is likened to Israel's eyes in this parable. This is striking in that eyes, as we have seen, are linked to insight and judgment and she is considered a judge, according to the text from Psalm 141. Aaron's role as priest is well symbolized by the cutting off of the hand, which performs the sacrifices, and Moses' functions as military and political leader are aptly embodied in the leg. Nonetheless, it is unexpected and instructive that Miriam is depicted as the discernment, vision, or light of the Jewish people while they wandered in the desert.

Until now, all the texts we have examined in this chapter have used one body to symbolize collective Israel. The next text is unique, not only because it uses a group of persons to symbolize Israel but because persons with disabilities here are represented as more fit to worship God than those without.

> R. Abba bar Kahana said in the name of R. Levi: [It is written, "And God said, Let the waters be gathered (*yikavvu*)" (Genesis 1:9). This means] the Holy One, blessed be He, said: Let the waters await me (*yikavvu li*) for what I will do with them in the future.

It is like a king who built a palace and settled in it residents who were mutes. They used to arise early and salute the king by gestures, and by [communicating with their] fingers and by [waving their] handkerchiefs. The king said: If these people [who are speechless salute me with their fingers, with gestures, and with handkerchiefs] were sensate (*pikchin*), how much more [lavishly would they greet me]! The king settled sensate residents in [the palace], but they rebelled and seized it, saying: This is not the king's palace, it is our palace! The king said: Let the palace return to what it was.

So, at the beginning of the creation of the world, the praise of the Holy One, blessed be He, ascended only from the waters: this is what is written: "From the voices of many waters, the mighty breakers of the sea" (Psalm 93:4). And what did they say? "The Lord is majestic on high" (Psalm 93:4). The Holy One, blessed be He, said: Now if these waters that have no mouth nor [power of] speech nor [ability to] talk praise Me so how much more [will I be praised] after I create humanity! But the generation of the Flood arose and rebelled against Him and the generation of Enosh arose and rebelled against Him and the generation of the separation [of tongues, i.e., the tower of Babel] rebelled against Him. [At that point,] the Holy One, blessed be He, said: Remove them, and let the waters return. Thus is it written: "The rain fell on the earth [forty days and forty nights]" (Genesis 7:12). (Genesis Rabbah 5:1 on Genesis 1:9; see also Genesis Rabbah 28:2 on Genesis 6:7)[8]

The midrash begins by expounding on a rare form of the word *yi-kavvu*, "gather," which is used in this exact form only in Genesis 1:9. That the root *kuf-vav-heh* is more frequently associated with the idea of hoping and waiting forms the basis of the pun here. The water that praises—the rolling waves with their movements (gestures and fingers) and white breakers (handkerchiefs)—is seen as preferable to the human beings who, though they can use language, rebel against God. Thus, the waters, which recede at the beginning of creation, need merely wait for God to become fed up with humanity to reassert their primacy in praising God. This story allows us to see another metaphor embedded in our texts. Torah is frequently likened to water in rabbinic literature—free to everyone, purifying, eternal, priceless, and so on (see Sifre D. Piska 48)—and the sages to the well containing that water. But perhaps most significant in the context of our investigation is that persons with speaking disabilities are depicted here as quite sensate and able to communicate effectively; indeed, their way is preferable to the manner of those who have verbal speech.

The dominant metaphorical extensions regarding vision that we have considered so far are from sight to insight and from blindness to lack of insight. Another metaphorical extension is from sight to sexuality, and conversely, from blindness to impotence. The relationship between sight and sexuality is the dominant one in the story in which the *yetser hara*, the evil impulse of all Israel, is embodied and then disabled. It appears in a long passage about the destruction of the Temple, caused by the evil desire for idolatry within the Jewish people. This urge toward idolatry, which yielded such massive destruction yet still "danced" among the Jewish people, was as strong as a lion lodged in the heart of the entire Israelite enterprise—that is, the Holy of Holies in the Temple—from whence it came forth like a lion of fire.

The desire for idolatry is linked to other desires, notably sexual ones. For once the Evil Inclination is given into the custody of the sages, something is missing in the world: "He [God] said to them [the sages]: See that if you kill him [the Evil Inclination], the world will fail. They imprisoned him [the Evil Inclination] for three days, then looked in the whole Land of Israel for a fresh egg and could not find it. [Thereupon] they said: What shall we do? If we kill him, the whole world would fail. We [cannot] ask for half mercy because Heaven does not give half mercy. They put out his eyes and let him go" (B. Yoma 69b). The Evil Inclination is here quite literally embodied in the form of a human being. Killing him is impossible, as the world could not go on without sexuality and procreation; the sages prove this by their experiment. God could not help the sages in this regard, for prayers for half mercy are not granted. Thus, it is left to the sages to disable the Evil Inclination by blinding him, making him impotent.[9] In that way, they wound him most yet still allow him to function. This is significant not only because of the relationship of sight and sexuality but because blindness is the disability that although clearly a burden would still allow a sage to function in his role. Merely laming the Evil Inclination would not have disabled him enough. Too much of his force would remain intact. Causing him to become deaf, or mentally disabled, may not have been options for two reasons: it may not be as easy to deafen a person or make them mentally ill as it is to put out their eyes, and the Evil Inclination could not have functioned well enough to do his "job" if so wounded.[10] While sight can lead to insight, this passage reminds us metaphorically that sight can be dangerous as well—the first step toward sexual activity.

The passages we have examined in this chapter, when taken together, present the following associations and metaphorical extensions: Eyes/Sight > Insight/Sexuality > Sages/Well > Torah/Water > Rebellion > Eyes/Sight. The sages, as the eyes of Israel, must finely balance their insight, and its resulting sexual energy, so that they can be fitting vessels for the water of Torah and not uncontrolled, rebellious waters whose power cannot be contained and usefully channeled.[11] The sages are precariously poised as the organ of Israel's body that can do the most harm, or the most good, to its collective soul. It is surely no accident that the sages portray themselves in this way: as the fulcrum of Israel's life, as much the focus and purpose of Israel as Lady Liberty's torch is to her presence.

4

Disabilities, Atonement, and Individuals

"Once upon a time . . ." This phrase raises our expectations that a story will follow in which good prevails and evil is punished. Such tales—fairy tales, literary tales, traditional narratives of every kind—can tell us much about the culture that produced them, regardless of how factual they may or may not be. In the previous chapter, we saw how a person with disabilities could serve as a symbol of collective Israel. In this chapter, we will examine narratives in which disabilities actually allow individuals to function more effectively than they could have done otherwise. This situation occurs often, though not always, because the disability atones for a sin or allows the individual to show how divine power trumps human power. The atonement that disabilities can bring in these stories, and the symmetry that atonement restores, is called in rabbinic literature *bamidah she'adam modeid ba, mod'din lo*—"With the measure that a person measures shall they mete [out] to him"—or, more colloquially, *midah k'neged midah*, simply "measure for measure." As the symmetry of heaven and earth was crucial in the Temple, so the symmetry of sin and punishment is operative here.

This principle is at work in our earliest sources. The life story of Jacob, son of Isaac, is one of great narrative and moral symmetry shaped by disabilities in some of its characters. Jacob is able to steal his twin brother's birthright because his father's eyes have grown dim (Genesis 27:1). Poor eyes will then almost immediately set Jacob up for a fall. After fleeing his angry brother, Esau, he comes to his uncle, Lavan. Jacob, looking at Lavan's daughters, disdains the elder because of her poor eyes: "And Leah's eyes were weak; but Rachel was of beautiful form and appearance" (Genesis 29:17). Having disregarded the rights of an elder sibling (his brother) once, Jacob now attempts to disregard them again, wanting to marry Rachel, the younger sister, before Leah. Lavan, Leah, and Rachel collude to marry off Jacob to Leah. When Jacob confronts Lavan, his uncle pointedly remarks, "It must not be done so in our place, to give the younger before the firstborn" (Genesis 29:26). As Jacob tricked his father and brother, exploiting the opportunity of his father's poor vision, so he is tricked in turn by a father and a sister because of his repugnance at Leah's poor eyes. Jacob himself is blinded by his lust for the birthright and for Rachel.

In another part of Jacob's story his punishment is likewise meted out "measure for measure." When Jacob is born, he emerges holding onto his brother's heel (in Hebrew, the word for heel is *akeiv;* this is the source of Jacob's name, *Ya'akov*). Just before he is about to meet his brother, Esau, after a long separation, Jacob struggles with an angel, probably Esau's representative spirit (Sarna 1989, 403–4). This spirit wrestles with, wounds, and finally blesses Jacob, renaming him Israel (Genesis 32:25–31), reflecting symmetrically the struggle of the boys in Rebecca's womb and their blessing decreed by God (25:22–23). When Jacob fled from his brother, he ran fearfully into the setting sun. As the sun rises, Jacob greets Esau again after many years, limping and unafraid, with a new identity won fairly instead of stolen (32:32–33).

Jacob's disability is accompanied by a blessing. His flawed moral state has finally been made manifest in his physical state and he is, somehow, released from his sin of tricking his father and brother. At this point, he can assume a new name and a new role as patriarch of a family in the land of Israel. Israel, then, in its first incarnation is physically disabled.[1] In this case the disability itself, by finally becoming physically manifest and fulfilling the narrative's demand for symmetry, allows Jacob to move forward as a character and a nation. In a sense, then, Jacob's disability actually heals him as it signifies that his competition with his brother at last is over: he has been appropriately punished for stealing the birthright and may move on with his life.

In a similar way, a disability actually helps Samson attain his goal of slaughtering as many Philistines as possible. In Samson's story, sight and sexuality blind the judge to what is right. Even Samson's name, *Shimshon* in Hebrew, hints at the importance of light, enlightenment, and sight in the story, for it is derived from the same root as the word "sun," *shemesh*. He follows his eyes, quite literally: "And Samson went to Gaza, and *saw* there a harlot, and went in unto her" (Judges 16:1). Subsequently, the harlot Delilah harasses Samson until he finally tells her that his strength derives from his Nazirite vows, one of which is a prohibition against cutting his hair. She cuts his hair, and he loses his strength, is taken captive, and is blinded (16:21). Yet his blindness and presumed helplessness enable him to kill 3,000 Philistines at the end of his life (16:27)—a great triumph over his enemies. Had he not been blinded, this opportunity would not have been his. Like Jacob's wounding, Samson's physical disability brings symmetry into the protagonist's life and actually enables him to act potently again.

In a different story, a person's overly clever machinations are rewarded, measure for measure, with mental illness. King Saul makes war against the Amalekites and should have utterly destroyed them. Instead, he takes pity on their king, Agag, and allows his people to take booty instead of destroying everything (1 Samuel 15:4–9). God rejects Saul for this action (16:1) and David is secretly anointed king by Samuel (16:13). Once Saul is no longer truly king, he becomes mentally ill: "Now the spirit of the Lord had departed from Saul, and an evil spirit from the Lord terrified him" (16:14). As P. Kyle McCarter (1980, 280) points out, the ancient understanding of an "evil spirit" bears almost no similarity to modern conceptions of mental illness: "In ancient tradition a person once touched by divine spirit can never again be free. When Saul loses place to David and Yahweh's spirit falls upon the young Bethlehemite (16:13), an evil spirit arrives in Gibeah as though rushing into the vacuum Saul's loss of favor has created. Another way of saying this is that the infusion of spirit is never neutral. It may endow with special powers, or it may breed misery; and indeed the spirit now torments Saul." It is significant that Saul's sin precedes his mental illness and that it comes after, if not directly as a result of, his great transgression. Because Saul thought to outwit God's law by sparing Agag, and perhaps because he identified too closely with an earthly king rather than with the divine one, God's spirit leaves Saul forever. This punishment also serves a narrative purpose: it brings David into Saul's tent, quite literally, to play the lyre when the "evil spirit" is afflicting him (1 Samuel 16:22–23).

Blindness also allows the prophet Ahiya to function more potently than he could have done had he been sighted. His story, in 1 Kings 14:1–18, pits a righteous prophet against a king characterized as evil (13:33) and his wife. King Jeroboam's son is ill and he sends his wife, pretending to be someone else, to the prophet to find out if the child will live. The prophet, forewarned by God that the woman is coming, is not fooled and delivers a stinging prophecy to the king through his wife. Jeroboam is thus shown that God and God's true prophet deliver justice and can overcome physical limitations, while he, the faithless king, cannot bring healing to his child without obedience to God's will. Ahiya's blindness makes the entire exchange possible. Presumably if the prophet had not been blind, Jeroboam's wife would not even have bothered to visit him, fully expecting to be recognized immediately and condemned. Lack of sight, in this case, does not connote lack of insight. The text is careful to attribute Ahiya's blindness to old age and not to any sin (14:4).

The Mishnah is well aware of the principle of symmetry established in the Tanach. Only two passages in the entire Mishnah speculate on the causes of disabilities and they both utilize the idea of *midah k'neged midah*, "measure for measure." Such relative lack of consideration is not surprising, for the Mishnah is far more often interested in the questions "who?" "what?" "where?" "when?" and "how?" than in knowing "why?" However, in these passages the Mishnah portrays disabilities as part of the grand order of God's creation. In both cases, sin leads to disability in that faculty with which the sin was committed. The passages (M. Sotah 1:8–9) are brought as a commentary on a mishnah that relates to tractate Sotah's main topic: the trial by ordeal of a wife suspected of adultery. This ordeal is outlined in Numbers 5:11–31 and describes a process whereby a woman suspected of adultery is made to drink a potion that, if she is guilty, causes her thigh (probably meaning her reproductive organs) to fall and her belly to swell.[2] The Mishnah notes that this punishment is fitting: "With the measure that a person measures shall they measure [out] to him. She adorned herself for sin; God made her repulsive. She exposed herself for sin; God exposed her [to public contempt by having the priest stand her at the Nicanor Gate]. With her thigh did she first begin her transgression and afterward, [with her] belly; therefore her thigh will be smitten first and afterward [her] belly, and the rest of [her] body shall not escape" (M. Sotah 1:7).[3] This mishnah begins by noting that a person's measure is meted out to him- or herself. Here, it is the person who acts first, herself (the Hebrew here is emphatic and repetitious: she adorns herself, *atsmah*; she exposes herself; etc.), and God who responds in kind. The mishnah then goes on to demonstrate that there are many examples of this phenomenon in Scripture:

> Samson went after his eyes, therefore the Philistines gouged out his eyes, as it is said, "And the Philistines took hold of him, and put out his eyes" (Judges 16:21). Absalom was [overly] proud of his hair, thus he was suspended by his hair. And because he had intercourse with ten of his father's concubines, thus they put ten javelins into him, as it is said, "And ten young men that bore Joab's weapons surrounded Absalom and smote him and killed him" (2 Samuel 18:15). And since he stole three hearts [i.e., deceived three people]—the heart of his father and the heart of the Court and the heart of Israel, (as it is said, "and so Absalom stole the hearts of the men of Israel" (2 Samuel 15:16)) thus three darts were thrust into him, as it is said, "And he took three darts in his hand, and thrust them through Absalom's heart" (2 Samuel 18:14). (M. Sotah 1:8; see also Mechilta, Tractate Shirata 2, on Exodus 15:1)

Suffering comes as a consequence of, and in similar fashion to, sin. Reward, likewise, comes as a consequence, and in similar fashion to, the righteousness enacted:

> And thus [it also happens with regard to] a matter of goodness. Miriam delayed [and watched over] Moses one hour, as it is said, "And his sister stood afar off" (Exodus 2:4), therefore Israel were detained for her seven days in the wilderness, as it is said, "And the people journeyed not until Miriam was brought back" (Numbers 12:15). Joseph merited [the privilege of] burying his father, and none of his brothers was greater than he, as it is said, "And Joseph went up to bury his father, and there went up with him both chariots and horsemen" (Genesis 50:9). Whom have we greater than Joseph, since none but Moses occupied himself with [burying] him: Moses merited [burying] the bones of Joseph and there is no one in Israel greater than he, as it is said, "And Moses took the bones of Joseph with him" (Exodus 13:19). Who is greater than Moses, [seeing] that none save the Almighty occupied Himself with [burying] him, as it is said, "And He buried him in the valley" (Deuteronomy 34:6). And not only of Moses have they spoken [of this reward] but also of all the righteous [people] as it is said, "And your righteousness shall go before you; the glory of God shall gather you" (Isaiah 58:8). (M. Sotah 1:9)

Above all else, what we have here are examples of the acute literary analysis to which the sages subjected Scripture. Each of these stories is carefully crafted to provide the symmetry pointed out in these mishnayot. The sages transform this literary principle into an ethical one: just as the stories of the Tanach reflect symmetry, so life will imitate them. Samson sins with his eyes (Judges 16:1) and is therefore blinded. Rewards come to those who practice righteousness, even if they suffer a disability because of sin. The case of Miriam is illustrative. Miriam and Aaron rebel against Moses' authority. Miriam is stricken with leprosy as a result and then healed by Moses' impassioned prayer (Numbers 12:1–13). She must be isolated from the camp for seven days because of her temporary state of ritual impurity. The Torah states explicitly that the entire camp waited for her during this seven-day period and did not resume their journey until she could rejoin the camp. Despite her great disability (particularly in a priestly family; her brother Aaron is the high priest), the entire camp is with her in spirit, supporting her. As Tosefta, commenting on this passage, points out, the measure of reward for goodness is 500 times greater than the measure of retribution for sin (T. Sotah 4:1). According to Tosefta, which supports this position with many examples (T. Sotah 3:1–4:19), punishment is distributed with an even hand but reward for good deeds is dispensed generously.

The principle of measure for measure is applied explicitly to disabilities in the other passage from Mishnah that speaks of disabilities' causes. Here is addressed the question, "Who is entitled to help themselves to *peah*, the corners of the fields which are to be left unharvested so that the poor might glean them?" (Leviticus 19:9–10, 23:22). The answer, logically, depends on how much money the person has. If the person has fifty large coins (called *zuzim*) that are being used actively to pursue business, he or she is deemed not to be needy enough to take from these corners of the fields.

> One who possesses fifty *zuzim* and trades with these must not take [*peah*]. And anyone who is not in need of taking and does take will not pass from the world before he will become dependent on other [people for charity]. And anyone who is in need of taking and does not take will not die of old age before he will support others from his own [wealth] and of him Scripture says, "Blessed is the man who trusts in God and God shall be his trust" (Jeremiah 17:7). And thus [it is also true of a] judge who judges according to the true law. And anyone who is not lame or blind or limping and makes himself [appear to be one of these] will not die of old age until he becomes like one of them, as it is said, ("And he who seeks evil, it shall come to him"; and it is [further] said,) "Justice, justice shall you pursue" (Deuteronomy 16:20). And any judge who takes bribes and perverts justice will not die of old age before his eyes have grown dim, as it is said, "And a bribe you shall not take, for the bribe blinds the seeing" (Deuteronomy 16:19). (M. Peah 8:9; see also Mechilta Kaspa 3 on Exodus 23:8; Sifre D. 144; B. Ketubot 105a–b)

The cause of disabilities, suggests this mishnah, can be found in the principle of *midah k'neged midah*. Not only will the abuse of public charity cause one ultimately to rely on it but one is rewarded for not taking this charity, even when one is entitled to it. Moreover, trying to abscond with such charity through the ruse of pretending to have disabilities leads to one eventually developing those very disabilities. Similarly, injustice, or turning a blind eye to the truth, eventually leads one to become blind. Here, the correspondence is clear: sin leads to disability.

Tosefta, in commenting on this mishnah, demonstrates the lengths to which Jews are to go to practice the concept of *midah k'neged midah* in their charity. They should restore persons to their former state, no matter how exalted. If a person would eat bread before they became poor, one feeds them bread. If a person ate a pound of meat every day before he became poor, true charity is to give him a pound of meat each day (T. Peah 4:10). Tosefta sees charity as a sort of replacement for the Temple.

> From whence [do we know] that charity and [deeds of] loving-kindness are a great intercessor and [bring] great peace between Israel and their Father in heaven? As it is said, "Thus said God, Do not enter into the house of mourning [neither go to lament nor bemoan them. For I have taken away my peace from this people, says the Lord, both love and mercy]" (Jeremiah 16:5). "Love"—this is [deeds of] loving-kindness. "And mercy"—this is charity. [This] teaches that charity and [deeds of] loving-kindness are great [makers of] peace between Israel and their Father in heaven. (T. Peah 4:21; see also B. Baba Batra 10a)

In the verse from Jeremiah, the two halves of the last verse are equated; that is, peace *is* love and mercy. Love here is *chesed*, related to the words *g'milut chasadim*, deeds of loving-kindness, a category of mitzvot that encompasses charity (charity is monetary giving only, while *g'milut chasadim* are deeds of kindness, including charity). In this passage, charity is a way of re-creating the connection between Israel and God that was formerly found only in the cult, which was, as we have already seen, the greatest intercessor in Jewish life while it stood.

How could one properly atone once the cult, with its sacrifices, had been destroyed? Tosefta suggests that suffering, and that includes disabilities and their attendant suffering, can effect atonement for sin.

> One [who] has violated a positive commandment and repented, does not move from [his place] before they forgive him. . . . One [who] violates a negative commandment and repented, repentance suspends [the punishment] and the Day of Atonement effects atonement. . . . One who violates [a commandment for which the punishments are] excisions [from the community] or deaths [meted out by] a court and repented, repentance and the Day of Atonement suspend [the punishment], and suffering (*yisurin*) effect atonement. . . . But one through whom the Name of Heaven is profaned and who repented, repentance does not have power to suspend [the punishment], nor the Day of Atonement to atone, but repentance and the Day of Atonement atone for a third, suffering on the rest of the days of the year atones for a third, and death wipes away [the sin]. (T. Kippurim 4:6–8)

This passage outlines four different kinds of sin, from least to most serious, and describes how one can atone for them after the Temple's destruction. Transgression of a positive commandment (such as "Give charity!") is forgiven as soon as one repents and gives to charity. Transgression of a negative commandment (e.g., "Do not eat pork!") can be atoned for only through the Day of Atonement after one has repented and, thereby, suspended the punishment. One who is liable to execution (e.g., one who committed murder) must repent, but only that person's suffering on other days of the year (the fasting on Yom Kippur will not suffice) will wipe away the sin. But one who sinned and caused others to sin (e.g., worshiped idols and caused others to worship idols) endures his punishment right away—repentance cannot suspend it—and the Day of Atonement cannot atone for it. Repentance and the suffering of the Day of Atonement can atone for some, suffering during the rest of the year can atone for more, and death can end it, since this obviously stops the person from sinning further. Suffering, then, which might be fasting, or might be the pain of disease or disability, effectively atones for sin.

The interrelationship of the cult, charity, and atonement is found in the midrash collections as well. Sifra, the tannaitic midrash on Leviticus, likens the giving of *peah*, and other forms of charity, to offering the sacrifices in the Temple:

> Why did Scripture place [the passage about *peah*, i.e., leaving the corners of a field unharvested so that the poor might gather crops there] in between the [passages about] Pesach and Shavuot and between Rosh Hashanah and the Day of Atonement? To teach that everyone who practices [the precepts of] gleanings [allowing the poor to glean after the reapers], forgotten sheaves [the poor are allowed to harvest sheaves forgotten in the fields], and *peah* and the tithe for the poor, it is accounted to him as if the Temple stood and he had brought his sacrifices within it. And anyone who does not practice [the precepts of] gleanings, forgotten sheaves and *peah*, and the tithe for the poor, it is accounted to him as if the Temple stood and he did not bring his sacrifices within it. (Sifra, Parshat Emor, 13:12)

This passage asks a logical question: "Why is the orderly account of the holidays, and the recounting of the sacrifices Israelites were to bring on each one (Leviticus 23:1–44), interrupted by the injunction to give *peah*?" (23:22). Sifra does not entertain the notion that the theme of the harvest, which immediately precedes 23:22, leads logically to the insertion of a verse about harvest. Instead, Sifra indicates that charity is redemptive: it has the quality of sacrifices in the Temple.

Given this overall framework for the sages' understanding of the giving of charity, it is logical that sins in charity will in an equal, measured fashion cause blemishes. This is, in fact, another extension of the priestly ideal, although so subtle and attenuated that it is almost invisible. The progression is from the Temple/sacrifices, to charity, to righteousness, to reward, to wealth, to the ability to bring more offerings, and finally to the closer conjunction of heaven and earth. Conversely, inattention to cult leads to sinfulness, to punishment, to blemishes, to disqualification from cult, and finally to a greater disjunction of heaven and earth. In this scheme, disabilities result from sinfulness and make it more difficult to atone through charity, which is the primary replacement of the cult.

The reinterpretation of the cult goes even further in the later midrash collection on Leviticus, Leviticus Rabbah. There, Metsorah 16 and 17 explore the theme of physical ailments as a punishment for evil deeds.[4] The sages often consider leprosy to be a physical symptom of a moral illness.

> "This shall be the law of the leper (*metsora*)" (Leviticus 14:2). [This is linked to] what is written, "Six are the things which the Lord hates and seven which are an abomination to Him" (Proverbs 6:16). . . . And these are they:
>
> 1. Haughty eyes,
> 2. A lying tongue,
> 3. Hands that shed innocent blood,
> 4. A heart that devises wicked thoughts,
> 5. Feet that are swift to run to evil,
> 6. A false witness that breathes out lies, and
> 7. One who sends forth discord among brethren. (Proverbs 6:16–17)
>
> R. Yochanan said: All these are punished by leprosy. (Leviticus Rabbah Metsorah 16:1)

This exposition plays on the sages' pun on the word *metsora*, "leper," as *motsi shem ra*, "one who gossips." The identification of the two allows Leviticus Rabbah to focus on ethical behavior rather than on the physical symptoms of leprosy presented in the Torah text, thus illustrating a classic difference between rabbinic and priestly approaches: intellect versus body, righteousness versus purity. Priests see the body's ability to become a source of ritual impurity as its most negative feature. The sages see the body's most negative characteristic as its ability to sin. The focus here is on the ways that major parts of the body can sin with words, the sages' very stock-in-trade. The body, specifically the tongue, is not only the locus of sin in this system: it is the locus of punishment as well. Consequences of sin committed through the body are experienced through the body; for these sins, the punishment is leprosy.

Another, quite lengthy tale in which disabilities play a role is told in Leviticus Rabbah 34:14. The rhetorical setting is an essay on the merits of giving charity. A great sage, Rabbi Yose HaGalilli, had an awful wife whom he could not afford to divorce. The community of sages made it possible for him to pay her settlement and to divorce her. The text then states that because of her sins (*g'ramin hovaya*) she married a watchman. After a little time, sufferings (*yisurin*) came upon her new husband and he went blind—a particularly crushing disability for a watchman. This pair became beggars; and one day during a period of drought, they had an argument on Rabbi Yose HaGalilli's street. The sage took pity on his former wife and gave her some coins. This rather scandalous-appearing behavior was reported to another sage who, on examining the circumstances, chastised God. If Rabbi Yose HaGalilli could be so merciful to his starving, nasty ex-wife who has no moral or legal claim on him, why cannot God be compassionate upon His covenant people? At this, rain immediately began to fall from the sky and the drought was broken.

The principle of *midah k'neged midah* is beautifully illustrated in this story. The evil wife received her divorce settlement, and yet she becomes impoverished. On the positive side, Rabbi Yose HaGalilli shows mercy above and beyond the call of duty and this brings forth a like response from God, that is, the rain. (In rabbinic literature, a drought is taken as a sign that the community has sinned. The standard response is a series of fast days that foster repentance.) Here, suffering is explicitly labeled as a consequence of sin, and the suffering is not the sinner's (i.e., the wife's) alone. But this suffering brings forth a redemptive act of charity, one that then benefits the entire community.

Cruelty to those with disabilities brings an appropriate punishment, also following the principle of *midah k'neged midah*. In the following story, a blind sage displays insight and enlightenment, as well as great abilities to affect others.

Rav Sheshet was blind. Once all the people went out to see the king, and Rav Sheshet arose and went with them. A [certain] heretic met him and said to him: The whole pitchers go to the river, but where do the broken ones go? He [Rav Sheshet] said to him: Come [along] and see that I know more than you.

The first troop passed by and a shout arose. Said the heretic: The king is coming. Rav Sheshet said to him: He is not coming. A second troop passed by and when a shout arose, the heretic said: The king is coming. Rav Sheshet said to him: The king is not coming. A third troop passed by and there was silence. Said Rav Sheshet to him: Now the king is coming. The heretic said to him: How did you know this? He [Rav Sheshet] said to him [the heretic]: Because the earthly royalty is like the heavenly royalty. For it is written: "Go out and stand on the mount before God. And behold, the Lord passed by and a great and strong wind rent the mountains, and broke in pieces the rocks before the Lord; but the Lord was not in the wind; and after the wind an earthquake; but the Lord was not in the earthquake; and after the earthquake a fire; but the Lord was not in the fire; and after the fire a still small voice" (1 Kings 19:11–12).

When the king came, Rav Sheshet said the blessing over him. The heretic said to him: You, who cannot see, say the blessing [upon seeing a king]? What happened to that heretic? Some say that his companions put his eyes out. Others say that Rav Sheshet cast his eyes upon him and he became a heap of bones. (B. Berachot 58a)

First of all, this story uses the concept of a symmetry between heaven and earth: the royal retinues of both spheres share some characteristics. Second, it contains great irony, as it implicitly negates simplistic thought. Thus the heretic thinks noise signals the king's arrival when, in fact, awestruck silence is his greatest tribute. The heretic thinks that physical sight is a prerequisite for insight whereas Rav Sheshet demonstrates just the opposite. (There is, of course, a dimension of animosity between Judaism and the heretic's religion, which is clearly bested by Rav Sheshet's wisdom.) Finally, as the heretic insulted Rav Sheshet about his blindness, so his eyes are put out or, as an alternative, Rav Sheshet curses him with the power of his insight and takes the life out of him. In its composition as well as its content, this story underscores the importance of the principle of measure for measure.

Nahum Ish Gamzo

One of the most striking examples of suffering, specifically disabilities, atoning for sin is brought as a commentary to the mishnah from Peah discussed above. It focuses on Nahum Ish Gamzo and exemplifies not only the idea that suffering atones for sin but also that it may come through disabilities dispensed measure for measure. Nahum Ish Gamzo is an exceptionally righteous individual who is also the teacher of Rabbi Akiba.

Indeed, this sage's name reflects his righteousness: Nahum is related to the idea of divine comfort (*nehamah*), and the reason he is called Ish Gamzo is that he is the man (*ish*) who always says, "This, too (*gam zo*), is for the good" (B. Sanhedrin 108b–109a), taking a positive attitude about any misfortune. The following account comes near the end of a long passage emphasizing how far one must go to be considerate of those who need charity, even if they are deceptive individuals. It is framed by two stories that bear on our tale and thus are also included.

> Nehemiah, a man [from the village of] Shichin, met a man from Jerusalem who said to him, "Deal kindly with me [and, through charity, give me] a chicken [to eat]." Said [Nehemiah] to him: "Go [take this] money and buy [cheap] meat." [The man took the money, bought cheap meat] ate it and died. And he [Nehemiah] said, "Come and mourn the one killed by Nehemiah!"
>
> Nahum, Ish Gamzo, was taking a gift to his father-in-law. A man afflicted with boils ran into him and said, "Deal kindly with me [and give me, through charity,] some of that stuff you have with you?" [Nahum] said to him, "When I return, [I shall give some to you]."

But when he returned, he found the man had died. [Nahum] said to those who rebuked him, "May the eyes that saw you and did not give to you go blind. May the hands that did not extend to give [charity] to you be cut off. May the legs that did not run to give [charity] to you be broken." And so it came to pass.

[One time] Rabbi Akiba came [to visit] him [Nahum]. [Rabbi Akiba] said to him, "Woe is me that I should see you in such [a state]!" [Nahum] said to him, "Woe is me that I do not see you in such [a state]!" [Rabbi Akiba] asked, "Why do you curse me?" [Nahum] said to him, "And why do you rebel against [divine] punishment (*b'yisurin*)?"

Rabbi Hoshaya the Elder had, for his son, a teacher who was blind and he would eat a meal with him every day. One time, others were with him [Rabbi Hoshaya] and [so] he [the blind teacher] did not eat with him [Rabbi Hoshaya]. In the evening, [Rabbi Hoshaya] came to him and said to him, "Don't be angry, my master. Because others were with me [at the meal] I did not want to waste the time of my master [i.e., you] and therefore I did not eat with you today. [The teacher] said to him, "You have appeased one who is seen but does not see. May the One who sees but is not seen [i.e., God] accept your apology [also]."

[Rabbi Hoshaya] said to him, "From whence do you [know this beautiful blessing you just bestowed upon me]?" [The teacher] said to him, "[From] Rabbi Eliezer ben Jacob [about whom it is told that] a blind man entered his city and Rabbi Eliezer ben Jacob sat [this man] below him [as if he were a student of his]. [The people of the city] said, "If this were not such a great man, Rabbi Eliezer ben Jacob would not have seated him below himself." And they treated him with respect [and gave him a sum of money for his maintenance]. He [the blind man] said to them, "Why [are you treating me with such respect and generosity]?" They said to him, "Rabbi Eliezer ben Jacob sat you below him." Then [the blind man] prayed for him [Rabbi Eliezer ben Jacob] and said, "You have shown kindness to one who is seen but does not see. May the One who sees but is not seen receive your [every] apology and deal kindly with you." (Y. Peah 8:9, 21b; see also B. Hagigah 5b)

All three stories drive home the point of the mishnah on which they are commenting: there is symmetry in goodness and in sin. The first and last stories are far more realistic, and less dramatic, than the one about Nahum Ish Gamzo, which occupies the prominent, central part of the composition. The first and second stories are tied together through wordplay. The names Nehemiah and Nahum come from the same three-letter root, *nun-chet-mem*, denoting comfort. In addition, Nehemiah is called a man from Shichin and the man who approaches Nahum has boils—in Hebrew, *sh'chin*, almost the same word. Both men commit the offense of not performing the act of charity properly and both take responsibility for it in their own way: Nehemiah by acknowledging that he has killed the man and Nahum by not only acknowledging his guilt but bringing suffering on himself to atone for it.

Nahum's suffering is not a punishment from God. Nehemiah, whose sin was very similar to Nahum's, suffers nothing like the same afflictions. Nahum brings these punishments on himself in order to atone for his sin and to ease some of his guilt: he curses himself with blindness and with physical disabilities in his hands and feet, following the principle of *midah k'neged midah*. He does not, however, curse himself with deafness, muteness, or mental illness—disabilities that would have stigmatized him in the sages' system—although such curses could have followed the same logic: he could have cursed his ears that did not hear, or his mouth that did not answer correctly, or his mind that was not more thoughtful.

The interchange between Rabbi Akiba and Nahum suggests that Rabbi Akiba does not yet understand the efficaciousness of sufferings in atonement and the importance of recognizing the principle of measure for measure. Rabbi Akiba does, indeed, eventually understand this relationship because he suggests to another of his teachers, Rabbi Eliezer, on his deathbed, that sufferings are precious (Sifre D., Piska 32; see also B. Sanhedrin 101a). In addition, at the end of his own life, when he is most cruelly tortured to death, Rabbi Akiba recites the Shema, the ultimate testament of faith in Judaism (Y. Berachot 9:5, 13b; see also Y. Sotah 5:7, 20c; B. Berachot 61b), and explicitly states that he is not rebelling against suffering but is embracing it as a redemptive experience.

The third story demonstrates the same principle, but now in a positive sense. It recognizes that a blind man may be disabled but that he may also be well-qualified to serve as a teacher. Rabbi Hoshaya seems to be quite sensitive to the blind teacher's need for dignity and is punctilious in showing him respect through inviting him to dine and through explaining why the normal routine was disrupted in a way that affirms the honor due him. In this way Rabbi Hoshaya merits a blessing, measure for measure. God, in this story, is linked to the blind man. By showing honor to the one who cannot see, one also shows honor to the One who cannot be seen. Rabbi Eliezer ben Jacob similarly earns a blessing because he treats a blind man with honor and indicates that this man is worthy of community support by positioning him as his disciple. In turn, Rabbi Eliezer ben Jacob earns blessings from God.

These three stories comment on the final mishnah in Peah, which serves as a theologically inspiring ending to the entire tractate. The Gemara to this mishnah likewise forms the conclusion of the tractate and, as such, is meant to inspire righteous behavior that goes beyond the letter of the law. In other words, only a minimum level of behavior can be legislated; desired behavior can only be encouraged through inspiring stories and the promise of great divine rewards. Nahum Ish Gamzo and, of course, Rabbi Akiba were exceptional individuals who could achieve far greater righteousness, and bear far more suffering, than the average person. The prefacing of Nahum's story with Nehemiah's shows that an ordinary person may feel guilt while only an extraordinary person need take on great suffering to atone for sin.

The Bavli retells Nahum Ish Gamzo's story in an even more exaggerated way. It is placed in tractate Taanit, which describes how communities would fast and suffer in order to appease God and cause rain to fall on their parched land. Nahum's story is set among many other tales of miracles wrought as reward for righteousness, all of which reflect the principle of measure for measure. For example, a fire spreads through a city but does not affect one neighborhood, because a woman in that neighborhood allowed her neighbors to use her oven (heated by fire) on Shabbat so that they might all have hot meals. As she was righteous in her use of fire so she, and her whole neighborhood, were spared from fire (B. Taanit 21b). The mishnah on which we will concentrate mentions dilapidated walls and buildings that may pose a hazard to the community. According to stories told in the Gemara, totally righteous persons were not afraid of having the wall of such a building fall on them, as their merit protected them from disaster (e.g., B. Taanit 20b).

It was said of Nahum Ish Gamzo that he was blinded in both his eyes. His two hands were cut off. His two legs were amputated and his whole body was covered with boils (*sh'chin*) and he was lying in a dilapidated house on a bed the feet of which were standing in bowls of water in order to prevent the ants from crawling onto him [since he was unable to drive them off his body himself]. His students sought to remove his bed [from the house] and afterward take out the utensils [from thence]. He said to them, "My sons, take out the utensils and afterward take out my bed for I assure you that all the time that I am in the house, the house will not fall." They took out the utensils and afterward took out his bed and the house [immediately] fell down.

His students said to him, "Rabbi, you are [clearly] a thoroughly righteous person [so] why has [all this suffering] happened to you?" He said to them, "I brought it on myself, for one time I was walking on the way to the house of my father-in-law and I had with me three asses, one laden with food, one with drink, and one with all kinds of dainties. One poor man came and stood in my way and said to me, "Rabbi, sustain me [with something to eat]." I said to him, "Wait until I unload [something] from the ass. And I did not succeed in unloading [something] from the ass before he died [from hunger]. I went and fell upon his face and I said, 'My eyes, which did not have pity upon your eyes, may they become blind. My hands, which did not have pity upon your hands, may they be cut off. My legs, which did not have pity on your legs, may they be amputated.' And my conscience (*da'ati*) was not quiet until I said, 'May my whole body be covered with boils (*sh'chin*).'" They [his students] said to him, "Alas for us that we should see you like this." He said to them, "Alas for me if you did not see me like this!" (B. Taanit 21a)

First, consider the differences between this version of the story and the Yerushalmi's. There, Nahum promises to feed the beggar when he returns from his visit; here he promises to feed the beggar as soon as he begins to unload his beasts of burden. There he is taking an unspecified gift; here he is bringing a veritable caravan of treasure. There, he is chided by onlookers and only then curses himself with blindness, amputation of his hands, and lameness. Here, no one chides him and he curses himself with all the disabilities mentioned in the Yerushalmi and with boils as well. There, he chides Rabbi Akiba for not comprehending how suffering can atone for sin. Here, he accepts the questioning of his suffering by his disciples and explains it to them.[5] There, no mention is made of his utter righteousness. Here, it is made explicit that though disabled, he need not be a sinner. Indeed, so righteous is he that he can be sure a building will not fall upon him—one of the highest levels of righteousness one can achieve, a level that many sages do not attain (B. Taanit 20b).

Perhaps the most important difference between the two versions of Nahum's story is the larger discussions in which they are placed. Both are set in discussions of *midah k'neged midah*, but in the Yerushalmi the context is the giving of charity and in the Bavli the context is miracles being wrought for the righteous. Significantly, the story here is immediately followed by one in which Nahum is traveling on his way to present a bag of jewels to the emperor in order to save the Jewish people. On the way, he is robbed of the jewels by some innkeepers who put earth in his bag, instead. When he discovers the robbery, he exclaims that this, too, is for the best. When he goes to court and presents the bag of earth, the emperor becomes insulted and imprisons Nahum. The prophet Elijah appears and suggests that the earth may have magic powers, which indeed it does. Nahum is released from prison and rewarded with a bag full of jewels. On his way home, Nahum stays at the same inn where he was originally robbed. The innkeepers are, needless to say, surprised to see him alive. They ask what he took to the emperor and Nahum replies that it was the earth he took from the inn that was so precious to the emperor. The innkeepers thereupon tear down their inn, take the earth from under it, and present the bag of dirt to the emperor. It is found ineffective and the innkeepers are put to death.

The two stories fit together, both shaped around a central observation: Nahum consistently maintains an attitude of acceptance by saying, "This, too, is for the best." The parallel construction may be represented schematically:

'This, too, is for the best!"

suffering accepted	stolen jewels accepted by Nahum
puts punishments on self	imprisoned
encounters man on road	Elijah appears
house stays up for Nahum	justice is achieved

This deliberate literary composition underscores two elements that are key for understanding the stories. First, as the second half of the piece is manifestly a fairy tale, so too should the first half be taken. And second, Nahum's story is told not to suggest a general way of regarding disabilities but to describe the special case of an exceptionally righteous man and his acceptance of misfortune that goes well beyond anything the average person is required to do. These two stories, and their contexts, point to the importance of the principle *midah k'neged midah*. This is a theological insight that can be illustrated but not legislated.

The passages we have examined in this chapter fall mainly in the category of folk tales, statements not of what is but of what ought to be. Unpunished wrongs create tension in individuals and societies. The concept of *midah k'neged midah* demonstrates how God brings justice into human situations, often using the human body to achieve that end.

5

Body, Soul, and Society

THINK OF all the variety of glasses there are, and how each fits form to function. There are brandy snifters that hold the scent of the spirit, champagne flutes that conserve bubbliness, and shot glasses for efficient transfer of alcohol. What each glass is meant to contain affects its shape. Culture also strongly influences the shape of each glass and dictates what to do in case it chips or is broken. This concept of container and contained can be used to frame our understanding of body (the container) and soul (the contained).

In the idealized environment of the Temple, death, decay, disorder, and disease could be banished so that a static, perfect environment of blemishlessness was achieved. However, the human body is itself not static, and the basic processes of human life involve disease, decay, and ultimately death. The way that Jewish texts dealt with these universal phenomena was affected by surrounding cultures: our sources did not develop in a vacuum. And while they share many traits in common with sources from Egyptian, Greek, Roman, and Christian cultures, they also express a distinctive outlook that emphasizes God's importance in the functioning of the human body.

The Social Nature of Illness and Disability: Body and Soul

Disability and illness are always part of a cultural complex of beliefs and practices in which metaphor and social power play large roles. As Arthur Kleinman explains:

Cultural systems are grounded in concepts and sources of legitimated power in society. . . . Knowing a culture's chief sources of power (social, political, mythological, religious, technological, etc.) allows one to predict its beliefs about the causes of illness and how it treats illness. In a metaphorical sense, we can speak of socially legitimated power as the active principle fueling health-care systems and of social reality determining what that power is (witchcraft, fortune-telling, science) and how it is to be applied (rituals, injections, psychotherapy), while symbolic reality lays down the pathways by which the application of that power may be effective. (1980, 44)

These culturally determined attitudes toward illness, and we may extend this paradigm and add "toward disabilities," are manifest in all cultures; they can readily be seen in Jewish and non-Jewish sources.

Ancient conceptions of health and illness in many cultures demonstrate a link between the body and soul, between society's need for order and the good health that results when that order is fostered. For example, Plato (ca. 427–347 B.C.E.), creating an ideal state consistent with his philosophical views in the *Republic*, prescribed the following course of action to regulate those sick in body or soul: "This then is the kind of medical and judicial provision for which you will legislate in your state. It will provide treatment for those of your citizens whose physical and psychological constitution is good; as for the others, it will leave the unhealthy to die, and those whose psychological constitution is incurably corrupt it will put to death. That seems to be the best thing both for the individual sufferer and for society" (1987, 173 [3.409e–410a]). Clearly, mental and physical disabilities were not to be tolerated in Plato's ideal state.

While the body might be born deformed, or decay through time, the soul, according to Plato, was unaffected by the body's travails: "We must maintain that the soul remains quite unaffected by fever or disease or injury, or even by the body being cut to fragments—unless, that is, someone can prove to us that any of these experiences makes the soul more unjust or wicked than it was" (Plato 1987, 442 [10.610b]). Like most Greek philosophers, Plato deemed the body and soul separate. Greek thinking on these topics had a profound effect on Roman culture.

Roman ideas of decorum, which had a direct impact on health and disability, served to undergird Rome's social hierarchy. At the top of this ladder stood men who were free citizens, "either orphans or legally emancipated sons, who, married or not, were 'fathers of families' and who possessed a patrimony" (Veyne 1987, 30). In addition, these men were to be physically (and fiscally) fit (see Veyne 1987, 136). Slaves were not eligible for this elevated status, nor were women, who were deemed "failed males" (P. Brown 1988, 10). Those not included in this upper class were apt to be made into amusing stock characters of comedy and art: "Genre sculpture, which decorated the homes and gardens of the wealthy, depicted conventional types. . . . Old age and poverty are here nothing but a spectacle for the diversion of indifferent aesthetes; the onlooker does not penetrate beneath the surface, nor does he ever put aside his fundamental disdain. Physical deformity is an occasion for smiles, like looking at midgets and giants at a carnival. Roman naturalism was full of condescension, without scruples" (Veyne 1987, 134). A member of this elite could maintain his status only by following a demanding regimen: an upper-class man had to maintain rigid control of his body and emotions, or risk losing face. The Stoic philosophers, who had far more influence among the Romans than the Greeks, urged that this emphasis on control of the body should begin at birth: "Says Seneca, 'parents subject the still malleable characters of their children to what will do them good. Let them cry and struggle as they will, we swaddle them tightly lest their still immature bodies become deformed rather than grow up straight and tall' " (Veyne 1987, 16).

Indeed, the ability to maintain physical and emotional control of oneself was what set one apart from the unruly masses. The body was deemed unruly, needy, liable to overrun the control of one's mind and soul, thus interfering with the Roman citizen's correct deportment. The Roman was to control his body and its appetites. Such heavy emphasis on control of one's body and emotions was this society's response to a dangerous world. Death and disorder were hardly tamed forces in the Roman world: few men or women lived past fifty, and all believed in the unseen dangers of demons and spirits (P. Brown 1988, 6; MacMullan 1981, 82). Order and continuity of the generations could only be achieved through the seemingly uncontrolled act of sexual intercourse. Romans therefore sought to control this behavior and its outcomes. They believed that birth defects could be minimized by conducting sexual intercourse with the proper solemnity: "Intercourse itself, if conducted in the right frame of mind—in effect with correct decorum—would have a positive effect on the character and the sex of the ensuing child, and certainly that the neglect of such decorum might produce offspring worthy of shame and pity" (P. Brown 1988, 20). We will find similar attitudes in Jewish sources. In Roman culture, in order to forestall such horrifying outcomes, medicine prescribed regimens of voluntary and rational conduct that regulated diet and the unruly act of sexual intercourse. The aim of such discipline was to cure the effects of illness in body and soul; in Galen's day, it was believed that "The ills of the body and those of the soul can communicate with one another and exchange their distresses: . . . the bad habits of the soul can entail physical miseries, while the excesses of the body manifest and maintain the failings of the soul" (Foucault 1986, 56).

On the one hand, Roman thought took a basically negative attitude toward the body, especially when compared with the soul. On the other hand, in the philosophical poem *On the Nature of the Universe* by the Epicurean Lucretius (ca. 100–55 B.C.E.), the senses, and hence the body, are lauded as the locus of true knowledge:

> You will find, in fact, that the concept of truth was originated by the senses and that the senses cannot be rebutted. The testimony that we must accept as more trustworthy is that which can spontaneously overcome falsehood with truth. What then are we to pronounce more trustworthy than the senses? Can reason derived from the deceitful senses be invoked to contradict them, when it is itself wholly derived from the senses? If they are not true, then reason in its entirety is equally false. Or can hearing give the lie to sight, or touch to

hearing? Can touch in turn be discredited by taste or refuted by the
nostrils or rebutted by the eyes? This, in my view, is out of the question. Each sense has its own distinctive faculty, its specific function.
There must be separate discernment of softness and cold and heat and
of the various colours of things and whatever goes with the colours;
separate functioning of the palate's power of taste; separate generation of scents and sounds. This rules out the possibility of one sense
confuting another. (Lucretius 1988, 145 [4.478–96])

A disabled person, whose experiences of the senses might be dulled
or defective would then, according to Lucretius, not have access to
the most basic raw materials from which to construct reason.

The attitudes of Greek and Roman cultures toward decorum also
appear in Jewish sources. For example, the Wisdom of Ben Sirah,
also known as Ecclesiasticus, was written by Joshua ben Elazar ben
Sirah, a professional scribe or sage of Jerusalem, during the first
quarter of the second century B.C.E. (Nickelsburg 1981, 55).[1] Ben
Sirah, a scribe, holds the cult in high esteem; as George Nickelsburg
(1981, 62) points out, "In his catalogue of heroes he devotes twice as
much space to Aaron as he does to Moses." This is a work of wisdom
literature, directed toward young persons from well-off, cultured
families (Gilbert 1984, 297), and apparently it was accepted by Jews
in the land of Israel by the first century B.C.E. and often cited in rabbinic literature (though according to Y. Sanhedrin 10:1, 28a, it is included among the works Rabbi Akiba banned on pain of exclusion
from the World to Come). It does not discuss disabilities in any
great depth, although a fool is described at length and bodily control
and decorum are also advocated. Ben Sirah's fool is one who disdains
Torah and the wisdom it contains.

In the following passage, Ben Sirah values moral attainments
over intellectual achievements. In addition, he attributes to a fraud-
ulent character the mimicking of a deaf person.

All wisdom is the fear of the Lord and includes the fulfilling of the
law. The knowledge of wickedness is not wisdom, nor is there good
sense in the advice of sinners. There is a cleverness that is loathsome,
and some fools are merely ignorant. Better to be God-fearing and lack

brains than to have great intelligence and break the law. A meticulous cleverness may lead to injustice, and a man may make himself offensive in order that right may prevail. There is a scoundrel who stoops and wears mourning, but who is a fraud at heart. He covers his face and pretends to be deaf,[2] but when nobody is looking, he will steal a march on you; and if lack of strength prevents him from doing wrong, he will still harm you at the first opportunity. Yet you can tell a man by his looks and recognize good sense at first sight. A man's clothes, and the way he laughs, and his gait, reveal his character. (Ecclesiasticus 19:20–30)[3]

The body transmits a great deal of information about the person. A sensible man is identifiable immediately due to his correct dress, gait, and emotional demeanor. And the corresponding signs identify a scoundrel: he stoops instead of standing straight, wears clothes of mourning instead of everyday clothes, covers his face instead of having an open disposition, and pretends to be deaf rather than being open to communication. The scoundrel, then, is one who cunningly manipulates those categories that close off a person from social contact in order to gain strategic advantage against his enemies. He also plays on categories that would normally evoke pity or concern in order to take advantage of the gullible. Note that the scoundrel *pretends* to be deaf; he is not actually disabled. Were he deaf, it is implied, he truly would be cut off from societal contact.

Some of Ecclesiasticus's most pejorative metaphorical images describe the fool, that is, the one who chooses not to pursue wisdom through Torah. Ben Sirah's characterizations of this fool are vivid:

A fool's mind is a leaky bucket: it cannot hold anything it learns. . . . A fool's wisdom is like a tumbledown house; his knowledge is a string of ill-digested sayings. (Ecclesiasticus 21:12, 21:18)

Prepare what you have to say, if you want a hearing. Marshal your learning and then give your answer. The feelings of a fool turn like a cartwheel, and his thoughts spin like an axle. (Ecclesiasticus 33:4–5)

Not only is Ben Sirah's fool intellectually disorganized, he seems to be emotionally unbalanced as well. This could be an example of how a category—here, "fool"—comes to incorporate within it many connected concepts. (Ben Sirah also makes use of the metaphor, a commonplace in rabbinic literature, equating the Torah and water; see Sifre D., Piska 48; B. Taanit 7a–b; B. Baba Kamma 82a; B. Kiddushin 30b. A corollary to this metaphor makes the mind and soul containers for Torah, or ground that Torah might fructify as rain fructifies. In other words, Torah is the purpose, the enlivening agent, of the soul and mind.) Though Ben Sirah apparently speaks of a fool, he attributes to this person actions characteristic of mental disability and mental illness (e.g., disorganized thought processes and inappropriate affect).

The fool exhibits inappropriate social behavior that is metaphorically described with physical imagery: "The fool says, 'I have no friends, I get no thanks for my kindnesses; though they eat my bread, they speak ill of me.' How everyone will laugh at him—and how often! Better a slip on the stone floor than a slip of the tongue; and the fall of the wicked comes just as suddenly" (Ecclesiasticus 20:16–18). The foolish person does not know how to relate to others, here apparently expecting to be able to buy friendship. He hosts persons with his bread and is disappointed when they speak ill of him, not realizing that a friendship is based on respect, for each party's wisdom cannot be bought. This foolish behavior is likened to a slip on a stone floor: a sudden, embarrassing, and painful experience that induces laughter in others. The foolish and the wicked are paired in this metaphor, further reinforcing the image of a foolish person as one lacking the fear of God. Just as a foolish person makes ridiculous statements that suddenly cause others to laugh, so a wicked person's (the same person's?) downfall can come painfully and quickly.

For Ben Sirah, the wise person manifests wisdom not only in his intellectual and moral stature but in his physical demeanor through proper decorum and control over his body and appetites: "If you are sitting at a grand table, do not lick your lips and exclaim, 'What a spread!' Remember, it is a vice to have a greedy eye. There is no greater evil in creation than the eye; that is why it must shed tears at every turn" (Ecclesiasticus 31:12–13). Previously, sight was metaphorically extended to refer to insight and good judgment. Here, sight is paired with an overactive appetite. Paradoxically, then, the eye symbolizes both insight, Ben Sirah's supreme good, and sexual and physical appetites, which may be a wise one's undoing. Within this symbolic system, blind persons actually achieve some advantage in their pursuit of wisdom, for they are not diverted by that which entices the physical eye. Such persons can focus on the light of insight, instead of being drawn toward what their eyes behold.

Like pagan and earlier Jewish works, Christian sources emphasize decorum and control of the body and its appetites. Peter Brown (1988, 106) notes that "Second-century thinkers invariably regarded the human person as a microcosm of the universe." Thus the relationship of husband and wife represented the ideal balance and harmony of society as a whole (P. Brown 1988, 57). The body, in Christianity, became a thing that had to be closely controlled in order to enable the soul within to come closer to God. These rules of propriety extended to almost every sphere of bodily activity. For example, at table we find the Christian "Keeping the hand and couch and chin free of grease-stains; possessing the grace of the countenance undisturbed, and committing no indecorum in the act of swallowing. He must burp gently, sit correctly, and refrain from scratching his ears" (Clement, *Paidagogos* 2.1.13.1:I, 2.2.33.4, 2.7.60.2:I; cited in P. Brown 1988, 128). So the ideal Christian evinced supreme bodily control and decorum in his behavior.[4]

How did disabled persons, who presumably had less control of their bodily functions, fit into this worldview? For without doubt such persons were a large part of society at that time. That in the Justinian Code (529 C.E.) deaf and mute persons constitute a legal category (along with minors) suggests that they existed in considerable numbers (see "History" in Van Cleve 1987, 2:41). Later Christian writings begin to express the idea that disabilities and illness are manifestations of a battle between good and evil; monk-physicians described cases of demonic possession (apparently such diseases as manic-depressive illness and epilepsy; see Rouche 1987, 458). So, the body in Christian thought comes to be regarded as troublesome. In these later works, as in earlier ones, the body is seen as an entity to be controlled if one aspires to participation in the elite group among Christians.

We can see the same sorts of attitudes about body and soul in Jewish sources that we found in Greek, Roman, and Christian sources. In one of the most salient passages for understanding the Torah's theology of disabilities, Moses protests to God that he cannot lead the Israelites from slavery to freedom because he has a speech impediment—perhaps a stutter, as Les Gruber (1986, 5–13) suggests: "And Moses said unto the Lord: My Lord, I am not a man of words, neither yesterday nor the day before nor ever since you have spoken to your servant, for I am slow of speech and slow of tongue. And God said to him, 'Who puts a mouth in a person? And who makes him mute or deaf or seeing or blind? Is it not I, the Lord?'" (Exodus 4:10–11). The first part of God's retort directly addresses Moses' concern. Just as God has made Moses "slow of speech," God can cure him, too. But the second part of God's reply does not bear directly on Moses' case and may be taken as a general statement that God is the provider of *all* the faculties. Speaking, hearing, and seeing are grouped together here, possibly as the faculties Moses needed most when leading the Israelites to freedom.

Rabbinic literature, like Christian and pagan literature, was very concerned with the relationship between the body and the soul. Leviticus Rabbah Vayikra 4 has as its theme the nature of the soul.[5] As part of its exploration of this topic, the relationship of the soul to the body is delineated. In this essay, the body and soul are portrayed as bound together, yet the body serves the soul; the soul is superior to the body: "Ten things serve the soul: the gullet for food, the windpipe for the voice, the liver for anger, the lungs for drinking, the stomach to grind [the food], the spleen for laughter, the maw for sleep, the gall for jealousy, the kidneys think, and the heart decides; and the soul is above them all. The Holy One, blessed be He, says [to the soul]: 'I have made you above them all, and you go forth and rob and act violently and sin!'" (Leviticus Rabbah, Vayikra 4:4). The body is designed to serve the soul, and thus the *soul* is held responsible for making the body sin.

In an example of "argumentation"—that is, the purposeful introduction of several different points of view in the same document—the very next passage of this exposition suggests the opposite: the body and soul cannot be judged separately. They share responsibility for each person's sins.

> "Speak unto the children of Israel, saying: When a soul sins, etc." (Leviticus 4:2). R. Yishmael taught: This may be compared to the case of a king who had an orchard containing fine early figs, and he placed there two watchmen, one lame and one blind. He said to them: "Be careful with these fine early figs." [After some] days the lame man said to the blind one: "I see fine early figs in the orchard." Said the blind man to him: "Come let us eat them." The lame man said to him: "Can I walk?" Said the blind man: "Can I then see?" The lame man rode astride the blind man, and they ate the early figs and [then each] sat down [again] in his place. [After some] days the king came into that orchard and he said to them: "Where are the fine early figs?" The blind man said: "My lord the king, can I see?" The lame man said: "My lord, the king, can I walk?" That king was sharp-witted (*pikeiach*). What did he do to them? He placed the lame man astride the blind man and they began to move about. [He] said to them: "Thus have you done, and eaten the early figs."
>
> So, in the future to come, the Holy One, blessed be He, will say to the soul: "Why have you sinned before Me?" And the soul will say before Him: "Master of the Universe, I have not sinned, but the body is the one that sinned. From the moment I left you I have been a pure bird flying through the air. What [sin could] I have committed before You?" [God will also] say to the body: "Why have you sinned before Me?" And the body will say before Him: "Master of the Universe, I have not sinned, but the soul is the one that sinned. From the moment it left me, I am cast about like a stone and thrown upon the ground. What [sin could] I have committed before You?" What will the Holy One, blessed be He, do to them? He will bring the soul and cast it into the body, and judge both as one. (Leviticus Rabbah, Vayikra 4:5)

This parable emphasizes the unity of a person in body and spirit. The body and soul work in a partnership to form a complete human being. A body without a soul is as disabled as a soul without a body. It is significant that the conscious literary choice is made to use blind and lame persons as symbols: a body without a soul can't see; a soul without a body can't act. The body and soul work in concert. Paradoxically, if they did not, there would be no sin, but there would also be no life.

Disabilities can come as a product of old age, without sin. This may be an inevitable part of life and is therefore *not* an atonement for sin; indeed, it may be part of the expected workings of the body over time.

> R. Shimon ben Halafta went to greet Rabbi [Yehudah HaNasi] every new moon. When he had grown old he was no longer able to go. One day he did go. [Rabbi] said to him: "What is the matter that you have not been coming up to me as you used to do?" He [R. Shimon] said to him: "Distant [things] have become near [ones] and near [ones] have become distant [ones]. Two have turned into three and that which makes peace in the home no [longer] functions." (An explanation [of the foregoing]: "Distant [things] have become near [ones]"—these are the eyes which used to see at a distance do not now see even [when] things are near. "And near [ones] have become distant [ones]"—these are the ears which heard the first time, do not now hear even at the hundredth time [of speaking]. "Two have turned into three"—[one walks only with] a stick in addition to two legs. "That which makes peace in the home"—this is [sexual] desire which brings peace between a man and his wife.) "Because man goes to his eternal home" (Ecclesiastes 12:5). It says not "eternal home," but "*his* eternal home" which teaches us that every righteous person has an eternity of his own [making]. (Leviticus Rabbah Metsora 18:1)

The meaning of this story is clear. A sage bemoans the decay of his body and its faculties. His vision, hearing, physical mobility, and sexual abilities have all decreased dramatically. While disease or disability can be seen as punishments for sin when they occur in youth or in the prime of life, when they appear in old age disabilities are viewed quite differently. In fact, the midrash is quick to reassure the righteous listeners that though they may suffer bodily decay now, they will have their eternal reward.

God is perceived as responsible not only for the proper functioning of the body but for those aspects which mark it as living:

> Our Rabbis taught: There are three partners in a person, the Holy One, blessed be He, his father, and his mother. His father sows the white [substance, i.e., semen] out of which [come the child's] bones and sinews and nails and the brain in his head and the white in his eye; his mother sows the red [substance, i.e. blood] out of which [come the child's] skin and flesh and hair and blood and the black of the eye. And the Holy One, blessed be He, gives him spirit and breath and beauty of face and seeing eyes and hearing ears and walking legs and understanding and insight. When the time comes for him to depart from the world, the Holy One, blessed be He, takes away His portion and leaves the portions of his father and mother with them. (B. Niddah 31a; see also B. Kiddushin 30b)

God is an integral partner with man and woman in the genesis of a human body. What God contributes are the faculties: the ability to see, hear, speak, walk, and understand—in other words, what makes a human being unique among God's creatures. The contributions of man and woman reflect the physical body flows with which they are associated: white/semen from men and red/blood from women.[6] One might infer from this passage that cognitive and sensory disabilities represent the withholding by God of the gifts of the faculties.

The following passage expresses similar beliefs regarding God's gift of the faculties:

> "And Hannah spoke in her heart (*al libah*)" (1 Samuel 1:13). Rabbi Elazar said in the name of Rabbi Yose ben Zimra: She spoke about the workings of her heart (*al iskei libah*). She said before Him: Master of the Universe, everything that You created in a woman has a purpose: eyes to see and ears to hear, a nose to smell, a mouth to speak, hands to do work, legs to walk with, breasts to nurse with them. These

breasts that You have put over my heart (*al libi*), are they not to nurse [with]? Give me a son, so that I may nurse with them. (B. Berachot 31b)

The sages who attribute these words to Hannah play on the assumptions expressed in B. Niddah 31a. It is taken as a given that God created each organ for a reason and that a person, as God's partner, should be allowed to use each organ for its designated purpose. To be sure, those purposes are not as obvious as they seem. Hands might have been destined for something other than work, a mouth might have been made to pray, and so on. The exposition plays on the somewhat odd phrase from Scripture *al libah*, which could either mean "silently" or "about her heart." Hannah is portrayed here as using God's own logic. Knowing herself to be blameless, she plays on God's own scheme for the body, and its use, in her demand that God give her a son. This passage is relevant for our purpose in that it identifies what each organ is to do, and in that it is understood that the organs are assigned these tasks by God.[7]

The Bavli strongly discourages any sort of indecorous sexual intercourse by linking it to birth defects. The correlation between decorum during sexual intercourse and positive outcomes in terms of fetal development was a widely held notion in the surrounding cultures as well (see above; and P. Brown 1988, 11, further cites Plutarch *Praecepta conjugalia* 48.145e–f, which specifically finds fault with women's unrestrained thoughts). While this passage speaks of improper sexual actions, they are nonetheless not sins.

Rabbi Yochanan ben Dahavai said: The Ministering Angels told me four things: People are born lame because they [their parents] overturned their table [during intercourse]; mute because they kiss "that place"; deaf, because they converse during intercourse; blind, because they look at "that place."

An objection is raised [to this teaching]. Imma Shalom was asked: Why are (20b) your children so very beautiful? She said to them: Because he [my husband] does not "converse" with me at the beginning of the night nor at the end of the night but [only] in the middle of the night. And when he "converses" he reveals a handbreadth and conceals a handbreadth, and he resembles one who is possessed by a demon. And I said to him, "What is the reason [for choosing midnight for intercourse]?" And he said to me, "So that I may not look at another woman and my children would be like illegitimate children. There is no difficulty: this teaching of Imma Shalom about speaking during intercourse refers to] speaking about intercourse [while it is happening]; the teaching that one should not talk during intercourse lest one's children be born mute refers to] speaking about other matters [during intercourse].

Rabbi Yochanan said: These are the words of Rabbi Yochanan ben Dahavai. But the sages said: The halakhah is not according to Rabbi Yochanan ben Dahavai. Rather, each person may do what he wishes with his wife [regarding intercourse]. It is like meat which comes from the butcher shop. If he wishes to eat it salted, he eats it; broiled, he eats it; cooked, he eats it; boiled, he eats it. And [it is just] so with fish that comes from the fish shop.[8] (B. Nedarim 20a–b)

This passage asserts that sexual intercourse conducted without the proper decorum results in disabled children. This is certainly as strong a sanction as one could imagine against a behavior considered to be undesirable. Inserted into the discussion is the story of Imma Shalom, who had exceedingly beautiful children and, it would stand to reason, engaged in exceedingly correct sexual behavior. Imma Shalom was a member of an aristocratic family: her brother was Rabban Gamliel II and her husband was the eminent Rabbi Eliezer ben Hyrkanos; both were extremely wealthy and learned men. If anyone would personify correct sexual behavior, it would be this woman. The story related here concerns the proper time and manner for sexual intercourse and whether conversation is acceptable at such a time. When the passage then returns to Rabbi Yochanan ben Dahavai's contentions, they are dismissed; because men are not constrained in their marital relations with their wives, his words must be discounted. However, the public is urged to conduct their marital relations as the sages recommend. While the sages could not legislate the most decorous sort of behavior during sexual intercourse, they could encourage it by the most strenuous means.

Blessings for Persons with Disabilities

Disabled persons, or persons who simply have a distinctive appearance, are considered part of God's creation and the emotions one feels on seeing such persons are consecrated with blessings. M. Berachot 9:1–3 outlines blessings for various occasions, such as seeing remarkable things (M. Berachot 9:1). Tosefta adds to these blessings one to be said on seeing a person with a remarkable physical constitution and one to be said on seeing a person who has become disabled or is afflicted with sickness.

> One who sees an Ethiopian, or an albino, or [a man] red-spotted in the face, or [a man] white spotted in the face, or a hunchback, or a dwarf (or a *cheresh* or a *shoteh* or a drunk person) says, "Blessed [are you Lord our God, Ruler of the Universe who creates such] varied creatures."
>
> [One who sees] an amputee, or a lame person, or a blind person, or a person afflicted with boils, says, "Blessed [are you Lord our God, Ruler of the Universe] the true Judge." (T. Berachot 6:3)

The implication here is that all these persons are part of God's creation and that any feeling experienced upon seeing them should be consecrated with a blessing. One whose condition simply makes him or her physically distinctive is one of the wide variety of creatures created by God and should not be considered judged. However, one who is visibly disabled or ill—that is, one to whom the "true judge" blessing applies—*is* deemed adjudged by God (the blessing that ends "the true Judge" is said on hearing bad tidings of any sort; M. Berachot 9:2). This distinction does not quite match the one offered by the Bavli (58b), which separates the disabled into those that have their conditions from birth and those that acquired their conditions later in life.

The Yerushalmi refines Tosefta's categorization system, reflected in these blessings, in a manner consistent with the Bavli. The concept of disabilities as a judgment from God can be seen in the rationale given for the blessings one says on seeing disabled persons: "This teaching [to say the blessing, 'the True Judge'] applies [to those who see persons with disabilities who were born] whole and later were changed. But if [one sees a person who] was born that way he says, 'Blessed [are you Lord our God, Ruler of the Universe who creates such] varied creatures'" (Y. Berachot 9:1). If one is born without disabilities and they later develop, then the disabilities are a judgment from God. Those born with disabilities, however, are simply among God's varied creations. The treatment in Tosefta is more straightforward: there, the difference was drawn between conditions that were physically distinctive and afflictions. But the Yerushalmi, despite adding the complication of the issue of timing, gets to the heart of a disability's meaning for the person who has it: it can be experienced either as one of a number of "normal" conditions or as a punishment.

Infanticide

While we have seen many similarities between the sages' attitudes and those of the peoples that surrounded them, we can find one area in which the Jewish attitude toward the body and soul is markedly different. Infanticide, the killing of unwanted or nonviable infants, was held in some cultures to be an appropriate response to the presence of birth defects. One such culture was that of late classical Sparta (fifth c. B.C.E.), where physical perfection was held in high regard because it enabled one to serve as a soldier, the most important activity in that society. An exercise regimen was prescribed by law for men who performed military service; a man could even lose his citizenship for failure to keep physically fit (see Xenophon *Spartan Constitution* 3.3, 3.7, 12.5, 10.7; cited by MacDowell 1986, 52, 68, 69). Women also had to maintain their physical fitness. Their task was to bear soldiers for the state, and healthy women were probably less likely to die during childbirth. In general, bodily control was emphasized and encouraged.

Given this philosophy, which valued physical fitness and military ability above all other attributes, the Spartan attitude toward children with birth defects is hardly surprising. By ancient custom, such infants were disposed of by communal authorities:

> The father did not have authority to rear the baby, but he took it to a place called a *leskhe*, where the eldest members of the tribe sat and inspected the child. If he was well-built and strong, they ordered him to rear it, allocating to it one of the 9,000 lots; but if he was ill-born and unshapely, they sent it away to the so-called *Apothetai*, a place like a pit near Taygetos, believing that it was better both for itself and for the city that it should not live if it was not well-formed for health and strength right from the start. (Plutarch *Lycurgus* 16.1–2; quoted in MacDowell 1986, 52)

We may infer that often a baby with obvious birth defects was exposed by the Spartan father without waiting for the verdict of the elders (MacDowell 1986, 54). It is the legal, communal nature of infanticide in Sparta that was unique, not the fact that it took place. Exposure of unwanted infants was a common practice throughout Greece, but outside Sparta it was normally done only on the parents' own initiative.

Soranus was a Greek physician who practiced medicine in Rome at the time of the Emperors Trajan (98–117) and Hadrian (117–138), dying about the time Galen was born. He wrote many books, and his work *Gynecology* represented ancient gynecological and obstetrical practice at its height (Temkin 1956, xxv). Soranus clearly outlines the criteria for deciding which infants should live and which should not.

> 10 [79]. Now the midwife, having received the newborn, should first put it upon the earth, having examined beforehand whether the infant is male or female, and should make an announcement by signs as is the custom of women. She should also consider whether it is worth rearing or not. And the infant which is suited by nature for rearing will be distinguished by the fact that its mother has spent the period of pregnancy in good health, for conditions which require medical

care, especially those of the body, also harm the fetus and enfeeble the foundations of its life. Second, by the fact that it has been born at the due time, best at the end of nine months, and if it so happens, later; but also after only seven months. Furthermore by the fact that when put on the earth it immediately cries with proper vigor; for one that lives for some length of time without crying, or cries but weakly, is suspected of behaving so on account of some unfavorable condition. Also by the fact that it is perfect in all its parts, members and senses; that its ducts, namely the ears, nose, pharynx, urethra, and anus are free from obstruction; that the natural functions of every [member] are neither sluggish nor weak; that the joints bend and stretch; that it has due size and shape and is properly sensitive in every respect. This we may recognize from pressing the fingers against the surface of the body, for it is natural to suffer pain from everything that pricks or squeezes. And by conditions contrary to those mentioned, the infant not worth rearing is recognized. (Soranus 1956, 79)

A child with a visible disability would not be considered worthy of rearing and would quickly be exposed.

Roman children who were born with birth defects were more than likely exposed, for even healthy infants were often exposed in those days. The reasons were numerous: the parents might be too poor to raise the child or they might want to give a decent inheritance to their surviving heirs. Indeed, exposure of infants with and without birth defects was so common that the Greeks and the Romans thought it peculiar that Egyptians, Germans, and Jews did not expose any of their children (Veyne 1987, 9).

The Bavli considers infanticide unacceptable, attributing such behavior to heathens (e.g., B. Avodah Zarah 26a). However, we should note that though this behavior was deemed unacceptable, it may still have occurred, just as it occasionally does today. That seems to be the background against which the following incident occurred: "Mar son of Rav Ashi said: Even if the child died [the remarriage of the mother] is forbidden, for perhaps she killed it so that she might marry. It once actually happened that a mother strangled [her child so she could remarry]. This is [no proof of the general statement]. That woman was a *shotah* for [sane] women [generally] do not strangle their children [and proof cannot be deduced from so anomalous a case]" (B. Ketubot 60b). This passage appears in a discussion about the length of time a woman must wait after being widowed or divorced before remarrying. If she has an infant whom she is still nursing, she is not permitted to remarry, lest she conceive another child and diminish the first child's supply of milk. Even if the child dies, she must wait at least three months before remarrying. In this connection, it is reported that a woman actually did strangle her child in order be able to remarry more quickly. The evaluation of this woman's behavior is significant: she is deemed a *shotah*, since normal women simply do not behave in such a manner. She is not *pikachat*, one who sharp-wittedly manipulates legal categories for her benefit. Rather, she is lacking in *da'at* and is, in a word, insane. Her act of infanticide is the proof. Life is considered by the sages, and by the priesthood before them, to be God's most precious gift. Given that attitude, all children are to be treasured in Jewish society.

While disabilities can have symbolic meaning, often related to punishment for sin, they can also be evidence in humanity of God's vast range of creativity, according to the sages. While birth anomalies were tied to indecorous sexual intercourse in Judaism, as in the non-Jewish surrounding cultures, they do not constitute permission to kill a child once born, as was the case in many other ancient cultures. Disabilities may be the outcome of life processes and may reflect nothing about the righteousness of the person who has them.

To hearken back to the analogy with which this chapter began, in Judaism the body, a glass vessel that may not have been blown quite properly or may have become chipped over time, can still serve its function as a container for the soul. And though there are contexts that demand a perfectly blown, unchipped glass (i.e., the Temple and priestly activities), usually one with an air bubble in the glass or one with a crack will do quite well.

6

Categorization, Disabilities, and Persons with Disabilities

THE QUESTIONS of the playground plague us for life. "Who's in?" "Who's out?" "Who's the prettiest?" "Who's the best athlete?" "Who's the last person to be picked for the team?" These questions of inclusion and exclusion, and the issues of categorization on which they rely, are extremely important ones for our sources with regard to persons with disabilities.

In our examination of priestly culture and its characterizations of disabilities, we saw how any sort of blemish caused human beings and animals to be banished from the cult. This was possible in the small, controlled environment of the Temple. However, persons with disabilities were most certainly not banished from everyday life in the rest of the Jewish community. As we have seen, the sages struggled to make sense of the symbolic and theological significance of disabilities and the persons with disabilities in their midst. Now we will examine the system the sages developed that outlines the way such persons were to be treated and how they were to be allowed to function (or not to be allowed to function) within the sages' vision of Jewish society.

In what follows, it is most important to remember that the sages' promulgation of a certain attitude toward a given group of persons with disabilities should not, by any means, be taken as proof positive of how that group was, in fact, treated. The sages generally had little power to coerce obedience or to enforce their opinions. And, of course, we learn almost nothing about the ways persons with disabilities viewed themselves. That history, most likely, can never be recovered.

Unlike the priests and their domain, open only to those who possessed the proper lineage, physical blemishlessness, and a state of ritual purity, the sages' culture depended on *da'at:* cognition and the oral transmission and discussion of received traditions. Therefore, the "most disabling" disabilities in rabbinic culture were those which prevented a person from participating in that culture and from being able to recognize its orally transmitted rules and norms: that is, deaf-muteness, mental illness (insanity), and mental disability (retardation). These disabilities, in rabbinic literature, led to the stigmatization of those persons who bore them. Blind and physically disabled persons, however, were considered disabled only when their disabilities prevented them from fully participating in a specific way in rabbinic culture's activities: for example, a blind person's inability to perceive sunlight or a lame person's need to use prosthetic devices on Shabbat. The categorization scheme that the sages developed reveals how they saw persons with disabilities fitting, or not fitting, into their society and may serve to describe how the sages responded to persons with disabilities.

The Nature of Categories

Categorization is a central activity of human reason. Understanding the cognitive and sociolinguistic bases of categories will help us understand the categorization system that the sages developed regarding persons with disabilities.

Categories are complex entities. Some have clear boundaries; others do not. Some categories contain a "best example," which sociolinguist George Lakoff calls a "prototype" (1987, 7). This prototype, Lakoff predicts, will be a "basic-level category." In a taxonomy of trees this would correspond to the genus level—an oak or a maple, for example. A sugar maple would be at the level of a species, at one level of specificity from the basic level, and a "leaf-bearing tree" would be in an intermediate category, one level of generalization above the basic-level category (Lakoff 1987, 33). Basic-level categories are cognitively and psychologically important because they are easily learned and psychologically prominent. They are also, as Lakoff puts it, "human sized": "They depend not on objects themselves, independent of people, but on the way people interact with objects: the way they perceive them, image them, organize information about them and behave toward them with their bodies. The relevant properties clustering together to define such categories are not inherent to the objects, but are interactional properties, having to do with the way people interact with objects" (51). Basic-level categories are embedded, then, in the body. The terms for persons with disabilities in Hebrew, such as *cheresh* (a person with hearing and speaking disabilities) and *shoteh* (a person with mental illness or disability), are basic-level categories.[1]

Since basic-level categories, according to Lakoff, depend on the way people interact with the items in them, it is reasonable to assume that the ways that the sages related to persons with disabilities helped form the categories used in the documents we will consider. For example, in the era before sign language, persons with hearing or speaking disabilities may have been engaged through an unsystematized set of hand signals, or through simple force or constraint. Mentally ill or disabled persons may also have been physically managed or constrained. Blind persons may have been spoken with and led around by hand. Physically disabled persons may have been aided in specific tasks. We might note that these are all ways in which adults interact with children at different times and in different situations. And, in fact, children are often grouped with disabled persons in the Mishnah. *Da'at*—most often translated "knowledge," though it has many meanings, almost all related to cognitive ability—may be the underlying factor that characterizes the intermediate category *cheresh, shoteh v'katan* (the deaf-mute person, mentally ill or mentally disabled person, and a child); but we should not ignore the possibility that another, equally important factor ties these basic-level categories together. That is, the sages relate to these three

groups of persons in a basically unified way: by directing and con-
straining them. In other words, the *cheresh, shoteh v'katan* are linked
not by something intrinsic in them but rather by the common way
others relate to them.

Often, categories are understood in terms of abstract ideals that
are, of course, culturally determined and that become the prototypes for these categories (Lakoff 1987, 87). These prototypes may
then form the centers of what Lakoff calls "radial categories": "Like
other categories, a radial category is represented structurally as a
container, and its subcategories are containers inside it. What distinguishes it is that it is structured by a center-periphery schema.
One subcategory is the center; the other subcategories are connected to the center by various types of links. Noncentral categories
may be 'subcenters,' that is, they may have further center-periphery
structures imposed on them" (287). This concept of a radial category will be especially useful as we explore conceptions of mental
illness and mental disability in our sources. We will witness the
metaphorical extension of terms relating to mental health and ability, or the lack thereof, such as *shoteh, da'at,* and *pikeiach* (a fully sensate individual).

For example, from the central meaning of the word *shoteh*—that
is, one who has no *da'at*—one might find radiating out other meanings, as the word is applied to the mentally disabled, the mentally ill,
an idolater (and, by extension, an ingrate), one who practices the
sages' system poorly, and one who can't be interrogated.

Categories, then, are intimately tied to the body and to our bodily
experiences. Even the category "God" is affected by the human
body. The priests experienced God through blood, smoke, fire, sacred procession, and procedure. The sages experienced God
through precept, prayer, and recited Scripture.

Liminality and Stigmatization

The existence of a category, metaphorically understood as a container, implies that a given item is either in or out of it. Reality, of

course, is rarely so neat. Indeed, persons with disabilities challenge neat categorical systems. Sometimes it seems that they are clearly included in society, except in those instances in which their disability precludes full participation. At other times they may be imagined to be stigmatized, that is, utterly discredited within the sages' idealized vision of society and excluded from the category "full member of society." In yet other instances, persons with disabilities may seem somehow betwixt and between, neither clearly in a category nor clearly out of it. This ambiguous status is called "liminality."

Victor Turner's is still the classic definition and discussion of liminality (1967, 93–111). He developed the concept, which applies to what he described as an "interstructural situation," in relation to puberty rites of passage in Africa during which neophytes are separated from their normal lives and become structurally "invisible" in their society. In this state of transition they are stripped of their former identity and molded with the authoritative "*gnosis*" of their society (102). The initiation process

> stamp[s] into the neophytes the basic assumptions of their culture. . . . Thus the communication of *sacra* both teaches the neophytes how to think with some degree of abstraction about their cultural milieu and gives them ultimate standards of reference. At the same time, it is believed to change their nature, transform them from one kind of human being to another. It intimately unites man and office. But for a variable while, there was an uncommitted man, an individual rather than a social *persona*, in a sacred community of individuals. (Turner 1967, 102)

If a person enters adult life without internalizing his or her culture's truths, he or she may be considered to be in a perpetually liminal position. In the sages' system, persons with hearing, speaking, and mental disabilities (i.e., persons without *da'at*) were deemed unable to receive, retain, and retrieve the *sacra* of the culture. Such persons were stigmatized, while those who might have been able receive the *sacra* but could not act on them consistently (e.g., women and slaves) were considered to be in a perpetually liminal state.

The term "liminal" may accurately describe the position of some persons with disabilities in the sages' system. Like Turner's neophytes, persons with some disabilities were experienced in the sages' culture as neither fully dead nor fully alive. Therefore, they are "structurally 'invisible' (though physically visible) and ritually polluting. They are very commonly secluded, partially or completely, from the realm of culturally defined and ordered states and statuses. . . . They have physical but not social 'reality,' hence they have to be hidden, since it is a paradox, a scandal, to see what ought not to be there!" (Turner 1967, 98). In addition, liminal individuals lose some of their rights over their physical property: "[they] *have* nothing. They have no status, property, insignia, secular clothing, rank, kinship position, nothing to demarcate them structurally from their fellows. Their condition is indeed the very prototype of sacred poverty. Rights over property, goods, and services inhere in positions in the politico-jural structure. Since they do not occupy such positions, neophytes exercise no such rights" (98–99). In the system the sages developed to describe their vision of Jewish society, the category *nashim, avadim, k'tanim,* "women, slaves, minors," is the one that embodies liminality. Turner (1967, 96) notes that liminal persons are not yet classified and that this is "often expressed in symbols modeled on process of gestation and parturition. The neophytes are likened to or treated as embryos, newborn infants, or sucklings by symbolic means which vary from culture to culture." Women and slaves are explicitly equated to children as liminal individuals. These persons are human beings with *da'at,* cognition, but they cannot freely act on that *da'at* because they are owned in some way; others bear responsibility for them. They are therefore betwixt and between full personhood and nonpersonhood.

By way of contrast, those in the category *cheresh, shoteh v'katan* were stigmatized in the sages' system. Erving Goffman's classic work, *Stigma* (1963), traces the history of the concept through the ages in a fashion similar to this book's treatment of terms referring to persons with disabilities:

The Greeks, who were apparently strong on visual aids, originated the term *stigma* to refer to bodily signs designed to expose something unusual and bad about the moral status of the signifier. The signs were cut or burnt into the body and advertised that the bearer was a slave, a criminal or a traitor—a blemished person, ritually polluted, to be avoided, especially in public places. Later, in Christian times, two layers of metaphor were added to the term: the first referred to bodily signs of holy grace that took the form of eruptive blossoms on the skin; the second, a medical allusion to this religious allusion, referred to bodily signs of physical disorder. (1)

A stigma is visible, perceptible, evident to the "normals" in the culture; it serves to spoil the stigmatized person's social identity, discrediting that person in society (Goffman 1963, 48, 19). To be stigmatized is to be seen as failing in some way. Paul Higgins (1980), in his sociological study of deaf persons, asserts that the stigma of deafness constitutes a "master status" that serves to homogenize the perception of the persons who share it. This is as true in the sages' system as it is today.

Another issue relevant to stigma is "extension," that is, the assignment of additional (often negative) characteristics and limitations based on the original "failing":

> Those who create and control the larger social world often treat the "failing" of outsiders as a master status. It is the particular stigma, the failing, which organizes people's behavior toward outsiders, and not the individual characteristics of those outsiders. . . . Not only does the larger social world emphasize the "failing" of the outsiders, but it also treats those with the same 'failing' as if they were the same. . . . The hearing world regards deafness (and its visible indication, signing) as a master status. (Higgins 1980, 131)

Because the stigmatized individual is seen as less than human, social distance may be created between this person and the rest of society. As Goffman (1963, 18) puts it, "We [normals] may try to act as if he were a 'non-person,' and not present at all as someone of whom ritual notice is to be taken." All of these aspects of stigma—the "master status," the "spoiled identity," the issue of "extension," and the social distance created in relation to the stigmatized person—will characterize rabbinic literature's approach to deaf-mute and mentally ill and disabled persons.

As we have already seen, disabilities had a symbolic importance in Jewish culture. According to Goffman, stigmas often have such meanings:

> The information of most relevance in the study of stigma has certain properties. It is information about an individual. It is about his more or less abiding characteristics, as opposed to the moods, feelings, or intents that he might have at a particular moment. The information, as well as the sign through which it is conveyed, is reflexive and embodied; that is, it is conveyed by the very person it is about, and conveyed through bodily expression in the immediate presence of those who receive the expression. Information possessing all of these properties I will call here "social." Some signs that convey social information may be frequently and steadily available, and routinely sought and received; these signs may be called "symbols." (1963, 43)

Persons who were deemed to lack *da'at* (cognition and purposeful action) were not seen by the sages to be liminal but rather stigmatized. Those who had *da'at* but could not act on it, being controlled in some way, were counted by the sages as liminal persons. Other disabled persons (i.e., persons with visual and physical disabilities) were treated as occupying neither stigmatized nor liminal positions. The sages accepted them as full participants except insofar as their disability hindered them from performing specific actions. As the priestly system was based on lineage, the sages' system was based on *da'at*, or cognition: acquiring, expressing, and imparting it.

Da'at

As mentioned above, *da'at* seems to mean more than its usual translation of "knowledge" would indicate. In the Bible, the word appears most frequently in Proverbs, Job, and Ecclesiastes—that is, in Wisdom literature—though it is also used in narratives and prophetic literature. *Da'at* is more than cognitive ability, although, to be sure, it involves cognitive skills. It is also moral insight, and it is a characteristic of purposeful action. Let us consider some examples.

Da'at is clearly equated with discernment—the ability to differentiate (a cognitive skill) between good and evil (i.e., to make moral evaluations that are culturally determined)—in Genesis 2:9 and 2:17, which describe the "tree of the knowledge of (*da'at*) good and evil": "And the Lord God caused every tree to spring from the ground that was pleasing to the sight and good to eat and the tree of life was in the midst of the garden and the tree of knowledge (*eits ha-da'at*) of good and evil" (Genesis 2:9). Here, in the first use of the term *da'at* in the entire Tanach, it is clear that *da'at*, if possessed, is what makes a person an adult human being. Eating the fruit of this tree leads to expulsion from the idyllic, protected, childlike existence of the garden into the world of adult independence. This *da'at* may be connected to sexuality as well as cognition. One medieval commentator, Ibn Ezra, argues that it is sexual in nature, since immediately after the expulsion Adam is said to know his wife (*yada*, from the same root as *da'at*) and she conceives and bears a son (Genesis 4:1). But the two may not be mutually exclusive. As we saw regarding priests, evidence of sexual maturity was paired with potential competence to perform the priestly role. Nahum Sarna (1989, 31), commenting on Genesis 4:1, notes that "'Knowing' in the Bible is not essentially intellectual activity, not simply the objective contemplation of reality. Rather, it is experiential, emotional, and, above all, relational. . . . The Hebrew stem *y-d-'* can encompass a range of meanings that includes involvement, interaction, loyalty, and obligation. It can be used of the most intimate and most hallowed relationships between man and wife and between man and God. Significantly the verb is never employed for animal copulation." *Da'at* signals maturity. Moral maturity, the ability to distinguish between good and bad, is paired with sexual maturity in the Garden of Eden narrative. The phrase "to know good and evil" is used again in this exact form only in Deuteronomy 1:39, where the absence of the ability denotes innocence: "And your babies, of whom you said, they will become prey. And your children who did not know today good and evil, they shall go there and to you I will give [the land] and they shall inherit it" (Deuteronomy 1:39). Since these children were too young to know the difference between good and evil, they could not have taken any conscious role in the desert rebellions and so will be allowed to enter and inherit the land.[2]

While *da'at* is something that a wicked person lacks, in a leader it goes hand in hand with empathy and caring. For example, Yehoyakim is chastised by the prophet Jeremiah because he lacks the knowledge of God that his father, the righteous King Josiah, possessed: "Shall you reign, because you strive to excel in cedar? Did not your father eat and drink and do justice and righteousness? Then it was well with him. He judged the cause of the poor and needy (*dan din oni v'evyon*); then it was good. Is this not what it is to know Me (*hada'at Oti*)? says the Lord. But your eyes and your heart are not but for your unjust gain, and for shedding innocent blood and for oppression and for violence, to do it" (Jeremiah 22:15–17). King Josiah reformed his nation, cast out religious syncretism, reestablished the covenant of justice with his society's most vulnerable members, and enlarged the territory of Israel. The son, manifestly, acted nothing like the father. *Da'at* is related, then, not only to empathy with the poor but to discernment, judgment, and the ability to lead. It is not, however, a trait that only leaders might or need possess.

The main way to gain access to *da'at* is through the study of God's teachings: "My people are destroyed for lack of knowledge (*hada'at*); because you have rejected knowledge (*hada'at*), I will also reject you, that you shall be no priest to me; seeing that you have forgotten the Torah of your God (*Torat Elohecha*) I will also forget your children" (Hosea 4:6). Since the people of Israel abandoned God's knowledge, God's template for truth and loving-kindness (Hosea 4:1), God will abandon the Israelites. This verse not only gives us an example of the ultimate source of *da'at*, that is, God's teachings, but also shows what happens, measure for measure, when that teaching is despised. The

Israelites, portrayed as priests to the world, shamed God by abandoning divine teachings; so God will shame the Israelites by abandoning them.

There is one more, quite specific, use of the word *da'at* in the Tanach, which is a metaphorical extension of the primary meaning of *da'at* as discernment and judgment—that is, the quality of acting intentionally: "Then Moses set apart three cities on this side of the Jordan toward the rising sun; that the slayer might flee there, who killed his neighbor unaware (*bivli da'at*)" (Deuteronomy 4:41–42; see also Deuteronomy 19:4; Joshua 20:3). *Bivli da'at* here quite simply means "without intention."

So we find that *da'at* has several meanings and implications in the Tanach. Its primary meaning, "knowledge," embraces a complex combination of cognitive and cultural skills involving the ability to discern the difference between right and wrong and an insight, born of familiarity with God's teachings, that allows for a comprehension and judgment that is greater than the senses. In addition, *da'at* can indicate that an action is performed with intention. *Da'at* is, in sum, a divine quality of which human beings may partake in some limited form.

Da'at in rabbinic literature is a both a prerequisite for and product of participation in the learning advocated by the sages: the study of Torah and the sages' own teachings. There is almost nothing one could do in the society that the Mishnah envisions without *da'at*. In addition to the meanings that word has in the Tanach, in the Mishnah it has been extended to have other meanings as well, as listed here.

Da'at As Innate Moral and Cognitive Insight and Excellence, As Well As Something Learned in the Sage's Culture

This meaning is attested to in several passages. For example, M. Berachot 5:2, in its discussion of the placement of the blessing for the new week in the Amidah, alludes to the fourth blessing of the Amidah, which thanks God for graciously bestowing *da'at* on humanity. This is the very first of the daily petitions made to God, which demonstrates how important the sages considered *da'at* to be. *Da'at* is the foundation of the sages' relationship with God and is therefore the first thing requested in the Amidah.[3]

Da'at As Purposeful Action

This meaning of *da'at* arises in a mishnah concerned with blemishes in firstborn animals. Normally, firstborn animals were sacrificed in the cult if blemishless and could be ritually slaughtered otherwise. Priests who owned such animals could only slaughter them to consume them after some blemish naturally arose in them. The priest was not permitted to intentionally inflict a blemish on a firstborn animal in order to circumvent these rules so he could eat it. One mishnah reports two instances in which firstborn animals were impulsively inflicted with wounds, once by a non-Jew and once by children, and the sages permitted these animals to be slaughtered and eaten. However, when these same parties inflicted more wounds on firstborn animals deliberately, in order that they might be eaten, the mishnah responds with the following rule: "This is the rule: if it be [done] deliberately (*kol shehu l'da'ato*) it is prohibited [to slaughter], but if it not be [done] deliberately (*v'shelo l'da'ato*) [the slaughtering is permitted]" (M. Bekorot 5:3). If the wound was inflicted on the animal on purpose, to make it possible to eat that firstborn, then the animal may not be slaughtered. The rules may not be so crudely circumvented. However, if the wound was inflicted not as part of some systematic plan but as a mistake or on impulse, then the animal may be slaughtered. There is no mistaking the meaning of this term here: *da'at* is the performing of an action purposefully.

Da'at As Consent

Da'at comes to have a social component in this sense. To be able to effect an agreement with mutual consent, both parties must be familiar with the rules that are to govern their transaction and must be able to agree to abide by those rules. For example, when discussing the building of a fence between two gardens, the Mishnah characterizes mutual consent as *"im 'asu mida'at shneihem,"* literally, "if they did it according to the *da'at* of both of them" (M. Baba Batra 1:2). Similarly, with regard to rebuilding a house that collapsed, it must be rebuilt exactly as it was unless the lessee and the owner agree "*mida'at shneihem*" (M. Baba Metsia 8:9).[4]

Da'at As Opinion

Da'at can be used to describe the result of knowing the sages' corpus of learning; that is, a judgment or opinion. For example, opinion and vision are paired in the following mishnah:

> [The size of] the egg of which [the sages] have spoken [refers to one] that is neither large nor small, but applies to one of average [bulk]. Rabbi Yehudah says [to determine this medium measure] they should get the largest [egg possible] and the smallest [egg possible] and place [them both] in [a vessel full of] water and divide [into two equal parts the volume of] the [overflowing] water, [then one half will be the measure of a middle size egg]. Rabbi Yose said, But who can tell me which [egg] is the largest and which is the smallest [egg]? [But rather] every [such matter] shall be according to the opinion of the viewer (*hakol l'fi da'ato shel ro'eh*). (M. Keilim 17:6)

An "egg's worth" (about two fluid ounces) was a standard measure in the sages' system. Such a quantity of food is the smallest amount that could convey ritual impurity. The question addressed in this mishnah is "Exactly how much is an egg's worth, since eggs come in a variety of sizes?" Rabbi Yehudah suggests a scientific method for determining the measure, while Rabbi Yose suggests that each person use his or her eyes and intellect to make a judgment. Not everything can be exactly prescribed, even in the Mishnah's idealized system.

Da'at As Temperament and Social Appropriateness

One's *da'at* can also refer to one's degree of engagement in social customs related to politeness and emotional affect. This is a natural extension of a meaning of *da'at* that we found in the Tanach: the internalization of the Tanach's teachings—for example, the ability or inability to distinguish between good and evil—may quite naturally affect one's temperament and public demeanor. From there it is but a short metaphorical step to use the term *da'at* to apply to personality and to public demeanor in and of themselves. Thus *da'at* may refer to one's physical constitution. A person may behave grossly, without proper limits on his appetites and manners:

> Rabbi Yehudah said, Rabbi Yishmael asked Rabbi Joshua when they were going on a journey and said to him, Why have they [the sages] prohibited the cheese of idolaters? He said to him, Because [they make cheese] by curdling [the milk] with rennet [taken] from the carcass (*n'veilah*) [of an animal not ritually slaughtered]. He said to him: But is not the rennet from a burnt offering more stringently prohibited than the rennet from a carcass (*n'veilah*), and [nevertheless] they have said, A priest who is robust (*sheda'ato yafah*) may suck it out raw. (M. Avodah Zarah 2:5)

Rennet, a coagulating agent used in the making of cheese, is derived from the stomach lining of animals. A strict view of the Jewish dietary laws says that only rennet from animals slaughtered according to Jewish law may be used; thus it cannot come from an animal that simply died in the field rather than being slaughtered. Rabbi Yishmael objects to this stringency by attempting to show that rennet is not considered part of an animal—it is merely refuse. He points to the example of the burnt offering, the uses of which are strictly limited. Yet a priest can suck out the rennet of a burnt offering raw, not considering the rennet a true part of the animal. And the sort of person who sucks up the rennet from a freshly slaughtered animal is someone not overly squeamish, whose *da'at* is *yafah*, perhaps best translated here as "robust."

By way of contrast, the phrase *n'kiyei hada'at* refers to those who are fastidious both socially and in their implementation of the sages' system:

> If they wrote a letter of divorce in Hebrew and its witnesses [signed] in Greek, [or] in Greek and its witnesses [signed] in Hebrew, [or] if one witness were a Hebrew and another witness a Greek, [or] if the scribe signed [together with] one witness, it is a valid [divorce docu-

ment]. [If he signed it] "John Doe, witness," it is valid. [If he signed it] "The son of John Doe, witness," it is a valid [divorce document]. [If he signed it] "John Doe the son of John Doe," and he did not write "witness" [after his name] it is valid. And this [last mentioned method] was how the fastidious minded (*n'kiyei hada'at*; literally, "clean of mind") in Jerusalem would do [their witnessing]. (M. Gittin 9:8)

These last-mentioned persons were, it seems, endowed with especially refined *da'at*. They did not sign "witness" after their names, assuming that anyone with any *da'at* at all would be able to adduce that information. The context in which is found the only other appearance of this term in rabbinic literature throws a bit more light on the subject:

> "[You shall not utter a false report;] put not your hand with the wicked [to be an unrighteous witness]" (Exodus 23:1). If John Doe said to you, "Someone owes me two hundred dinars and I [only] have one witness. Come and testify for me and take one *maneh* [= one hundred dinars] and I'll take one *maneh*. Thus [to apply to just such a situation] it is said [in Scripture], "put not your hand with the wicked, etc." . . . So the pure minded (*n'kiyei hada'at*) in Jerusalem would act: None of them would go to a banquet until he knew who would go with him and he would not sign a divorce decree until he knew who would sign with him. (Mechilta Mishpatim, Masekhet Kaspa, chap. 20, on Exodus 23:1; see also B. Sanhedrin 23a)

This passage helps explain our mishnah. These men were being most scrupulous to observe the verse in the Torah, guarding against aligning themselves with a wicked witness. In this sense, then, *n'kiyei hada'at* means "one with a clear conscience." Moreover, they were careful, even in social situations, not to associate with persons of questionable repute.

The term *da'at* in these passages refers to control (or relative lack thereof) of one's affect. This is a logical extension of the idea of *da'at*: it leads to a righteous life, to an empathic nature, to insight, and to refinement. In other words, *da'at* has moral, psychological, cognitive, and social components.

Da'at As the Ability to Ask and Answer Questions

The ability to communicate verbally, and specifically the ability to ask and to answer questions, is central to the sages' enterprise. Legal and religious issues were settled through the sages' questioning of witnesses and the witnesses' replies. The equation of *da'at* with the ability to communicate verbally, then, is not surprising. This is clearly the meaning of the use of *da'at* in these two passages:

> A *cheresh, shoteh v'katan* who were found in an alley, wherein was *tum'ah* (ritual impurity), behold, these are assumed to be ritually pure. And anyone of sound senses (*pikeiach*) is assumed to be ritually impure. And anyone who is incapable of being questioned, (*sh'ein bo da'at l'hishael*), [where there is a] doubt [about his state of ritual purity] he is [assumed] to be ritually pure. (M. Tohorot 3:6; see also Sifrei Numbers 5:14 Naso, Piska 7)[5]

> They poured out for him the second cup. And here the child asks his father, and if the child has insufficient understanding (*ein da'at baben*), the father instructs him [i.e., prompts him to ask the four questions of the Passover service]. (M. Pesachim 10:4)

In both cases, the inability to discern information and to answer or formulate questions about that information is conceived of as a lack of *da'at*. In our first passage, the *cheresh, shoteh v'katan* are equated with those who are incapable of being questioned about their contact with impurity and are assumed to be clean. A *pikeiach*, on the other hand, who can be questioned and who can provide information to clarify the matter is assumed to be unclean if there is any doubt. One is reminded of the sages' concept that a broken or incomplete item cannot accept ritual impurity (e.g., M. Keilim 5:10). Because the *da'at* of the *cheresh, shoteh v'katan*, the ability to be interrogated, is in a sense broken, they cannot accept ritual impurity and are thus considered clean. The case of the son and his father at Pesach is clear, although obviously limited to that specific ritual moment. If the son knows the four questions, he shows his understanding. If not, the father feeds him his lines.

Since *da'at* is a prerequisite for, and characteristic of, full participation in the culture that the Mishnah outlines in its characteristically utopian way, those who lack cognitive, cultural, moral, auditory, or oral skills will be deemed nonparticipants in that culture insofar as their impairments reduce their *da'at*. In addition, because the Mishnah develops a scheme of categorization according to which "the sages assume that everything can be classified in principle and that every category has a polar opposite" (Wegner 1988, 7), those with *da'at* were deemed participants in the system the Mishnah developed, and those who were considered not to have *da'at* were deemed nonparticipants.

Shoteh

Like the term *da'at*, the word *shoteh* has multiple meanings. When many cognitive models combine to form a complex cluster that is psychologically more basic than the models taken individually, Lakoff (1987, 74) calls these "cluster models." Within these cluster models, there may be one concept that is the prototype for the category: "Many categories are understood in terms of abstract ideal cases—which may be neither typical nor stereotypical. . . . A lot of cultural knowledge is organized in terms of ideals. We have cultural knowledge about ideal homes, ideal families, ideal mates . . . , etc. Cultural knowledge leads to prototype effects" (87). We will see such a "cluster model" and a "prototype effect" in the related categories that are referred to by the term *shoteh*.

Shoteh = One Lacking *Da'at*

The prototype of the category *shoteh* is a person who is profoundly mentally ill, for example, schizophrenic, or a person who is mentally disabled, for example, of extremely low intelligence. Such persons are stigmatized, that is, discredited. Their identity as a *shoteh* is used as a master status: they are regarded as basically like each other and they are considered to be outside the system of "normals." The word *shoteh* may be found in this use in Y. Sanhedrin 11:2, 30a, and Y. Ketubot 7:6, 31c.

In the Mishnah, the verb *shafah* describes relief from hard labor pains (M. Niddah 4:4) and the Bavli, too, uses it in this manner (B. Niddah 37b; B. Sanhedrin 87b). The verb *nishtafah*, from the same root, also describes a *shoteh* who recovers his senses. For example, in B. Yebamot 113a, the *cheresh* is described as *nitpakeiah* on recovering, that is, on becoming sensate once more, while the *shoteh* is described as *nishtafah* (see also B. Gittin 23a; B. Baba Kamma 40a; B. Baba Batra 128a; B. Arachin 18a). Anyone who has been, or been with, a woman in labor will appreciate the metaphorical extension that has taken place here. The pain of the contractions may cause a woman to behave somewhat irrationally, or at least behave out of character, while they last. When they are over she returns to a comparatively normal state. The recovery of a person who is intermittently mentally ill is similar. This metaphorical extension tends to reinforce the observation that when the *shoteh* is lucid, he or she is not stigmatized.

The term *shoteh* is used in other ways. When used in isolation and not included in the category *cheresh, shoteh v'katan*, it may refer to someone who might be called a fool. Such a person is not mentally ill or disabled but simply fails to follow the path of learning to a meaningful life, lacking *da'at* in the fullness of that term's meaning (see M. Sotah 3:4; M. Avot 4:7; M. Eduyot 5:6; T. Shabbat 11:15).

The use of the word *shoteh* is recorded in a folk saying which suggests that popular opinion counted a person with mental disabilities or illness almost as good as dead: "A *shoteh* cannot be stricken [by feeling insult] and dead flesh does not feel a scalpel" (Y. Taanit 3:8, 66d; see also B. Shabbat 13b). Of course, this proverb, and its explicit pairing of a *shoteh* with a corpse, certainly supports the notion that a person with mental illness or disability was stigmatized—as much a nonparticipant as a corpse. In the Yerushalmi, this saying is used to describe a person so dense as to be completely unaware of his great sin, while in the Bavli, it describes a community unable to appreciate God's greatness. Both rely on metaphorical extensions of the primary meaning of the term *shoteh*.

Shoteh = Idolater = Fool

The term *shoteh* can also refer to those who do not recognize the truth of Judaism. For example, idolaters are referred to as *shotim*: "[Some idolaters] asked the elders [when they were in Rome], 'If [your God] does not want idolatry, why does He not abolish it?' They said [to the Romans], 'If it was something the world didn't need that was worshiped, He would abolish it. But [people] worship the sun and the moon and the stars and the planets. Should He destroy His world because of *shotim*?'" (M. Avodah Zarah 4:7; see also Mechilta, Tractate Bachodesh 6, on Exodus 20:5). Rabban Gamliel, Rabbi Elazar ben Azariah, Rabbi Joshua ben Hananiah, and Rabbi Akiba are the elders who visited Rome in 95 C.E. Rome, of course, is the conqueror, the antithesis, of Jerusalem. Given the relative rareness of stories in the Mishnah, we may gather that demonstrating the superiority of Judaism over idolatry was important to the compilers of this document.

The idolaters, who worship the power inherent in different gods, want to know why, if the Jewish God was all-powerful, that God didn't display power. In answering that God can't destroy creation just because some people appreciate it in perverted ways, the sages make a subtle dig at the capriciousness of pagan gods. A person could make an offering to one of these gods and they might, or might not, grant the request that accompanied the offering. However, God's relationship with Israel and the world is one of faithfulness and reciprocity. God promised not to destroy creation again no matter how badly humans misbehaved (Genesis 8:21). In this sense, God, while omnipotent, has agreed to let a covenant made with Noah limit divine power.

Here the word *shotim* cannot refer to persons who are literally mentally ill or disabled, since the idolaters in this mishnah are apparently carrying on an extended, sophisticated debate with the sages. Rather, it refers to those who either cannot or will not understand that God is the creator of the world. By using the term *shoteh* to refer to idolaters, the sages liken idolatry to mental illness or disability—that is, one would have to be foolish to the point of insanity or mental disability not to realize that God is the Creator—in another metaphorical extension of the word's prototypical meaning (see also, e.g., B. Berachot 17b).

Shoteh = A Fool Who Observes the Sages' System Idiosyncratically

One other ingrate is deemed a *shoteh*: the stubborn and rebellious son who is a trial to his parents and to society: "'A stubborn and rebellious [son]' (Deuteronomy 21:18). . . . 'Rebellious': *shoteh*" (Sifre D., Piska 218). Sifre D. wonders what the word "rebellious," *moreh*, comes to teach in addition to the designation "stubborn." One possibility is that the son is a *shoteh*, an unappreciative fool. This is a bilingual play on words. The word *moreh* resembles the Greek *mōros*, "stupid," "foolish," which corresponds to the *shoteh*, according to the sages. This stubborn and rebellious son is brought to trial, held accountable for his deeds, and can be sentenced to death for them. He, therefore, cannot be the mentally incompetent *shoteh* who could not be made to stand trial; in this case, the *shoteh* must be mentally competent but morally incompetent.

These *shotim* are all fools of one sort or another and are all stigmatized: they are discredited from the sages' point of view. The idolater is so foolish that he cannot understand the sages' most self-evident truth: God is the one Creator. Therefore, this sort of *shoteh* is outside the sages' system. Those who idiosyncratically, with inappropriate affect or intent, subscribe to the sages' system are likewise discredited (as, e.g., in M. Avot 4:7; M. Eduyot 5:6; M. Sotah 3:4). What these uses of the term *shoteh* have in common is an inability to participate reliably in the sages' system of norms and obligations. If one has failed to internalize the sages' cultural *gnosis*, or has internalized it inappropriately or incompletely, one is stigmatized in the Mishnah's system of thought and labeled a *shoteh* of one sort or another.

Shoteh = Prophet

In the following passage, the *shoteh* is one, who, like a child, is utterly guileless and speaks without motive or a desire to knowingly influence a situation. It is for precisely this reason that such persons are given prophecy: they can be direct conduits for God's word because God's message will not be tainted by any attempt on their part to shape it.

> R. Yochanan said: From the day the Temple was destroyed, prophecy has been taken from prophets and given to young children (*tinokot*) and *shotim*. How [do we know it was given to *shotim*? From what happened to] Mar son of Rav Ashi. [One day] he was standing in the arena of Mahuza when he heard a certain *shoteh* who said: The head of the Academy in Mata Mehasya [will be the one who] signs [his name] Tavyumi. [Rav Ashi] said: Who among the rabbis signs [his name] Tavyumi? I do. I deduce from this that my time has come. (B. Baba Batra 12b)

Mar was so sure of the *shoteh*'s prophetic decree that he would succeed his father, Rav Ashi, as the leader of the Academy in Mata Mehasya that he hastened thither and unseated Rav Aha.

In terms of prophecy, *shotim* can function as God's mouthpiece because they are unaware of the consequences of their words and are thus trustworthy; they have no stake in their utterances. This is part of the *shoteh*'s stigmatization, as Goffman (1963, 5) reminds us: "The person with a stigma is not quite human. . . . We tend to impute a wide range of imperfections on the basis of the original one, and at the same time to impute some desirable but undesired attributes, often of a supernatural cast, such as 'sixth sense,' or 'understanding.'" The *shoteh* who prophesies is paired with a child who was thought to have little or no controllable *da'at*. However, this child must be at least two or three years old as he or she must be able to speak, if only in an apparently meaningless fashion.

The passage continues with an example of how prophecy was given to a child: "Rav Hisda's daughter would sit in her father's lap and [one time] Raba and Rami bar Hama were sitting before him. He [Rav Hisda] said to her: Which of these would you like [to marry]? She said to him: Both of them. Said Raba: I [want to be] the last!" (B. Baba Batra 12b). Rav Hisda's daughter does, indeed, marry both men: first Rami bar Hama and then, after his death, Raba. We can easily imagine a three- or four-year-old girl sitting in her father's lap and blithely saying she wants to play with both fellows. It is somewhat less likely that a girl of eleven would sit on her father's lap and, old enough to be aware of the seriousness of what she was saying, make such a declaration. Indeed, the whole point of prophecy being given to children is that they do not understand the import of their words.

Pikeiach

While the word *pikeiach* almost always means "sensate" and is often contrasted with the category *cheresh, shoteh v'katan* (e.g., M. Yebamot 18; M. Baba Kamma 4:4),[6] it is also extended to mean sharp-witted, expert at manipulating Jewish law in order to achieve an advantageous result (e.g., B. Eruvin 41b; B. Pesachim 31a; B. Pesachim 86a, 89b; B. Menachot 72a).

In the sages' system, a person acquires an item at the moment of taking physical possession, not when money changes hands. The simplest means of acquisition is *hagbahah*, or "lifting up." If an item is too heavy to lift, the purchaser can drag it toward himself (*meshichah*) or the seller can push it toward the purchaser (*mesirah*). A mishnah examines different ways of acquiring produce: "[If] one sells produce to his fellow and [the customer] drew it to himself (*mashach*) and did not measure it, he has acquired [this produce]. If he measured it [into the customer's vessel] but [the customer] did not draw it to himself, he has not acquired [this produce]. If he were sharp-witted (*pikeiach*) he [the customer] would hire the place [where the produce lies or is measured out. Anything lying there would automatically be in the customer's possession.]" (M. Baba Batra 5:7). Obviously, using the act of drawing an object toward oneself to determine the moment of acquisition led to some ambiguities. These could be manipulated by a sharp-witted consumer who acquired the place wherein the produce was measured out and, thus, would automatically acquire everything in it. This *pikeiach* understands the rules and is able to use the conventions to make their application turn to his advantage.[7]

While in the Yerushalmi *pikeiach* appears mostly in explanations of the Mishnah's use of the term as "sharp-witted," there is one exception that makes the *pikeiach* not only sharp-witted but conceivably evil in the use of this superior intellect. The Mishnah (Kiddushin 4:11), in a discussion of which professions one should urge one's children to join, designates most ass drivers as evil, most camel drivers as decent, and most sailors as saintly. The Gemara then goes on to note, "The majority of illegitimate children are *pikchin*" (Y. Kiddushin 4:11, 66c). The commentary P'nei Moshe explains this cryptic observation by saying that the product of an adulterous union (the definition of an illegitimate child in Jewish law) will resemble its father, who is devious (because adultery involves deceit). Therefore, others should beware of illegitimate children.

One manuscript describes illegitimate children not as *pikchin* but as *kipchin*. The transposition of two letters results in a word that refers not only to robbery but to a person who is hunchbacked. This variant undergirds both the notion of the *pikeiach* as too quick-witted for his own good and the notion that illegitimate children suffer from physical disabilities because of their parents' sin.

Tipeish

The Mishnah uses one term, *shoteh*, to denote mentally ill, mentally disabled, and foolish individuals; nowhere does it use any form of the term *tipeish*, "ignorant." In Tosefta, which begins to employ a more differentiated vocabulary to describe such persons, we see *tipeish*, alongside *shoteh*, being used to denote the fool who has not well and fully internalized the knowledge the sages deem important (T. Pesachim 9:2; T. Baba Metsia 6:17).

A *tipeish* is contrasted with a *hakham*, a sage, while a *shoteh* is contrasted with a *pikeiach*. This is an additional differentiation in the characterization of mental abilities, corresponding to the distinction in English between the pairs "foolish" and "sagacious" and "insane" and "sane." All these terms describe affective and cognitive qualities, but the "foolish" and "sagacious" both fall within the range of normal affect and cognition, while "sane" and "insane" distinguish between the normal and the stigmatized. This use of more specific words, and a greater number of them, to describe the mental domain may signify its increasing significance to the sages. The *tipeish* is not stigmatized in Tosefta, as is the *shoteh*. The *tipeish* is a full, albeit undesirable, participant in the sages' system.

The halakhic midrashim describe the fool with a variety of terms. While some midrash collections do not use the term *tipeish* (Sifra and Sifre N.), others do. In addition to being designated a *shoteh*, the fool may also be described as *tipeish*. The word seems to mean the same as the "foolish *shoteh*," but without the metaphorical link that leads to the *shoteh*'s stigmatization. There is some subtle difference between these two terms, however. In general, the *shoteh* is offensive to God, particularly because the "foolish *shoteh*" does not appropriately appreciate God's nature and creations. The *tipeish* is simply stupid; though perhaps offensive to other people, in general he is not "theologically incorrect."

One passage that (in some versions) contains the word *tipeish* has become a well-known feature of the Passover ritual. A verse concerning the Exodus from Egypt seems to have a few superfluous words in it: "When your son asks you in the future, saying: What are these testimonies and statutes and judgments which the Lord our God has commanded you?" (Deuteronomy 6:20). The son could simply have said, "What are these laws?" Therefore, the sages reason, the multiplicity of words must each have a special meaning.

> You find that one [can] say [these extra words in Deuteronomy 6:20 can be related to] four sons: one wise (*hakham*), one ignorant (*tipeish*), one evil (*rasha*), [and] one who does not know how to ask (*sh'eino yodei'a lish'ol*). [The] wise [one], what does he say? "What are these testimonies and statutes and judgments which the Lord our God has commanded you?" (Deuteronomy 6:20). So you begin [to explain] to him the laws of Pesach and [continue] saying [these laws until you have explained] that [the group that has eaten the seder together] does not disband until after eating an *afikoman* [dessert] of [a piece of] the Paschal offering.

[The] ignorant [son] (*tipeish*), what does he say? "What is this?"
And you say to him, "With an outstretched hand God brought us out
of Egypt, from the house of bondage" (Exodus 13:14). (Mechilta
Piskha 18 on Exodus 13:14; see also Y. Pesachim 10:4, 37d)

Those familiar with the text from the Passover seder, the holiday
service conducted in the home, will be surprised to find the word *tipeish* instead of the word *tam* and to see that the ignorant son comes
before the wicked one.[8] Moreover, the answer given the *tipeish* in the
Yerushalmi is quite different than the one recorded in Mechilta or in
the seder: "The *tipeish*, what does he say? You teach him the laws of
the Paschal offering, that we don't end until the Pesach afikoman so
that he should not stand [and walk away] from this eating group [of
which he is a member] and enter another eating group" (Y. Pesachim 10:4, 37d). The last thing one must taste at the seder is the
Paschal offering. People bought "shares" in this offering and only a
member of the group could eat a piece of that particular offering.
Thus, it was important to stay with one's group in order to fulfill the
mitzvah. The impression one has of the *tipeish* here is not only that
he is ignorant of the most basic aspect of the seder—how to validly
eat a piece of the Paschal sacrifice—but that he might be prone to
wander around and take food without scruple. This could well describe the behavior of a child between the ages three and five wan-
dering about a kind of "campground," where many groups would be
roasting their lambs and telling the story of the Exodus from Egypt.

In this passage, and in Mechilta, the *tipeish* seems to be similar to
the *katan* who is grouped with women and slaves rather than the one
associated with the *cheresh* and *shoteh*. The *katan* linked with the latter group is preverbal—an infant, one or two years old. The *katan*
who is in the former group has verbal skills and is included in the
mitzvot in a flexible way as his abilities allow. Perhaps the *tipeish* corresponds to this *katan*, possibly designating a developmental stage,
a condition of ignorance that can be ameliorated. The *shoteh*, by contrast, is either temporarily or permanently hopeless, as unreachable
by reason as a preverbal baby.

In Sifre D., the *tipeish* is contrasted with the *hakham* in a passage that also draws on the metaphorical connection of light and enlightenment: "'For a gift blinds the eyes of the wise (*hakhamim*)' (Deuteronomy 16:19) and one need not [even] mention [that it blinds] the eyes of the ignorant (*tipshim*)" (Sifre D., Piska 144). If a bribe would blind a wise person, how much more would it distort the vision of an ignorant person? This midrash seeks to explain why the word *hakhamim* is used in the Torah here and not *pikchim*, which appears in the parallel passage in Exodus 23:8. Sifre D. interprets this variation to show the 'strength of a bribe: it can blind even a sage, and all the more so an ignorant person, the *tipeish*. Here, again, the *hakham* is explicitly contrasted with the *tipeish*.

Learning styles, and learning disabilities, were of great importance in the sages' culture. Leviticus Rabbah employs the word *tipeish* to describe someone who participates in the sages' system, but who does so in a foolish way. The context for the following passage is fitting, since the theme of chapter 19 is proper and improper ways of studying Torah and observing mitzvot.[9]

> R. Hanin of Seforis explained the text, ["His locks are in curls (*k'vutsotav taltalim*)" (Song of Songs 5:11);] this [refers] to a mound (*t'lulit*) of earth. One who is ignorant (*tipeish*), what does he say? Who can carry (*l'katsot*) this [away]? One who is sensible (*pikeiach*), what does he say? Behold, I will carry two baskets today [and] two baskets tomorrow until I have carried it all [away]. One who is ignorant (*tipeish*), what does he say? "Who can learn [all of] the [oral] Torah? [The order of] Nezikin has thirty chapters! [The order of] Keilim has thirty chapters!" One who is sensible (*pikeiach*), what does he say? "Behold, I shall learn two mishnahs today and two tomorrow, until I shall have learned the whole [oral] Torah."
>
> R. Ammi said, "Wisdom is too high for a fool [to attain]" (Proverbs 24:7). Rabbi Yohanan said: [This may be compared to] a loaf hanging high up in a house. One who is ignorant (*tipeish*) says: "Who is able to bring this down?" One who is sensible (*pikeiach*) says: "Didn't another hang it up? Rather, bring two rods and tie them together and bring it down." So one who is ignorant (*tipeish*) says: Who is able to learn [all] the Torah that is in the heart of a sage (*hakham*)? One who is sensible (*pikeiach*) says, "Did he [the sage] not learn it

from another?" Rather, behold, I will learn two mishnahs today and two mishnahs tomorrow until I have learned the entire [oral] Torah.

Said R. Levi: It is like a basket with a hole in it whose owner hired workers to fill it. One who is ignorant (*tipeish*), what does he say? "What does [my labor] profit me? I put [material] in here, and it comes out there!" One who is sensible (*pikeiach*), what does he say? "Do I not receive a wage for each bit I put in?" So one who is ignorant (*tipeish*), what does he say? "What does it profit me to learn Torah and forget it?" One who is sensible (*pikeiach*), what does he say? "Does not the Holy One, blessed be He, give reward for the labor [of Torah study, therefore I shall study even if I forget]?" (Leviticus Rabbah Metsorah 19:2; see also Deuteronomy Rabbah 8:3; Song of Songs Rabbah 5:11)

In this tripartite contrast between the fool and the sensible person, the fool is overwhelmed by the task of Torah study whereas the sensible person breaks the task down into manageable units.

The *tipeish* is contrasted with a *pikeiach* (the term that usually serves as the opposite of the *shoteh*) rather than a *hakham* in this passage. This may be because both are depicted as beginning their studies, so neither could possibly be a *hakham*. This passage seems to suggest that the terms belong on a continuum, running from least knowledge to most knowledge: from *shoteh* to *tipeish* to *pikeiach* to *hakham*. Alternatively, it may indicate that the terms *tipeish* and *shoteh* were still interchangeable when this midrash was composed. Since this is a non-halakhic context, their usage may have been less strictly limited than in a document such as the Mishnah.

The contrast between the categories *hakham* and *tipeish* is similarly employed in the following passage. Here, rather than simply indicating a person of wisdom, *hakham* has a more specific meaning, "a sage." In contrast, the *tipeish* is a person who pursues the activities of the sages in a foolish manner.

[The knowledge of] Torah is acquired only in group [study], as Rabbi Yose said [in the name of] Rabbi Hanina for Rabbi Yose said in the name of Rabbi Hanina said: What [is the meaning of what] is written,

"A sword is upon the idle talkers (*baddim*) and they shall become fools" (Jeremiah 50:36)? A sword is upon those who hate the students of the sages [that is,] those who sit alone (*bad bedad*) and study the Torah. Not only that, they become ignorant (*shemitapshim*) [through studying alone, i.e., such study does not avail them]. (B. Berachot 63b; see also B. Taanit 7a; B. Makkot 10a)

This person is studying; he is simply doing so in a way that is frowned on by the majority of sages, a way that will cause him to become ignorant. The exposition uses puns extensively. *Chavura*, "studying together," has basically the same letters as *cherev*, "sword." Likewise, the words for "idle talkers" and "those who study alone" are quite similar. In the system of disciple circles, with deep attachment to one's master teacher and fellow students, such an ethic is perfectly logical (see Goodblatt 1975). Becoming a sage has not only an intellectual component but a social one as well. Not attending to the latter causes the former to deteriorate. Here, the term *tipeish* refers to one who is not a sage, or who foolishly engages in the sages' pursuits.

The terms *tipeish* and *pikeiach* are also found in a parable that Rabbi Akiba uses to explain why he continued to teach Torah even after an edict was issued banning this activity:

I will tell you a parable. To what is [our situation] similar? [To a] fox who was once walking alongside of a river, and he saw fishes gathering [and going in a group] from one place to another. He said to them: From what are you fleeing? They said to him: From the nets cast for us by people. He said to them: Would you like to come up onto the dry [land] so that you and I can live [together] in the way that my ancestors lived with your ancestors? They said to him: Are you the one they call the most sharp-witted of animals (*pikeiach*)? You are not clever (*pikeiach*) but foolish (*tipeish*; Munich MS, *shoteh*). [If] we are afraid in the place in which we live, how much more [would we be afraid] in the place [where] we die! So it is [with] us. Now, when we sit and study Torah, of which it is written, "It is your life and the length of your days" (Deuteronomy 30:20), [we are killed] how much the more so [would we be killed] if we went and stopped studying it. (B. Berachot 61b; see also Tanhuma, Ki Tavo, 2:1)[10]

Torah, in a standard metaphorical extension, is likened to water: a free, purifying, safe environment that gives life. Pappos ben Yehudah suggests to Rabbi Akiba that he stop promulgating Torah since an edict has been issued that promises death to those who teach Torah. Pappos might appear to be wise, or even merely clever, but Rabbi Akiba explains to him that such a course of action would actually be foolish. In this context, the choice of the word *pikeiach*, rather than *hakham*, makes sense. Not studying Torah would be shrewd, but not wise. The fish, who see through the fox's machinations, call him *tipeish*, "foolish." The fox/Pappos has been given the great gift of Torah but does not understand its potency. This unappreciative fool can also be denoted by the term *shoteh*, which indeed appears in a manuscript variant of this passage.

Categorization of Persons with Disabilities in Rabbinic Literature

Categorization is an important activity in the Mishnah and, subsequently, much of rabbinic literature. One authority contends that the Mishnah's propensity to categorize is due most fundamentally to its origins in lists of items (Jaffe 1992, 70 n. 36). It could also be explained by the Mishnah's connection to the priestly literature, the categorizing writings on which much of this document is based and that may have appealed to the sages precisely because they were so systematic (see Eilberg-Schwartz 1986, 192). Alternatively, it could stem from the Mishnah's *purpose*.

Documents that provide operational information—in distinction to narratives, for example—may tend quite naturally to focus on categorization since it is such a basic human means of making sense of reality. Much of the Mishnah's material is theoretical in nature (e.g., various preposterous combinations of marriages between widows and their brothers-in-law, called levirate marriages, or rules regarding the Temple cult, which at that time lay in ruins). But even possibly applicable laws fall within the category of "operational laws" and will therefore be operational in nature, even if only in theory. Thus the fictional *Star Fleet Technical Manual* is written in the style of an actual operational manual, complete with guides to the rules and the equipment in the original *Star Trek* television series. Therefore, I am suggesting that the propensity of the Mishnah to categorize is due in part to its genre, not necessarily or solely to its affinity with, and elaboration of, the priestly school of thought.

Not surprisingly, categorization is a priority for the Mishnah with regard to disabilities and disabled persons. The Mishnah differs from the Tanach by consistently differentiating among disabilities, because, within its system, some disabilities are more disabling than others. Just as the priestly culture guarded its practitioners against dangerous contact with lethal holiness by barring blemished priests and those contaminated by ritual impurity from the cult, so rabbinic culture identifies those abilities that allowed a person to function within that culture and, hence, the corresponding disabilities that would make a person unable to participate. The sages developed an intellectual and spiritual system of Judaism that was cultivated in a communal, professional culture and transmitted with a great degree of orality. Thus, within this system one who could not communicate intellectual content orally was more disabled than any other individual.

Mental, hearing, and speaking disabilities compromised one's ability to participate in the sages' system. These sorts of disabilities are most often designated by the category *cheresh, shoteh v'katan:* the person with hearing and speaking disabilities, the person with mental disabilities or mental illness, and the minor. Such individuals suffer a common stigma, as their linked categorization serves as a "master status": no differentiation is made between, for example, a schizophrenic person and a normal one year old, or a deaf-mute person and one with an IQ of 40. All such persons are placed into a single discredited group; their performance of mitzvot is questioned and often discredited. However, as we will see, an individual may move from this category and become a full participant, if it can be proved that he has *da'at*, that is, has been impressed with the seal of his culture's *gnosis* and can form a legally actionable intention and act on it legitimately.

In contrast, blindness and such physical disabilities as lameness or a malformation of the hands compromised participation only in certain, limited aspects. With regard to most activities, blind and physically disabled persons are not even considered to be liminal: though visibly marred, they can function satisfactorily. They are fully credited participants in the sages' system, except in those limited circumstances for which vision or mobility is absolutely necessary. Virtually the only time we will find such individuals discredited is when the Mishnah's system recapitulates the priestly Writings or when the sages seek to disqualify as many persons as possible from an activity and use all disabilities as means of reducing the number involved.[11]

In this way, the Mishnah innovatively considered disabilities and redefined perfection. Perfection no longer means "zero defects," as it did in the priestly literature (although traces of that attitude can still be found). Instead, perfection is identified with intellectual functioning and communicative abilities. In rabbinic literature, these concepts are often related to the term *da'at*. There is almost no action that one can validly perform in the Mishnah's system without *da'at*.

The Theoretical Nature of Some Mishnaic Discussions

Before we begin our consideration of how persons with disabilities are categorized in the Mishnah, one point about the nature of the document must be made clear. To say that the Mishnah speaks with a unified voice about its world is not to imply that every passage of Mishnah should be understood in the same way. If theoretical or exegetical concerns are primary in a given mishnah, our understanding of the comments in it regarding disabled persons must take this into account. As Howard Eilberg-Schwartz (1986, 192) notes, "Many of the mishnaic cases which strike the contemporary reader

as bizarre or farfetched merely represent the sages' desire to ratio-
nalize their system, in the sense of carrying their legal principles to
their logical conclusions, and imagining all possible permutations
of a given situation." Several of the passages that touch on the role of
disabled persons in the Mishnah are logical or exegetical exercises,
rather than concrete legal prescriptions.

For example, in a long series of mishnayot in tractate M. Yebamot
(chapters 13 and 14) appears a description of the role of deaf-mute
men and women in relation to the obligation of levirate marriage:
that is, the duty of a man to marry his brother's childless widow or
submit to the ritual of *halitsah* by which the woman is released from
the obligation to marry one of her dead husband's brothers. In these
chapters, the various permutations of persons, relationships, and
categories of marriage are explored. Consider the following passage:

> [If] two brothers [with all their] sense (*pikchim*) were married to two
> sisters, one a *chereshet* and the other sound of hearing (*pikachat*), [and
> the one of] sound [hearing], the husband of the *chereshet*, died, what
> shall the one of sound hearing, the husband of her of sound hearing,
> do? She [the deaf widow] goes free since she is the wife's sister. [If the
> man] of sound hearing, the husband of her of sound hearing, died,
> what shall the other [husband of] sound of hearing, the husband of
> the *chereshet*, do? [He must] put away his own wife by a bill of divorce
> and [free] his brother's wife by [the ritual of] *halitsah*. (M. Yebamot
> 14:5)

The ritual of *halitsah* is outlined in the Torah:

> And if the man like not to take his brother's widow, then his brother's
> widow shall go up to the gate to the elders, and say: My husband's
> brother refuses to raise up a name in Israel for his brother. He will not
> perform the duty of a husband's brother for me. Then the elders of his
> city shall call him and speak to him and if he stand and say: I do not
> want to take her, then his brother's widow will come near to him
> before the elders and take off his shoe from his foot and spit in his
> face and she shall answer and say: So shall it be done to the man who
> will not build up his brother's house. And his name shall be called in
> Israel the house [of him that had] his shoe taken off. (Deuteronomy
> 25:7–10)

Clearly, this ritual was designed to humiliate the brother who was derelict in his duties to his brother's widow.[12] In its day, this legislation was designed to help childless widows. However, it could be problematic in practice, particularly when any of the participants lacked the requisite *da'at* to perform the ceremony adequately.

The sages allowed persons with hearing and speaking disabilities to marry, but their union is only a rabbinically permitted marriage, not scripturally permitted as would be the case between two persons with no such disabilities. To understand this passage, we also need to know that the Torah forbids relations between a man and his wife's sister: "And you shall not take a woman to her sister, to be a rival to her, to reveal her nakedness, beside the other in her lifetime" (Leviticus 18:18). Since the *chereshet* in our mishnah is married with a lesser degree of authority than is her widowed, hearing sister, she is divorced so that her husband can fulfill his obligations to his brother's widow as outlined in the Torah. However, he cannot marry the widow, since even after the divorce she remains his wife's sister. So he performs the ritual of *halitsah* for her and frees her to marry another. Here, a *chereshet* is used simply to make a point about the distinction between a rabbinically and scripturally permitted marriage. The actual *chereshet*, as a person, has no bearing on the discussion at all. Indeed, the "logical" outcome of this mishnah is absurd from a practical standpoint: in the end, *no one* is married—the exact opposite of the original intent of the rules of levirate marriage.

Another example of the theoretical nature of some discussions regarding persons with disabilities is seen in a mishnah describing the impact of becoming disabled, and overcoming disabilities, on the process of divorce:

> If a minor received [a *get*, a writ of divorce, from a husband and was commissioned to act as a messenger to give it to the man's wife] and then came of age [before delivering the document, or] a *cheresh* [received it] and recovered his senses (*v'nitpakeiach*) [before delivering the *get* to the woman, or] a blind man regained his sight, or a *shoteh* became sane, or a non-Jew converted, [the divorce document] is invalid. But [in the case of] one of sound senses who became a *cheresh*

and then recovered his senses, or one with sight who became blind and then regained his sight, or one who was mentally normal and became a *shoteh* and then recovered his mental health, [the divorce document] is valid. This is the general principle: [If at] the beginning and at the conclusion [the messenger performed his task] with [full] cognition (*b'da'at*), [the divorce] is valid. (M. Gittin 2:6)

While it is not inconceivable medically that a person should be blinded and then recover his sight, or become deaf and mute and then recover his hearing and speech, the possibility of either happening in the relatively short time it usually takes to deliver a document seems very remote. Here we have another example of how some passages of the Mishnah fully flesh out all the theoretical possibilities of the situation being considered. Note that the sages do not admit the theoretical possibility that a person who converts to Judaism again becomes a non-Jew. Once one has validly converted to Judaism, one may not rescind that decision.

It is important to gauge the rhetorical purpose of a given passage in the mishnah in order to understand it correctly. Out of context, these passages, especially the one from M. Yebamot, might be construed to be cruel to persons with hearing and speaking disabilities. Grasping the essential nature of such texts—their theoretical purport—allows the modern reader to avoid such errors of interpretation.

Women, Slaves, and Minors

The most salient mishnaic category we will study is the grouping of the *cheresh, shoteh v'katan*, which classifies persons with hearing, speaking, and mental disabilities with the minor. One of the greatest aids we have in understanding this category is another: that of women, slaves, and minors. While the former category epitomizes stigmatization, the latter embodies liminality. Women, slaves, and minors clearly had *da'at*—that is, had received the cultural *gnosis*—but were unable consistently to actualize their intentions. Therefore, they were not like the *cheresh, shoteh v'katan* who, the sages believed, had no *da'at*, but neither were they like free, grown, Jewish men who have *da'at* and could act on it: they were liminal. Because male minors are placed in both groupings, by contrasting the two we can see more clearly both the role of the minor and the ways minors are at different times similar to the other members of first one and then the other of these categories.

In short, we will find that the minor who is like the *cheresh* and *shoteh* is an infant who, while having his own will, does not have *da'at* in the sages' understanding of that word; the minor who is like women and slaves is an older, verbal minor who gradually becomes able to participate fully in Jewish life. The ideal Jewish participant in the sages' system—the grown, free male with functioning *da'at*—begins life as a stigmatized person, moves into a liminal position, and finally grows into a full participant. In this sense, then, everyone is disabled at some point in his or her life.

Shekalim

Who counts? This is the question a census answers literally by numbering those who, according to some determination, count. In the Torah, those who count are male Israelites over the age of twenty, that is, those who have reached the age of military service (Numbers 1:2–3). The command from God to take a census of such persons is related to the building of the Tabernacle in the wilderness.

> And God spoke to Moses, saying, When you take the sum of the children of Israel according to their number, then each man shall give atonement for his soul to God, when you number them so that there be no plague among them, when you number them. This [is what] they shall give, every one that passes among them that are numbered, half a shekel [according to] the shekel of the sanctuary: (a shekel is twenty *gerahs*) a half shekel shall be the offering to God. Everyone that passes among them that are numbered from twenty years old and above, shall give the gift to God. The rich shall not give more and the poor shall not give less than half a shekel when they give the offering to God, to make atonement for your souls. And you shall take the atonement money of the children of Israel and shall use it for the ser-

vice of the Tent of Meeting that it may be a memorial to the children of Israel before God to make atonement for your souls. (Exodus 30:11–16)

A shekel is a measure of gold or silver, and the sanctuary weight was heavier than the going merchants' weight. A shekel is about 11.4 grams and a *gerah* is about 0.5 grams (Sarna 1991, 196). The money collected in this census was used to construct the Tent of Meeting (Exodus 38:24–28).

Later, this shekel collection became a yearly tax to support the functioning of the Second Temple. Everyone that contributed thereby had a stake in the Temple's daily offerings. The Mishnah records who was to pay this tax and thereby participate in the cult: "From whom did they take pledges [of goods among those who had not yet given the half shekel]? Levites and Israelites, proselytes and freed slaves but not women, slaves, or minors. Any minor, for whom his father had begun to contribute [the half shekel], must not discontinue [making this contribution]. But they do not take pledges [from] the priests for the sake of peace" (M. Shekalim 1:3).

Let us examine these categories systematically. Bloodlines were extremely important in the functioning of the cult, as this is what makes a priest a priest or a Levite a Levite: his blood. Categorization of Jews along bloodlines breaks down Jewish society into ten genealogical groups who came from Babylonia to Israel after the destruction of the First Temple (586 B.C.E.) and subsequent exile:

People with recognized bloodlines:
1. priests
2. Levites
3. Israelites

People whose bloodlines impair them only with regard to the priesthood:
4. *chalalim:* the children of an interdicted priestly union (e.g., between a priest and a divorcee)

People whose bloodlines are irrelevant:
   5. proselytes
   6. freed slaves
People whose bloodlines are impaired in some way:
   7. *mamzerim*: the children of a union forbidden by death or excision from the community (e.g., an adulterous union)
   8. *Netinim*: a special group of proselytes, descended from the Gibeonites
   9. *shektuki*: those who know their mother but not their father
   10. foundlings: those who were found in the street and know neither their father nor mother (M. Kiddushin 4:1)

The rules of marriage for these different groups are as follows:

Those in groups 1, 2, and 3 can marry each other.
Those in groups 2, 3, 4, 5, and 6 can marry each other.
Those in groups 5, 6, 7, and 8 can marry each other.
Those in groups 9 and 10 cannot marry people in their own group, but they can marry people in categories 5, 6, and 8.

Any Israelite whose bloodlines were either normal or irrelevant was subject to the tax. For the purposes of this mishnah (M. Shekalim 1:3), the *chalal*, the person whose bloodlines are impaired for the priesthood, is simply considered an Israelite. The priests exempted themselves from paying this tax because some of their offerings had to be entirely burnt up and not eaten; if their money went toward the purchase of sacrificial animals, these animals could not be eaten (M. Shekalim 1:4).

The exclusion of women, slaves, and minors from the obligation to pay is not based on their bloodlines. After all, a minor child may have excellent bloodlines and may one day become a priest or Levite. Likewise, a woman may be the daughter of a priest. So participants in this tax must also be male, free, and mature; women, slaves, and minors are excluded because they are perceived of as unable to act consistently and freely as full, normal participants for the purposes of this tax. This makes them liminal, betwixt and between, as the mishnah shows. Once a minor, who will some day be liable to this tax, begins having the tax offered in his name, it is already taken as an obligation and cannot be omitted from that time onward.

In this instance, the disability of women, slaves, and minors need not be permanent. Children mature. A woman who was widowed or a slave who was freed would no longer be controlled by someone else. The sages recognized that women, slaves, and minors *could be* eligible for the tax, and hence for participation in and support of the cult. Therefore, the sages legitimized their paying this tax after the fact: "Even though they said that they do not exact pledges from women, slaves, or minors, [nevertheless] if they gave the half shekel, they accept it from them. If an idolater or a Samaritan gave the half shekel they may not accept it from them" (M. Shekalim 1:5). The category "women, slaves, and minors" is contrasted in this mishnah with idolaters and Samaritans. Idol worshipers might want to participate in the cult: they worshiped many gods and could have wished to worship the God of the Temple, too. However, the sages' prohibitions against idolatry are exceptionally strong and such persons' contributions would not be accepted. The sages would not even allow the contribution of Samaritans, Jews descended from the Joseph tribes (Ephraim and Manasseh) whose Judaism developed in a different manner than that of the Jews who suffered the Assyrian conquest (722/721 B.C.E.). These persons are disqualified because their intent is incorrect.

Women, slaves, and minors are included because even though they were not participants with the ability to act on their *da'at* at the moment, *they could be qualified* to act if their conditions changed. Their intention is assumed to be correct; it is their ability to act on it that is in question. And what of the *cheresh, shoteh v'katan*? They are not mentioned here or in the corresponding Tosefta, Yerushalmi, Midrash, or Bavli passages. The Mishnah and subsequent documents apparently assume that these people have no *da'at* and that therefore their participation is never a possibility; it needn't even be discussed. Though one might have surmised that this absence meant that the *cheresh* and *shoteh* were simply to give the half shekel, the prohibition against accepting the contribution of the idolater and the Samaritan make it manifest that the key here is intention. The *cheresh*, the *shoteh*, and the *katan* who was like them were considered to have no *da'at* and therefore no intention; hence they could not participate.

So, we may ask again, who counts? We have moved from the Torah's definition of militarily eligible men to the Mishnah's redefinition, which counts full-grown, male, free Jews with *da'at*. Persons who have *da'at* but who cannot reliably act on it—women, slaves and minors—are liminal: they do not automatically count but they are not automatically *dis*counted either. The *cheresh*, the *shoteh*, and the *katan* who is like them are totally discounted, not even worthy of mention with regard to this mitzvah that serves as a tax and a census.

Sukkah and Hagigah

The holiday of Sukkot, "Booths," is one that involves many different observances: a pilgrimage to Jerusalem, eating and sleeping in booths (sukkot) for the weeklong holiday, reciting psalms of praise called the Hallel (Psalms 113–18), and waving the *lulav* (palm, myrtle, and willow branches held together with a citron). Each of these important rituals involves the equivocal participation of minors, and our sources offer some significant clarification of a minor's role. The requirement to eat and sleep in the sukkah does not fall upon women, slaves, or *some* minors. The lead-in to the discussion of our liminal category considers a man whose head and torso are in the sukkah while the rest of his body is in the house (M. Sukkah 2:7). Here, the individual is quite literally on the threshold, and his case is followed logically by the following mishnah: "Women, slaves, and minors are exempt from the [obligation to sleep in the] sukkah, but a minor who no longer needs his mother is bound to observe the [precept of sleeping in the] sukkah. It once happened that the daughter-in-law of Shammai the Elder gave birth and he broke away some of the ceiling plaster and covered it with sukkah-roofing over the bed for the sake of the child" (M. Sukkah 2:8).

What are we to make of this behavior? To dwell in a sukkah is to live under an open roof covered with vegetation. Hence, by pulling away part of the roof and putting the proper vegetation on it, Shammai the Elder was creating a sukkah for this newborn. Shammai the Elder held that a *katan*, even one who manifestly has no *da'at*, is obligated to do this mitzvah. With this ruling, he was hearkening back to the Torah text itself, which commands: "You shall dwell in booths seven days; *all that are homeborn* in Israel shall dwell in booths" (Leviticus 23:42). The midrashic explanation of this verse states: "'The homeborn [*ha'ezrach*]' exempts women [since the word *ha'ezrach* is masculine]. '*Every* homeborn' [comes] to include minors. 'In Israel' [comes] to include proselytes and freed slaves" (Sifra, Parshat Emor, 17:9). Since this grandchild of his was "homeborn" and *all* the homeborn are commanded to dwell in booths, Shammai the Elder wanted his grandson to observe the commandment from the first possible moment.

Another observance of the holiday of Sukkot is the waving of the *lulav*; during that ritual, psalms of praise are recited. Our next mishnah considers the case of a man who needs others to recite Hallel for him, presumably because he is illiterate: "One who had a slave or a woman or a minor recite [Hallel] for him, he [must] repeat after them what they say, and it shall be a curse for him [that they had to coach him through it]. If an adult recited for him, he responds after him, 'Halleluyah' [but does not repeat the psalms line for line]" (M. Sukkah 3:10). This mishnah indicates obvious disapproval of a man needing help from a slave, woman, or child in reciting Hallel, while no such shame is attached to his reciting after another free, grown man. For our purposes, the definition of this minor is most interesting. Clearly, he cannot be the minor who is like the *cheresh*, since a *cheresh* (a person with hearing and speaking disabilities) would not be able to recite Hallel. The Yerushalmi clarifies how old this child might be: "'*Let it be a curse to him.*' And they said further,

'May a curse come upon a man of twenty [years] who needs a ten year old [to recite for him]'" (Y. Sukkah 3:9, 53d 3:11). This *katan* who can recite Hallel is ten years old, that is, soon to achieve puberty and, thus, his majority. But he is still, clearly, a *katan*. It is considered shameful that the twenty year old does not know how to recite Hallel but quite unremarkable that the ten year old can do so, just as this ability is not at all unexpected in the woman and slave.

The sages expect that the *katan* will also learn how to wave the *lulav* sometime before he reaches his majority: "A *katan* who knows (*yodei'a*) how to wave it is obligated [to perform the commandment of] the *lulav*" (M. Sukkah 3:15). Here, *da'at* is the clear differentiating factor. If the child knows (the verb here is from the same root as *da'at*) how to wave the *lulav*, he is obligated to perform this commandment. Both the Yerushalmi and Bavli further explore what it is that a *katan* should be taught to do according to his developing *da'at*. They base their comments on the following passage in T. Hagigah:

A *katan* [who needs his mother] goes out [on Shabbat] using his mother's *eruv* [her food used to extend the Sabbath boundaries]. And [if he doesn't need his mother] he is obligated [to perform the commandment of sitting] in a sukkah and they mix for him food for two meals for an *eruv t'chumin*.[13]

[If] he knows (*yodei'a*) how to wave [it] he is obligated [to wave] the *lulav*.

[If] he knows (*yodei'a*) how to wrap himself [in a tallit] he is obligated to wear *tsitsit* (fringes).

[If] he knows (*yodei'a*) how to speak, his father teaches him the Shema and Torah and the holy language [Hebrew]. And if [he does] not [know how to speak Hebrew] it would have been fitting that he had not come into the world.

[If] he knows (*yodei'a*) how to guard his tefillin [boxes containing holy texts that are worn during morning prayers], his father procures tefillin for him.

[If he knows how to guard his hands against ritual impurity, people may eat *terumah*, food which only priestly families may eat and which must be consumed in ritual purity, from his hands.]

How do they check him? They immerse him [in the ritual bath] and give him unconsecrated food [and tell him it is] *terumah* [which must be eaten in a state of ritual purity and they see if he treats it correctly]. [If] he knows (*yodei'a*) how to guard himself [from ritual impurity from corpses, for example,] they eat [items that must be] ritually pure [relying on his knowledge].

[If he knows how to guard] his hands [against ritual impurity, people] may eat *terumah* [which must be consumed in ritual purity] from his hands.

[If] he knows (*yodei'a*) how to fold his garment [to collect grain] they give him a portion [of *terumah*] on the threshing floor.

If he has *da'at* [with which] to be asked [questions about ritual purity, then] a doubtful item in a private domain [is considered] impure [and an item of doubtful purity] in a public domain, pure.

[If] he knows (*yodei'a*) how to slaughter, his slaughtering is valid.

If he is able to eat an olive's worth of grain, they remove his excrement and urine four cubits [from a habitation].[14]

[If he can eat] an olive's worth of roast meat, they slaughter a Paschal offering on his behalf.

Rabbi Yehudah says, They should never slaughter a Paschal offering on his behalf unless he knows (*yodei'a*) [how to] distinguish food [from what is not food]. What is "distinguishing food"? Anyone who, when they give him an egg he takes it [and eats it and they give him] a stone and he throws it away.

A girl [*tinoket*] that produced two [pubic] hairs is obligated for all the commandments stated in the Torah, whether *halutsah* [releasing her dead husband's brother from the obligation to marry her] or *yebamah* [marrying this brother].

And so [also] a boy (*tinok*) that brings forth two [pubic] hairs is obligated for all the commandments stated in the Torah, he is fit to be [condemned] as a stubborn and rebellious son. Once his beard has filled out, he is fit to become a public [prayer] leader, pass before the ark, and raise his hands [in the priestly benediction]. But he does not have a portion in the holy things of the Sanctuary until he brings forth two [pubic] hairs. Rabbi [Yehudah HaNasi] says, "I say until he will be twenty years old, as it says, 'The Levites from twenty years and older [were appointed] to superintend the work of the house of the Lord'" (Ezra 3:8). (T. Hagigah 1:2–3)

Let us look at the overall structure of this passage first and then analyze its component parts. First, we have the consideration of the *katan* in relation to the sukkah and the *eruv*. This is logical, since the child's first ritual step away from home would be sleeping in the sukkah, just outside the home, and then the extension of home boundaries through the *eruv*. The second section is concerned with the concrete expressions of the Shema: *tsitsit*, tefillin, and the actual recitation of the passage (Deuteronomy 6:4–9). The third section focuses on the *katan*'s ability to observe the rules of ritual purity; the fourth, his ability to eat and slaughter food in a proper way. Up to this point, Tosefta here has uniformly obligated the *katan* to do those mitzvot he can do and that are not expressly prohibited by a mishnah (e.g., the obligation to recite the Shema or don tefillin, M. Berachot 3:3). In our fifth section, the endpoint of the piecemeal approach to adulthood is defined: two pubic hairs on a girl or a boy qualify them to observe all the mitzvot. Once puberty has been reached, a girl can be an effective agent in transactions involving levirate marriage and a boy can be held responsible for his actions.[15] However, the last section of this passage shows that this achievement of mature status does not extend to those synagogue practices which are an adaptation of Temple rites. Only when the boy has reached the age of twenty and carries the visible sign of true maturity—a full beard—will he be fit for these duties, as he would have been considered a full participant among the officiants in the Temple.

In the case of a communal *eruv* for Shabbat, women, Hebrew slaves, and grown children all have an obligation to observe the mitzvah; thus all have a stake in it. A *katan*, however, in this case is likened to a Canaanite slave, who is considered to be chattel (see Flesher 1988, 54–55), as opposed to the Hebrew slave, who is an indentured servant.

> How do they [prepare] a partnership [*eruv*] in an alley? One sets down a jar [of wine or food] and says, "Behold this [*eruv*] is for all the persons of [this] alley." And he includes them through the agency of his grown son or daughter and through the agency of his Hebrew slave or slavewoman and through the agency of his wife. But he does not include them through the agency of his minor son or daughter nor through the agency of his Canaanite slave or his Canaanite slave woman because their hand is as his hand. (M. Eruvin 7:6)

The *katan* of this mishnah is utterly identified with the adult who raises him and who possesses him as the master owns the Canaanite slave, a quality of being owned from which even the wife and Hebrew slave, in this mishnah, are partially spared. However, in the matter of the *eruv*, this *katan* remains different from the *katan* who is grouped with the *cheresh* and *shoteh*: "[If] one sends his *eruv* through the agency of a *cheresh*, *shoteh*, or *katan* or through the agency of one who does not admit [the legality] of an *eruv*, it is not a [valid] *eruv*" (M. Eruvin 3:2). None of these people can validly perform a mitzvah because they are considered not to have *da'at*. The *katan* who is likened to the Canaanite slave has *da'at* but cannot perform the mitzvah himself because he is not able to carry out his intentions with independence and full agency; perhaps he goes out relying on his mother's *eruv*. In other words, this is not a preverbal toddler or infant, who is like the *cheresh* and the *shoteh*, but a person with *da'at* who cannot move about freely without either supervision or direction (the *katan*) and does not have the correct intention (the Canaanite slave).

The issues regarding the *katan* and ritual purity are somewhat complicated. Some foods, such as the gift of food to the priests called *terumah*, had to be eaten in a state of ritual purity. In order to be sure that the *katan* would treat *terumah* properly, his elders would have him purify himself in the ritual bath (*mikveh*) and would give him regular food but tell him it was *terumah* in order to see if he would deal with it properly. Furthermore, if this child is able to understand rules about ritual impurity and can answer cogently when questioned about his status, then we assume he is impure since he can explain otherwise.[16]

The importance of discernment as a defining characteristic of *da'at* is seen with regard to the Paschal sacrifice. The child must not only have the ability to eat roast meat, that is, have teeth, but also must have the *da'at* required to eat with intention. The sages were doubtless aware that in early childhood children tend to put everything in their mouths, while at two or three years old they begin not to do so.

Part of the Sukkot celebration, and indeed, part of almost every celebration, was public prayer and the reading of the Torah. The role of the *katan* here is liminal, quite obviously on the edge between marginal and full participation. "If he [the one who read *maftir*, the last portion of the Torah reading] was a *katan*, his father or his teacher passes [before the ark] in his behalf [instead of having the *katan* do it himself as one reading *maftir* would normally do]. A *katan* [may] read the Torah and translate, but he may not recite the Shema, nor go before the ark, nor raise his hands [in the priestly benediction]" (M. Megillah 4:5–6). At first, these restrictions on the *katan* might seem surprising. But perhaps passing before the ark and reciting the Shema, together with the priestly benediction, were all rites, or similar to rites, that were performed in the Temple; in that case, *da'at* alone does not determine who may participate in them.[17] If *da'at* were the only factor, then any *katan* who had sufficient *da'at* might perform these mitzvot as well as wave the *lulav* and secure ritual purity (as we saw above in T. Hagigah 1:2–3).

Even within the Temple, however, a Levite who had not yet attained his majority could participate on the edge of the Temple ritual:

> No fewer than twelve Levites [could] stand on the [priestly] platform, and they [could] infinitely add [to their number]. No minor could enter the Temple Court [to take part] in the service except at the time when the Levites would stand to sing; and [these Levite minors] did not [accompany their song] with lyre and harp, but with their voices [only in order] to add sweetness to the melody. Rabbi Eliezer ben Yaakov says, [These minors] did not go to make up the [required] number [of twelve Levites], nor did they stand on the [priestly] platform, but they stood on the ground so that their heads [could be seen] between the legs of the Levites, and they were called "the tormentors of the Levites." (M. Arachin 2:6)

The Levites provided the musical accompaniment to the Temple service and were themselves physically situated between the holy precincts of the Temple and its public courtyard. While Temple service was offered in utter silence, the Levites provided the words and music of the psalms that framed the sacrifices and confirmed their meaning to the worshipers. The "tormentors of the Levites" were boys whose voices had not yet changed; they would sing along, with high voices that the adult Levites could not match for beauty. T. Arachin 2:1 reports that the only time minors (Tosefta identifies them as the children of Jerusalem's nobility) appeared in the Israelite's Court (just below the Levite's platform) was when the Levites were performing their songs. Normally, women and children were relegated to the Women's Court, except women who were offering a sacrifice.[18] The Israelite's Court is just on the edge between the Women's Court and the plaza containing the altar where the animals were sacrificed. Male children were admitted there to contribute to the singing but not to fully participate until they had reached physical adulthood, as manifested by a full beard. Here, the liminality of minors is graphically portrayed. Their voices are between those of men and women. They are positioned between the Levites and the Israelites (and the Levites, themselves, are between the Israelites and the priests; on the Levites' mediating role, see Levine 1995, 48–55). These minors are moving toward full participation, almost on the heels of those who have already achieved full participatory status.

In sum, we see that the *katan* who is included in the category of women, slaves, and minors holds a liminal position relative to the full participants in the sages' system, who were free, grown, Jewish men. This *katan* is quite different from the one who is grouped with the *cheresh* and *shoteh*, to whom we now turn our attention.

The Category *Cheresh Shoteh v'Katan*

The *cheresh*, the *shoteh*, and the *katan* are grouped together as those whom the Mishnah considers to be stigmatized in almost every situation. Their lack of *da'at* provides them with a master status that makes their other abilities irrelevant to the sages. They have not been able to receive the sages' cultural *gnosis*, either because they are too young to do so (the *katan*) or because they lack the means to receive and transmit it accurately (the *cheresh* and *shoteh*). Therefore, they are considered incapable of participating in almost every action that the sages deem important.

Terumah: Separation and *Da'at*

The stigmatization of the *cheresh, shoteh v'katan* can best be seen in the context of the mitzvah of *terumah*. *Terumah* was separated from the harvest as a gift to the priests. Produce from which *terumah* and *ma'aser* (the tithe) have not been set aside is called *tevel* and may not be eaten by either the owner or by priests; food from which it is doubtful that the tithes have been separated off is called *demai*. The amount of *terumah* to be set aside was anywhere from one-sixtieth to one-thirtieth of the crop (M. Terumot 4:3). A blessing was said upon separating *terumah* and, ideally, the person reciting the blessing should be able to hear himself say it. Once it was separated, *terumah* could be consumed only by priests and their families in a state of ritual purity; this food could not revert to *hullin*, that is, food fit for consumption by ordinary folk or even by priests in a state of ritual impurity.

Some of the most important, and lengthy, discussions of disabilities are connected to separating *terumah*, an act that provides an excellent example of accomplishing something through intention, blessing, and action. By its very nature, that is, differentiating one thing from another, it epitomizes having *da'at*: one has the intention to differentiate, can verbalize this intention, and has the wherewithal, physically and materially, to act on it. It may be for this reason that we find so much material about persons with disabilities related to this activity. Moreover, these rules were of more than theoretical interest: people continued giving these tributes to the priests after the Temple's destruction.

The separation of *terumah* from the rest of a crop entails an understanding of the nature of the act and its consequences, the ability to be questioned about it, and the ability to maintain the separation once it had been made. Separation is obviously an important issue for the Mishnah in many spheres, not only in relation to *terumah* (separation of men and women at certain times, separation of pure from impure, etc.), but in its application to *terumah* it receives particular emphasis in this tractate. For example, later chapters examine the continued separation of *terumah* from other foods (e.g., a lay Israelite may not even use water in which *terumah* was boiled or preserved; M. Terumot 10:12). The ability to maintain all such distinctions in the sages' system through consistency of commitment and cognition was crucial. Since the *cheresh, shoteh v'katan* were thought to lack the *da'at* that would make this possible, they were excluded from this mitzvah: "Five [sorts of persons ought] not to separate *terumah*, and if they did separate *terumah*, it is not considered *terumah*: *hacheresh, v'hashoteh v'katan* and one who separates *terumah* from [crops] which are not his own, and a non-Jew who separated *terumah* from [crops] of a Jew even by permission, his separation is not [valid] *terumah*" (M. Terumot 1:1). Who, then, may separate *terumah*? First of all, such persons must have *da'at*, as the first exclusion of this mishnah makes clear. Thus, the separation of *terumah* by the *cheresh, shoteh v'katan* is not considered valid because it may not have been done with the intentionality needed to complete the transaction. They are stigmatized and their actions are not accepted, even when this might seem illogical—for example, when the action is performed correctly. As we will see, when it comes to a blind person, who is considered disabled in this matter (due to a presumed inability to separate the best of the crop for *terumah*), his separation is nevertheless considered valid after the fact. It is not stigmatized, as is that by the *cheresh, shoteh v'katan*. The Mishnah further states that one cannot separate *terumah* from crops that do not belong to him and a valid actor must be Jewish—part of the community for whom this is an obligation. The obligation to perform the action constitutes a large part of the requisite intention.

This mishnah is followed by one of the few explicit definitions of the exact nature of a *cheresh*'s disability: "A *cheresh* who speaks but cannot hear should not separate *terumah*, but if he did separate, his *terumah* is valid. The *cheresh* of whom the sages spoke in all cases is one who can neither hear nor speak" (M. Terumot 1:2). There seem to be two meanings that can be attributed to the term *cheresh*. It can refer both to one who cannot hear but can speak—who has, for example, lost the ability to hear in old age—and to one who can neither speak nor hear. The general rule is then stated that when the Mishnah speaks of a *cheresh*, it refers only to the latter.

T. Terumot 1:1–4 seeks to flesh out the definitions and historical conditions behind the Mishnah's ruling that the *cheresh, shoteh v'katan* be judged not to validly separate *terumah*, even ex post facto. These passages from Tosefta do not quote the Mishnah, but they clearly follow the categories mentioned in M. Terumot 1:1, discussing the *cheresh, shoteh, katan*, one who separates *terumah* from a crop not his own, and a non-Jew, in turn. In commenting on this mishnah, Tosefta does not treat *cheresh, shoteh v'katan* as an overarching category, but examines each term by itself.

R. Yehudah says, "A *cheresh* who separated *terumah*—that which he has separated is [valid] *terumah*." Said R. Yehudah: [The] story [is told about] the sons of R. Yohanan ben Gudgada [who] were *chershim*, and in Jerusalem all [of the foods requiring preparation in] purity were prepared under their supervision. They said to him, Is that proof [that a *cheresh* may separate *terumah*]? For [foods requiring preparation in] purity do not require [preparation with] intention (*machshavah*) and [therefore] may be prepared under the supervision of a *cheresh, shoteh v'katan*. [But] *terumah* and tithes require [separation with] intention (*machshavah*) [and therefore may not be separated by such individuals].

R. Yitschak says in the name of R. Elazar, "[That which has been separated as] *terumah* by a *cheresh* does not enter the status of *hullin* [even though it is not valid *terumah*] because it is a matter of doubt whether or not he has understanding (*safeik yeish bo da'at, safeik ein bo da'at*)."

What do they do for him? [Since his understanding is questionable, he may not separate his own *terumah*. Yet since he may have understanding, administrators may not separate *terumah* for him.]

The court appoints for him administrators [and] he separates *terumah* and they validate it on his behalf. [If the *cheresh* has understanding, the sanctity of the *terumah* depends on him alone. If not, the action of the administrators is sufficient to make the *terumah* valid.]

Rabban Shimon ben Gamliel says, "Who is the *cheresh* [whose *terumah* is not valid]?" Anyone who is a *cheresh* from birth. But if he was of sound senses (*pikeiach*) and became a *cheresh* [and wishes to separate *terumah*], he writes [indicating his intention to separate *terumah*], and they validate [the document] for him [and the sanctity of the *terumah* depends solely on the *cheresh*].[19] (T. Terumot 1:1)

[One who] hears but does not speak—that is a mute (*illem*). [One who] speaks but does not hear is a *cheresh*. And each of these is equivalent to a person of sound senses (*pikeiach*) in every respect. (T. Terumot 1:2)

Who is a *shoteh*? One who goes out alone at night, and who sleeps in a graveyard, and who rips his clothing, and who loses what is given to him. [If he is] at times a *shoteh* [and] at times lucid (*chalom*), this is the general principle: Whenever he is a *shoteh*, behold he is [considered] a *shoteh* in every respect, [but whenever he is] lucid (*chalom*), behold he is [considered] a person of sound mind (*k'pikeiach*) in every respect. (T. Terumot 1:3)

R. Yehudah says, "A *katan* whose father left him in a [cucumber] field, separates [*terumah*] and his father says on his behalf, "His *terumah* is [valid] *terumah*." They said to him: It is not he [the *katan*] who separated *terumah* but his father [who] validates it after him. (T. Terumot 1:4)

This passage illustrates the general tendency of Tosefta to take the broad categories of the Mishnah and break them down, not only into their component parts but into the categories within those parts. Tosefta admits to variability in a person's condition (e.g., the *shoteh* who is occasionally lucid) and defines disabilities much more finely than did the Mishnah. While we can probably never adequately answer the question of why this approach is taken, we can certainly judge its result. This passage explores the categories of stigmatization, makes them more precise, limits their impact, and even provides a mechanism whereby a *cheresh* can participate in the separation of *terumah*. Tosefta, the first document composed following the Mishnah's redaction, takes the first steps toward making the Mishnah's vision a workable blueprint for a functioning society that included persons with disabilities.

First, Tosefta counters the Mishnah's disqualification of *terumah* separated by a *cheresh* (M. Terumot 1:1) by citing a tradition in the name of R. Yehudah that considers it valid *terumah* once it has been separated. Three types of material elaborate this point: a specific example, a theoretical consideration, and a practical solution. We begin with the teaching about R. Yohanan ben Gudgada's sons who were *chershim* and supervised the preparation of ritually pure foods. (R. Yohanan ben Gudgada himself was apparently noted for taking special care to eat in a state of purity; see M. Hagigah 2:7.) We note that such actions by these *chershim* do not relieve their stigmatized condition, in theory. Their actions are considered valid, but so would be the actions of a robot if performed correctly in this situation.[20] An objection is raised by the sages to this example: such preparations do not require intention and so do not explain the acceptability of a *cheresh*'s *terumah*, since intention *is* needed for the separation of *terumah*.

Tosefta expresses doubt as to whether the *cheresh* has *da'at* or not and this throws the *cheresh*'s separation of *terumah* into doubt, as well. Is it discredited or not? Because Tosefta appears to be unable to decide one way or another, it is decreed that an executor validate the *cheresh*'s separation. This is a "belt and suspenders" solution: if the *cheresh* has *da'at*, then his intention is not discredited and his separation is valid; if he does not have *da'at*, the validation of the executors will make it valid *terumah*. Tosefta focuses on the power of the *cheresh*'s inner state to define reality.

T. Terumot introduces the opinions of Rabban Shimon ben Gamliel on the exact nature of different kinds of *chershim* and their statuses. Who is the stigmatized *cheresh*? The one deaf and mute from birth who was never impressed with the seal of the culture's *gnosis*. However, the *cheresh* (deaf and mute) who did experience this *gnosis* is considered by Rabban Gamliel to be a full participant in the sages' system. Accommodations are made for his inability to speak, and his separation of *terumah* is considered valid. The distinction is between stigmatization (not liminality) and acceptance. If this grown, free, male *cheresh* has *da'at*, then his actions are as acceptable as those of any other full participant in this system. Nothing is said here about a female *cheresh* or a slave *cheresh*, but we assume that the same basic rules apply. If they have *da'at*, even though *chershim*, the limited ways in which they are allowed to separate *terumah* will be valid. (T. Terumot 1:6 outlines their roles in separating *terumah*.)

T. Terumot 1:3 defines a *shoteh*. A *shoteh* is, in short, one who behaves in an insane manner, that is, one who is mentally ill or mentally disabled.[21] Recognizing that mentally ill persons may experience periods of rationality and that mentally disabled persons may exhibit adequate functioning in selected areas of behavior, Tosefta validates actions taken during those periods and in those areas. Again, the distinction being drawn is between stigmatization and acceptance. When the person is not behaving like a *shoteh*, that person is considered "abled," that is, *pikeiach*. According to Tosefta, the person's moments of insanity or mental disability do not serve as a master status when he is not exhibiting them. Only when such states are evident are his actions discredited.

The *katan* who might separate *terumah* is old enough to help his father with the harvest. This is a child of perhaps five or six, certainly not two or three. Like the *cheresh*, this child's *terumah* is validated by a person whose intention is recognized as valid. The father says the blessing and the child says, "Amen," that is, "I agree." This *katan* who is liminal, who can participate in separating *terumah* at the very least, is already somewhat independent and verbal. This is not a one year old, who cannot yet speak or help with harvesting. That *katan* is utterly stigmatized with regard to this mitzvah.

This emphasis on who may not separate *terumah* stems, suggests the midrash collection Tanhuma, from the following use of the word *terumah* in the Torah:

> Said Rabbi Shimon ben Lakish: And all these [exclusions from the ability to separate *terumah* come] from this verse: ["Speak to the children of Israel, that they shall take for Me an offering (*terumah*); from each man whose heart makes him willing shall you take My offering

(terumati)" (Exodus 25:2).] *"[The]* cheresh" *(M. Terumot 1:1):* as it is written, *"Speak* to the children of Israel," excludes the *cheresh* who neither hears nor speaks. *"And the* shoteh," as it is written: "each man whose heart makes him willing" excludes the *shoteh* for the *shoteh's* heart does not move him. *"And the* katan," as it is written: "from each *man*" excludes the *katan* who is not [yet] a man. *"The one who separates* terumah *from [crops] which are not his,"* as it is written: "From each man whose heart makes him willing shall *you take*." Take from [what is] yours. *"And the non-Jew who separated* terumah *from a Jew's [crops] even with permission,"* as it is written: "Speak to the children of *Israel*" excludes the non-Jew who is not [a part of] Israel. (Tanhumah Warsaw Terumah 3)

This exposition systematically links the exclusions listed in M. Terumot 1:1 with the verse in Exodus that mentions a *terumah*, although there the word refers to offerings to build the tabernacle, not to agricultural taxes. This midrash gives a relatively straightforward textual basis for the exclusions in M. Terumot 1:1.

The Yerushalmi to this Mishnah offers a variant of this exposition:

> *"Five may not separate* terumah" *(M. Terumot 1:1).*
> R. Shmuel bar Nachman derived [reasons for the exclusion of] each of these [five individuals] from this [verse, Exodus 25:1–2]: "[The Lord said to Moses], 'Speak to the children of Israel that they may take for Me an offering *(terumah)*.'" [This reference to "the children of Israel"] excludes non-Jews [from separating *terumah*].
> "From every *man*" (Exodus 25:2). [This] excludes the *katan* [from separating *terumah*].
> "Whose heart makes him willing" (Exodus 25:2). [This] excludes the *cheresh* and *shoteh*.
> "And this is the offering which you shall receive *from them*" (Exodus 25:2). [This] excludes [from separating the offering] one who separates the [produce] that belongs to someone else. (Y. Terumot 1:1, 40a)

In a fashion similar to Tosefta's, when the Yerushalmi agrees with the categorization it finds in the Mishnah, it provides scriptural justification for the Mishnah's rulings. This constitutes a tacit acceptance of the Mishnah's categorization scheme. The Yerushalmi accepts the stigmatization of the *cheresh* and the *shoteh*, affirming, by its use of this prooftext from Exodus, that their lack of *da'at* causes their stigmatized master status. Tanhuma used the prooftext in a different way. The exclusion of the *cheresh* there was based on his inability to hear and speak rather than on lack of intention. Though we should be careful about drawing conclusions from such limited evidence, the way the Yerushalmi uses this text seems to indicate that it considers the *cheresh* to be as mentally impaired as the *shoteh*; Tanhuma, however, appears not to make this connection.

The issue of separating *terumah* is an important one for exploring the stigmatization of the *cheresh, shoteh v'katan*. Most notable is the contrast between Mishnah and Tosefta. The Mishnah states the exclusion of this category unambivalently while Tosefta moderates the Mishnah's severity. Tosefta demonstrates that the number of persons who are truly stigmatized can be defined more subtly than is done in the Mishnah. It recognizes (1) the *cheresh* who received the sages' *sacra* and who can therefore separate *terumah* validly; (2) intermittent sanity in a *shoteh*, which is considered complete while it lasts; and (3) the *katan* who is liminal, not stigmatized, because of his gradually developing maturity, competence, and internalization of the sages' *sacra*. Tosefta underscores the Mishnah's underlying system through these refinements: having *da'at* and being able to act on it validly are the criteria by which the stigmatized are differentiated from the accepted.

Injury and Insult

As was the case with *terumah*, Tosefta will moderate the Mishnah's generalized approach with regard to injuring a *cheresh, shoteh v'katan*. We have seen that some of these persons' actions can be considered valid under the right circumstances. The sages also admitted their participation in the system of criminal and civil justice, albeit somewhat grudgingly: "[To take away anything] found [by] a *cheresh, shoteh v'katan* is a kind of robbery, because of the ways of peace. Rabbi Yose says: It is actual robbery" (M. Gittin 5:8). This is an especially interesting mishnah because this treatment of the *cheresh, shoteh v'katan* can only be justified by appealing to the principle *mipnei darkei shalom*, "because of the ways of peace." That justification, used in the Mishnah only in M. Sheviit 4:3, M. Gittin 5:9, M. Shekalim 1:3, and M. Gittin 5:8, tends to be applied to rules that lack any clear textual basis but that are simply acknowledged by the sages to be accepted practice (though they do not entirely approve). According to the strict interpretation of the rules the sages developed, the *cheresh, shoteh v'katan* could not legally acquire items that they found. They therefore could not be robbed of property they did not technically own. However, "because of the ways of peace," the sages did not allow thieves to steal from such persons without penalty. The sages do not validate the *cheresh, shoteh v'katan's* acquisition of a given object here but rather protect such persons from robbers.

While the *cheresh, shoteh v'katan* are not credited with intentionality and its concomitant responsibility, the sages did recognize that these persons experience injury: "Injuring a *cheresh, shoteh v'katan* is bad, [as] he who injures them is liable [to pay damages], whereas if they injure others they are exempt [from paying damages]. [So also] injuring a slave and a [married] woman is bad as he who injures them is liable [to pay damages], whereas if they injure others they are exempt [from paying damages]. But they [may] have to pay at a later time: [for if] the woman was divorced or the slave freed, they would [then] be liable to pay" (M. Baba Kamma 8:4). The *cheresh, shoteh v'katan* are not held responsible for the injuries they cause.[22] Women and slaves (and minors, as they mature) are also problematic, but not in the same way: they may become full participants in this part of the sages' system at a later date if that which makes them liminal (their "owned" status) changes. The contrast is clear: the two categories, the stigmatized and the liminal, are both difficult to deal with, but for different reasons because of the different nature of their characters (or characterizations).

Tosefta, commenting on this mishnah, analyzes the sorts of damages the *cheresh, shoteh v'katan* might collect of the five sorts available: that is, compensation for damage, pain, healing, loss of time, and indignity (M. Baba Kamma 8:1).

> He who inflicts injury on a *cheresh, shoteh v'katan* is liable for four things, but exempt [from making compensation for] indignity (*haboshet*), because they are not [subject to compensation for] indignity. Rabbi [Yehudah HaNasi] says, "I say a *cheresh* is subject to [compensation for] indignity. A *katan* is not subject to [compensation for] indignity. A person who inflicts injury on a *shoteh* is sometimes [obligated to make compensation for] indignity, and sometimes he is not [obligated to compensation for] indignity. [As to a] blind man, Rabbi Yehudah says, "He is not [to be compensated for] indignity." And sages say, "He is [compensated for] indignity." (T. Baba Kamma 9:13)

In this passage, we clearly see a difference of opinion. Can a person who has not been stamped with the seal of his culture's *gnosis* be deemed capable of feeling insult? (After all, an insulting hand gesture is only insulting if one understands what it normally means. One might otherwise assume it was a kind of waving or a random motion.) The *cheresh, shoteh v'katan* are not to be compensated for insult; Tosefta maintains their stigmatized position. Rabbi Yehudah HaNasi, however, asserts that a *cheresh* experiences insult and should therefore be compensated for it. This suggests that he believed that the *cheresh* had some sort of cognition. But the *katan* deserves no such compensation. For example, one may change a baby's diaper in public and the infant will experience no sense of diminished dignity. The *shoteh*, depending on his state of mind, may or may not experience indignity and this is to be judged, according to Rabbi Yehudah HaNasi, on an ad hoc basis. This ruling is in accord with T. Terumot 1:3. When the *shoteh* has been initiated into the culture and is experiencing its *gnosis*, he is deemed a full participant in the culture and is compensated for insult. When he is not experiencing its *gnosis*, he is stigmatized and his participation in the system is discredited.

Machshavah and *Kavvanah:*
Communication and Stigmatization

The Mishnah clearly regards the lack of reliable, communicable intention, related to the lack of *da'at*, to be the reason for the exclusion of a *cheresh, shoteh v'katan* from their system. Such persons also lack *machshavah*, the ability to have a recognizable plan, according to the sages.

> A [general] rule [regarding food needing] ritual purity (*toharot*) [is that] whatever is specially food [for a] person is [susceptible to] ritual impurity until it is rendered unfit to be food [even for] a dog, and any [food] that is not specially food for a person is [not susceptible to] ritual impurity until it is prepared [to be consumed as food] by a person. How [might an example of this distinction be shown]? If a [young] pigeon fell into the winepress [and died, thus being unfit for food], and one thought of bringing it up [to give it to] an idolater [to eat], it becomes susceptible to ritual impurity, [since it was categorized as food for a human being, but if his intention was to give it] to a dog [to eat], it is [insusceptible to] ritual impurity. Rabbi Yochanan ben Nuri [considers it susceptible to] ritual impurity.
>
> [If] a *cheresh, shoteh v'katan* formed [this] intention [to give it to an idolater to eat], it is [insusceptible to] ritual impurity, but if they brought it up, it is susceptible to [ritual impurity] for they [are credited with cogent] action but not [with] intention (*sheyeish lahen ma'aseh,v'ein lahen machshavah*). (M. Toharot 8:6)

Only whole items can become ritually impure. So food fit for a person (e.g., a roasted chicken) is susceptible to ritual impurity and cannot become insusceptible until it no longer fits into the category of "human food"—that is, is not even fit for a dog (e.g., the chicken is reduced to a stack of bones). Conversely, food that is not usually food for a person (e.g., a container of bird seed) is not susceptible to ritual impurity until it is made fit for a person (e.g., presented on a plate with fork and knife on a bed of lettuce). Now, if a bird, which could be fit food for a (non-Jewish) human or for a dog, had died, then it is the intention of the person who picks it up that defines whether the bird is human food or dog food. If he plans to give it to a human being, then it is human food. If he plans to throw it in the trash, then it is trash. The *cheresh, shoteh v'katan* can similarly affect the definition, and susceptibility to ritual uncleanness, of this bird, but *only* through their actions, *not* through their intentions. The Mishnah identifies the critical factor as *machshavah*, which Eilberg-Schwartz (1986, 7) explains as "the intention an individual formulates before he or she actually begins to act. . . . [*Machshavah*] serves to determine the classification of an object in a person's possession. When an Israelite formulates a plan to use an object for a particular purpose, he in effect places that object into a given category." According to our mishnah, the *cheresh, shoteh v'katan* do not have valid *machshavah*. The thought that proceeds action and that is recognized by the sages as *doing something*, as changing reality in some way, is not attributed to this category of persons. However, their *action* is credited as meaningful and accomplishing something. In this case, by tossing the bird to a non-Jewish human or to a garbage heap, the *cheresh, shoteh v'katan* have changed reality as effectively as might persons of sound senses. Their actions serve as their means of communication.

The *cheresh, shoteh v'katan* are credited neither with *machshavah*, the thought that constitutes a plan before action takes place, nor with *kavvanah*, the thought and purpose with which one performs an action. The Mishnah uses the presence or absence of *kavvanah* to determine whether a precept has been fulfilled or transgressed, as in this example:

> If one heard the sound of a shofar [on Rosh Hashanah] or the sound of the scroll [of Esther being read on Purim], if he had intention (*im kivvein libo*) [to fulfill the mitzvah with this hearing], he has fulfilled [it]. If he did not [have this intention] he has not fulfilled [the precept]. Even though both this one and the other one heard [this is not critical; rather the critical matter is that] this one had intention and the other did not.
> A *cheresh, shoteh v'katan* cannot fulfill an obligation [to do a mitz-

vah] for a group. This is the general principle: Anyone who is [himself] not obligated to perform an act [which is a mitzvah] cannot fulfill [the obligation to do it] for a group. (M. Rosh Hashanah 3:7–8)

Simply hearing the shofar (ram's horn) sounded on the Jewish new year, or hearing the story of Esther recited on the holiday of Purim, is not enough to fulfill the precept. One must *intend* to do so for the action to count. Hearing is an excellent test case for exploring this issue, since no overt action is required by the hearer. Functioning hearing and a correct inner state allow one to fulfill the commandment; no other action is required.

Because the *cheresh, shoteh v'katan* have no legally recognized *da'at* and, hence, no *kavvanah*, they are not held liable to perform those commandments which require intention (e.g., reciting the Shema, offering the prayer or *Tefillah*). This is elucidated by the Mishnah as a general rule that excludes the *cheresh, shoteh v'katan* from acting on behalf of the community in any matter needing intention; thus they are barred from leading the congregation in almost every liturgical act of Jewish practice.

Some actions did not require intention to be performed correctly in the sages' system of thought and, hence, the *cheresh, shoteh v'katan* might be able to carry out those actions validly (e.g., see T. Terumot 1:1). However, there had to be some way of verifying that these actions, not requiring *da'at* and only needing mechanical perfection, were correctly done. For the *cheresh, shoteh v'katan*, their inability to communicate constitutes a second sort of barrier to their participation in Jewish ritual life, even when *da'at* is not a requirement.

This factor comes into play in the first mishnah of tractate Hullin, which outlines who may slaughter meat in a way that makes it kosher, that is, proper for consumption by Jews:

All [persons may] slaughter and their slaughtering is valid, except a *cheresh, shoteh v'katan*, lest they spoil what they slaughter. [But if] any of [the persons in this category] slaughtered and others [of sound senses] saw them [do it], their slaughtering is valid. The slaughtering by an idolater is [considered] carrion [and is unfit for Jewish consumption] and it communicates ritual impurity by being carried. One who slaughtered at night and also if a blind man slaughtered [at any time]—his slaughtering is valid. [If] one slaughtered on Shabbat, or on the Day of Atonement, although he is guilty against his [own] soul, his slaughtering is valid. (M. Hullin 1:1)

The tendency in this mishnah is to validate the slaughtering done by any Jew, even one who is blind and unable to see the animal or the knife. That done by a non-Jew is invalidated because he might have dedicated the animal, and its blood, for pagan purposes; such an animal is therefore ruled off-limits. But even slaughtering done by a Jew at a completely inappropriate time, when slaughtering outside the cult is prohibited, is valid, albeit sinful. This mishnah affirms that the *cheresh, shoteh v'katan* are able to slaughter validly *if* someone else can testify on their behalf. The act does not require intention (unlike the separation of *terumah*) and need only be accomplished correctly. Therefore, the issue at stake here is acceptable testimony. While the *cheresh, shoteh v'katan* are stigmatized because of their inability to give such testimony, their kosher slaughtering is validated as legitimate. This emphasis on the mechanical action hearkens back to the Temple, where intention was not as crucial as it was in the sages' system. In the Temple, what mattered instead was accomplishing the rituals accurately. If we think of modern medicine, this distinction becomes clear. A mistake in an operating room is just as lethal whether it was performed intentionally or unintentionally. Likewise, a surgeon might be deaf and mute but if she can do the cutting correctly, her surgery will be considered valid and valuable.

The Mishnah records a conflict of opinion as to the status of slaughtering done by a *cheresh, shoteh v'katan*, based on witnesses who are able to reliably communicate what happened.

[If a] *cheresh, shoteh v'katan* slaughtered [a wild beast or a bird], and others saw them [and could testify that they had slaughtered correctly, one of the observers] is obligated to cover up [the blood]. [If the *cheresh, shoteh v'katan*] were by themselves [with no witnesses for their slaughtering, then the blood] is exempt from [the law of] covering up (Leviticus 17:13). And likewise, also, with the matter of [an animal] and its young (Leviticus 22:28). [If a *cheresh, shoteh v'katan*] slaughtered [correctly a cow or its young] and others saw [them and could testify that they had slaughtered correctly] it is prohibited to slaughter [the young or the cow, as the case may be, on the same day] after them. [If the *cheresh, shoteh v'katan*] were by themselves [with no witnesses for their slaughtering] Rabbi Meir permits the slaughter [of the other animal on the same day] after them, but the sages prohibit it. But [the sages] admit that if one did slaughter [the other beast on the same day], he is not punished [with] forty [lashes]. (M. Hullin 6:3)

This mishnah refers to two obligations outlined in the Torah: "And every man of the children of Israel, or of the strangers that live among them, who hunts [any] animal or bird which may be eaten, he shall pour out its blood and cover it with dust" (Leviticus 17:13); "And [whether it] be cow or ewe, you shall not kill it and its young [both] in one day" (Leviticus 22:28). Table 5 summarizes the views expressed here.

The Mishnah evinces some slight ambivalence regarding the unwitnessed slaughter of an animal by a *cheresh shoteh v'katan*. Rabbi Meir's view is actually the lenient one in this case, since it obligates one to observe fewer rules. However, the majority opinion also tends toward leniency in its hesitation to mete out punishment based on the (presumed) correct slaughtering of a *cheresh, shoteh v'katan*. Nevertheless, by not requiring that punishment be meted out if the mother is killed on the same day as a *cheresh, shoteh v'katan* slaughtered the young, the stigmatization of the category is maintained. Even though such slaughtering is prohibited, indicating a

TABLE 5. Slaughtering by a *Cheresh, Shoteh v'Katan* (M. Hullin 6:3)

Obligation	If Witnessed	If Not Witnessed	
		R. Meir	Sages
To cover blood	yes		no
Not to kill mother and young on same day	yes	no	yes (but no punishment incurred if done)

certain "better to be safe rather than sorry" attitude toward the To-rah, these persons are not punished for transgressing this ruling be-cause their unwitnessed actions do not have validity within the system.

If we contrast this mishnah with that concerning *terumah*, we be-gin to see more clearly the factors contributing to the stigmatization of the *cheresh, shoteh v'katan*. These exclusions can be represented as concentric circles, with the lack of *da'at* at the core. If *da'at* exists, there remains the question of whether there is *machshavah*, inten-tion. Finally, even if *da'at* and *machshavah* are assumed to exist, there must be a valid way of communicating their presence.

The Mishnah recognizes that communication need not be verbal: "A *cheresh* [may transact business by] gestures and be communicated with by gestures. Ben Beteira says, He [may transact business] con-cerning movable property with lip movements and be communi-cated with [regarding such commerce] by lip movements. Children [of six or seven years old, *hapa'otot*, 'talkers'] can [validly buy and] sell movable property" (M. Gittin 5:7). In this mishnah, we see that *chershim* could use nonvocal means of communication to participate in commerce.

The *cheresh* here is linked to a child of intermediate age who can speak and who is trusted to buy and sell movable property (but not real estate) on his own. This ruling was made so that the child might be able to acquire food for himself (Y. Gittin 5:8, 47b); because par-ents were not obligated to support their children after they reached the age of six (B. Ketubot 49b), these children had to have the legal ability to acquire food, a kind of movable property. The Bavli (B. Gittin 59a) puts the range for *pa'otot* as between six and ten years old, with the matter being judged according to the child's intellect. Here, the *cheresh* and this particular sort of minor are enabled to par-ticipate in the sages' system of commerce in their distinctive ways. The stipulation that children could not sell real estate was possibly a measure to protect them, lest they be taken advantage of.

This mishnah opens up a different perspective on the *cheresh*. Not grouped with the *shoteh v'katan* but likened to a child who can speak and function to the best of his abilities, this *cheresh* is allowed to validly function as his abilities permit. In this mishnah, and the commentary to it, there seems to be no stigmatization of either the *cheresh* or the *pa'otot*: they are both full participants, albeit somewhat idiosyncratic ones, in the act of selling movable objects.

Later Nuancing of the Category *Cheresh, Shoteh v'Katan*

In the Bavli, the category *cheresh, shoteh v'katan* almost always appears in a quotation from an earlier source. As an exception, the following passage is particularly interesting. It is in Aramaic rather than Hebrew, except for the terms *cheresh, shoteh v'katan* and the quotations, which suggests that it is an Amoraic composition. Here each component of the category *cheresh, shoteh v'katan* is evaluated separately.

Mishnah (24:1): If darkness falls upon a person on a road, he entrusts his purse to a gentile (nokhri), *but if there is no gentile with him, he places it on an ass. . . .*
Gemara: [If there is] an ass, and a *cheresh, shoteh v'katan* he [should] place it [his purse] on the ass, and not give it to the *cheresh, shoteh v'katan*. What is the reason? These [persons] are human beings (*adam*) and this [ass] is not [a human being].
[In the case of] a *cheresh* and a *shoteh*: [he should give it] to the *shoteh*. [In the case of] a *shoteh* and a *katan* [he should give it] to the *shoteh*.
The [sages] were asked: What [if the choice is between] a *cheresh* and a *katan*? According to Rabbi Eliezer there is no question, for it was taught: Rabbi Yitschak said in Rabbi Eliezer's name: **The *terumah* of a *cheresh* does not revert to *hullin* [unconsecrated status], because there is doubt [whether the *cheresh* has *da'at* or not]** (T. Terumot 1:1). The question is on the rabbis' view. For we learned: *Five [sorts of persons ought] not to separate* terumah, *and if they did separate* terumah, *it is not considered* terumah: hacheresh, v'hashoteh v'katan *and one who separates* terumah *from [crops] which are not his own, and a non-Jew who separated* terumah *from [crops] of a Jew even by permission, his separation is not [valid]* terumah (M. Terumot 1:1).
What [should be done about our original question]? [Should] he give it to the *cheresh* since the *katan* will arrive at understanding (*da'at*)? Or perhaps he should give it to the *katan*, because a *cheresh*

may be confused with an adult of sound senses (*pikeiach*)? Some say: He [should] give it to the *cheresh*. Some [others] say: He [should] give it to the *katan*. (B. Shabbat 153a–b)

This short passage seems to be an exercise in logic responding to the Mishnah's categorization of a Jew, a Gentile, and an ass. Here, the Bavli fills in the intermediary categories, adding the logical justification it perceives to be necessary. The result is a continuum that spans the range from "more like an animal" to "more like a 'normal' human being," moving respectively from ass to *shoteh* to *cheresh/katan* to sensate Jew. The *shoteh* is unambivalently stigmatized, as are the *cheresh* and *katan*: it is better for them to carry something on Shabbat than it is for a Jew who has *da'at*. For the sages, the issue is one of appearance: they assume that a *shoteh*'s disability is visible and that a *cheresh*'s is not. If the *cheresh* carries the purse on Shabbat, others might believe that a person with *da'at* is doing so; this would be demoralizing and shocking. An alternative argument is that the *katan* is developing *da'at* and it would be harmful to start the child on a sinning path by having him carry something on Shabbat. The issue remains undecided as nascent *da'at* is set against the appearance of breaking religious norms. It is almost as if the sages are weighing priestly values (appearance) against their own system of *da'at* as the great determiner of status, and they cannot disregard either.

One passage in the Bavli, which contrasts the mental functioning of the *cheresh* with that of the *shoteh*, expresses doubt about the *cheresh*'s true cognitive abilities. After exploring all the possibilities, the discussion ends without a definitive decision and with the word *teiku*, "let it stand."[23] The main topic here is marriage. The sages declared the marriage of a *cheresh* valid according to their rules even though it is not valid according to Pentateuchal law. This equivocal status of a *cheresh*'s marriage is likened to the eating of a fictitious animal called the *koy*, whose status the Mishnah had difficulty clarifying (M. Bikkurim 2:8–11). The sages could not determine whether the *koy* was a domesticated animal or not, whether its blood required consistent covering up on slaughter, and so forth. The Bavli makes a metaphorical connection between the eating of the *koy* and the unwitting adulterous union with the wife of a *cheresh*. In each case, something has been "consumed" and there is some doubt as to what sort of sin, if any, this constitutes. The sages often compared women in general, not just the wife of a *cheresh*, to a *koy*, for neither the *koy* nor the woman fit neatly into the sages' system of classification. Both, according to Judith Wegner, are anomalous:

> Depending on context, [the sages] sometimes identified women with Self and treated them as persons; at other times they viewed women as Other and treated them as chattels. This oscillation between two poles, arising from woman's ambiguous ontological character, makes her the outstanding anomaly of the Mishnah. For though the framers could not fit her consistently into either of the polar categories *chattel* or *person*, they declined to create a third, intermediate category to contain her. Here, we recall once more the case of the *koy*. The sages' reluctance to recognize a hybrid (stemming from their dislike of the excluded middle) forced them to place the *koy* sometimes in one and sometimes in the other of two polar categories, sometimes in neither and sometimes in both at once. (1988, 178)

This claim that women fall outside all categories is questionable, for there *was* a category of women, slaves, and minors, as we have seen. But the suggestion that the sages, like the Torah before them, see correspondences between human and animal appears much more defensible (see also Eilberg-Schwartz 1990, 115–40, on animal metaphors in Israelite society). We can outline the following metaphorical equivalences:

sacrificial animals	priests (blemishless, priestly, grown men)
kosher animals	full participants (free, grown Jewish men)
blemished kosher animals	blind, physically disabled Jewish men and hermaphrodites and androgynes
koy, doubtfully kosher animals	women, slaves, and minors (liminal)
nonkosher animals	*cheresh, shoteh v'katan* (i.e., nonparticipants)

Priests and sacrificial animals are blemishless and efficacious within the cult. Kosher animals are fit for Jews to eat but might not be perfect enough to be sacrifices. Just as blemished kosher animals are fit for consumption outside of the cult, so men with visual and physical disabilities and unclear gender are fit for almost every activity in Jewish life, as these conditions do not affect their *da'at*. Women, slaves, and minors, like the *koy*, are liminal, difficult-to-categorize entities with which the sages struggled. The *cheresh, shoteh v'katan* are analogous to nonkosher animals, which play no substantive role in Jewish religious life: they may neither be offered in the cult nor consumed by lay Israelites. Such animals (horses, hippopotami, etc.) are recognized to be part of the world and may be used in unconsecrated ways (e.g., for work), but they do not help further the relationship between Israelites and God as do animals fit for consumption or sacrifice.

The discussion begins by differentiating among marriages of *shotim, k'tanim,* and *chershim* (B. Yebamot 112b). *Shotim* have no means of marrying validly, either from Toraitic law or from the sages' authority, whereas the sages did legitimize the marriages of minors and *chershim*. This is in line with the ruling in B. Shabbat 153a–b, just examined, which stigmatized the *shoteh* to a greater extent than the *katan* or *cheresh*. The sages granted *chershim* the right to marry, but by what authority and, consequently, with what validity? Does transgressing the marriage bonds entail severe punishment for them? Once a marriage is entered into by a *cheresh*, it is, ex post facto, a rabbinically valid marriage. This sort of marriage is compared to a *cheresh*'s ability to separate valid *terumah*. Indeed, the topics are not unrelated. As we have already seen, to separate *terumah* is to make something holy and dedicate it for special use; to marry is to separate someone from others and relate to him or her in a special, holy way. Of course, both actions also require functioning *da'at*, as well. If a *cheresh* separates *terumah* (and he was observed by witnesses who could testify that he had done so correctly), though he was prohibited from separating it before the fact, nevertheless the produce is, after the fact, *terumah* and does not revert to unconsecrated status (*hullin*). In a like manner, the marriage of a *cheresh* is valid only by rabbinic edict, but once entered into, it is, in fact, a marriage; it is not discredited.

Transgression against the integrity of such a marriage has some similarity to the eating of fat from the *koy*. Rabbi Elazar holds that one must bring an *asham talui*, a "suspended guilt offering," for having done so; that is, there is the possibility, although not a certainty, that to eat such fat is a sin. Similarly, if one had intercourse with the wife of a *cheresh*, it might be a sin, although there is doubt regarding this issue, since the marriage is only valid rabbinically. The *asham talui*, which is described in Leviticus 5:17–19, is offered by a person who is in doubt as to whether a transgression has been committed with one of two items. For example, one could pick one of two available pieces of meat, only one of which was permissible. An *asham talui* would have to be brought in such a case. But the nature of the doubt regarding a *cheresh*'s wife is different, for only one doubtful "item"—that is, the *cheresh*'s wife herself—is involved. Indeed, since the marriages of *chershim* are valid only rabbinically and not according to Pentateuchal law, sleeping with a *cheresh*'s wife results in no transgression and no necessity to bring the offering. Nonetheless, some sages maintain that this offering would have to be brought, reasoning as follows:

> Rav Ashi asked: What is Rabbi Elazar's reason [for not allowing *terumah* that a *cheresh* has separated to revert to unconsecrated status, in line with his ruling in T. Terumot 1:1, and by extension, for requiring an *asham talui* for intercourse with a *cheresh*'s wife]? Does he simply believe that the *cheresh* has weak *da'at* [i.e., is mentally disabled]? In any case, he is in doubt if [the *cheresh*'s *da'at*] is lucid [in which case he will understand the proceedings] or not [in which case he'll never understand the proceedings] but he always has the same mental capabilities [i.e., the *cheresh*'s mental functioning is constant, unlike that of the *shoteh* who is occasionally lucid]. Or perhaps [Rabbi Elazar] simply believes that [the *cheresh*] is always mentally disabled and never lucid?
>
> [Rabbi Elazar's doubt] here is due to this reason: Because [the *cheresh*] may sometimes [function cognitively] in a normal state [for a

cheresh, that is with weak intelligence that stays at a constant level] and sometimes [have a lack of *da'at*] like a *shoteh* [whose mental state can change from one day to the next]. What is the practical difference [between these views]? [It makes a difference in respect to] releasing his wife by a letter of divorce. If you say that his mind is always [in the same condition], just as [his] wedding [is valid] so his divorce [would have the same validity]. But if you say that sometimes he is in a normal state and sometimes he is [as mentally disabled as] a *shoteh*, he would be capable of valid betrothal but he would not be able to grant a divorce [because he may be insane at the moment, in which case his divorce would be invalid]. What [then is the decision]? This remains undecided (*teiku*). (B. Yebamot 113a–b)

According to M. Gittin 2:6, when executing a divorce one must be in the same mental state as when one contracted the marriage. This is problematic in the case of the *cheresh* for, as we see, there is genuine confusion about his state of mind. It cannot be determined whether the *cheresh* is intermittently lucid and impaired (in which case, the divorce could not be executed), or in a constant state of impaired functioning (in which case, the divorce could be executed). This issue remains undecided. As the passage makes clear, the sages simply did not understand what sort of mental functioning a *cheresh* had.

Contrasting Categories: Persons with Visual Disabilities and the *Cheresh, Shoteh v'Katan*

Lack of *da'at*, as we have seen, had a drastic and wide-ranging impact on one's ability to participate in the sages' system. Not every disability, however, is associated with a lack of *da'at*. Unlike the *cheresh, shoteh v'katan*, persons with visual disabilities were barely considered to be disabled by the sages; indeed, several blind sages excelled in that culture. Blindness is presented as an impediment only in a few, specific situations in which vision is deemed necessary; it does not become a master status for the sightless person. Blind persons are more often categorized as "blemished" than as disabled or stigmatized. We can contrast the sages' views of the *cheresh, shoteh v'katan* with their views of persons with visual disabilities in two specific areas: the separation of *terumah* and liability for civil and criminal damages.

Terumah

In the matter of separating *terumah*, blind persons are considered impaired, but not completely so: "Five [sorts of persons should] not separate *terumah*, but if they have separated it, their *terumah* is valid *terumah:* The mute person (*ha'illeim*), or the drunk person, or the naked person, or the blind person, or the *ba'al keri* [a person who is in a state of ritual impurity because of a seminal emission] should not separate *terumah*, but if they have separated it, their *terumah* is valid *terumah*" (M. Terumot 1:6). Each person in this mishnah is disqualified because he lacks a requisite skill or condition for the proper separation of *terumah*. The *illeim* physically cannot say the blessing; a drunk person would neither be able to say the blessing correctly nor separate the best of his crops for *terumah*. Naked persons and one who had a seminal emission (*ba'al keri*) and consequently is ritually impure are prohibited from reciting a blessing. Blind persons were deemed unable to select the best of their crops for the priests' due. However, if such persons did separate *terumah*, it is acceptable *terumah* and does not revert to *hullin*. In other words, a blind person's *terumah* may not be of the best sort, but it fulfills the requirements of the category "*terumah*" nonetheless. Again, within the sages' structure the blind person does not occupy a liminal position, that is, an intrastructural position, but merely a position that is blemished. Once accomplished, the blind person's deeds are considered completely valid (as are the mute person's).

Tosefta provides the rationale behind the exclusion for each of these five categories of persons:

> Why did [the sages] say that a mute person may not separate *terumah*? Because he is not able to [recite] the blessing [with which the separation is accomplished].
>
> Why did [the sages] say a blind person may not separate *terumah*? Because he is not able to [distinguish when] choosing [between] the fine [produce] and the poor [produce].
>
> Why did [the sages] say a drunk person may not separate *terumah*? Because he has no *da'at*. Even though he is drunk, his acquisition is valid, his sale is valid, his vow is valid, his consecration [of a gift to the

Temple] is valid, and his [giving of] a gift is valid. [If] he commits a sin which requires a sin offering [for atonement] we obligate him to bring a sin offering. If [the punishment for the sin] is stoning, we obligate him [to suffer] stoning. The rule of this matter is that a drunk person is [considered to be] like a person of sound senses (*k'pikeiach*) in every way.

Why did [the sages] say a person who has had a seminal emission may not separate *terumah*? Because he is not able [to recite] the blessing [being unable to say God's name as he is in a state of ritual impurity].

Why did [the sages] say a naked person may not separate *terumah*? Because is not able [to recite] the blessing [since it is improper to utter God's name when naked]. But he [may] cover himself with straw, stubble, or any thing and [recite the] blessing. (T. Terumot 3:1–2)

The most remarkable statement in this passage is that the drunk person has no *da'at*. In the specific context of separating *terumah*, he may not choose the best produce or he may separate less than the required amount. If he separated his *terumah* in a state of drunken dementia his *terumah*, like that of the *shoteh*, is not valid even after the fact of his separation (Lieberman 1992, ad loc.).

This passage at first would seem to suggest that the drunkard is like the *cheresh, shoteh v'katan*, subject neither to mitzvot nor to the punishments that failure to follow them incurs. Tosefta, however, immediately goes on to deny this possibility, in the end saying that he is considered sensate in every respect. Although a thoroughly inebriated person may have no functioning *da'at*—may not experience the norms of the sages system, just as the *cheresh, shoteh v'katan* did not—Tosefta holds this person responsible for his actions since he *could* have had access to his *da'at* had he not disabled himself.

The Yerushalmi, quoting and adapting Tosefta, goes on to combine the five categories of persons into two groups:

Some of these [five sorts of persons may not separate *terumah*] because [they are not permitted to recite] the blessing [that accompanies the separation of *terumah*]. And some of them because they are not [to separate *terumah* because they are not] able to [distinguish between produce of better or worse quality in order to] separate *terumah* from the best [of their produce].

A mute person, a naked person, and one who has had a seminal emission [may not separate *terumah*] because [they may not recite] the blessing [through lack of speech, ritual impurity, or impropriety].

The blind person and the *shoteh*[24] and the drunkard [may not separate *terumah*] because they are unable to separate *terumah* from the best [crops]. (Y. Terumot 1:4, 1:6 40d)

The blind person does not lack *da'at;* his disability is merely a mechanical impediment to the proper separation of *terumah*. In contrast, the *terumah* of the *cheresh, shoteh v'katan* is not valid because the proper intention was not considered present when they separated it. The case of the drunkard makes the difference clear. The alcohol makes this person "blindly" unable to discern which are the best fruit, and though he may lack *da'at* at the moment, he is held responsible for having it and deliberately losing it. The blind person's *terumah* is, after the fact, valid *terumah*, albeit not the best sort, since he has intention and the ability to communicate that intention through the blessing.

Injury and Insult

Are blind persons accepted as full participants in the sages' culture, except on those infrequent occasions when their impaired vision prevents them from performing a specific commandment? Or are they stigmatized, like the *cheresh, shoteh v'katan?* Can there be a situation in which a blind person is treated the same as a sighted person? These issues are debated in the context of accidental murder and the protection the unintended murderer may seek. The laws that cover these eventualities are based in the Torah. Intentional murderers are to be put to death by blood avengers (Numbers 35:16–21). However, unintentional murderers can take refuge in designated cities: "But if he pushed him suddenly [i.e., accidentally], or threw upon him anything without lying in wait, or dropped upon him any deadly object of stone, *seeing him not*, and he died, and he was not his enemy, neither sought his harm; then the congregation shall judge between the killer and the blood avenger according to these laws" (Numbers 35:22–24). It would be possible to interpret this passage in a way that makes a blind person equivalent to a sighted person. If either killed a person unintentionally, it was because neither one saw the victim before dropping the rock.

Sifre N. fleshes out this notion: "'[Dropped] a deadly stone, seeing him not' (Numbers 35:23). [These words come] to include the blind man and the one who threw [a rock] at night. Rabbi Yehuda says, 'seeing him not': [these words come] to exclude the blind man [from the need to flee the blood avenger and to go to a city of refuge]" (Sifre N., *Eleh Mas'ei*, Piska 160). The same two viewpoints are also found in the Mishnah: "A blind person [who committed an accidental killing] does not have to flee [into exile to a sanctuary city]. These are the words of Rabbi Yehudah. Rabbi Meir says, 'He must flee [into exile]'" (M. Makkot 2:3). The question between Rabbi Yehudah and Rabbi Meir, here, is how to understand "seeing" in Numbers 35:23. On the one hand, if we follow Rabbi Yehudah's interpretation, the blind man is not at all responsible for an accidental death that he causes and need not even go to a city of refuge. This is consistent with Rabbi Yehudah's reasoning more generally, for he exempts blind persons from every precept in Torah (see Y. Makkot 2:5, 31d; B. Baba Kamma 86b–87a). Rabbi Meir's interpretation, on the other hand, suggests that the blind man is held responsible for the accidental killing and must proceed as would anyone else who committed unintentional manslaughter. In Rabbi Meir's understanding of the Torah verse, the blind man and the one who throws a rock at night are equal.

Rabbi Yehudah's opinion that blind persons are exempt from all the commandments of the Torah appears in the discussion of compensation for indignity inflicted on a person with visual disabilities. The Mishnah states that such persons are to be compensated: "One who insults a naked person, one who insults a blind person, or one who insults a sleeping person is liable [to pay compensation for indignity]" (M. Baba Kamma 8:1). The blind person is likened to other "normal" individuals who have a specific vulnerability; sightlessness is put on the same level as nakedness and unconsciousness.

It would be quite easy to subject any of these persons to indignity. Nonetheless, or perhaps particularly because of this, one is liable to pay compensation for any indignity inflicted upon them.

Insult is what people experience when they are aware that they have not been treated properly according to communal standards. One must experience the insult to be compensated for it. We saw this earlier in this chapter when considering T. Baba Kamma 9:13, where there was a debate over whether a *cheresh* or *shoteh* experienced the breaking of communal norms and whether they should be compensated for insult. In the following passage from the Bavli, the same question is asked about blind persons.

> **Rabbi Yehudah says, "A blind person is not [compensated for] indignity" (T. Baba Kamma 9:13).** So [in line with this ruling] Rabbi Yehudah exempts [the blind man] from all commandments (mitzvot) in the Torah.[25]
>
> Rav Sheishah the son of Rav Idi said: What [was the] reason Rabbi Yehudah [made this ruling]? Scripture said, "And these are the commandments (*hamitzvot*), the statutes (*hahukkim*), and the ordinances (*v'hamishpatim*)" (Deuteronomy 6:1). Anyone who is [obligated to observe the] "ordinances" is [also obligated to observe the] "commandments" and "statutes." And anyone who is not [obligated to observe the] "ordinances" is [also not obligated to observe the] "commandments" and "statutes."
>
> Rav Yosef [who was blind] said: At first, I would have said: [For the] one who would say the law is according to Rabbi Yehudah, who said that a blind person is exempt from the [obligation to observe the] mitzvot, I would have made a feast day for the sages [in honor of that ruling]. Why? Because not [being obligated] I [nevertheless] do the mitzvot [and would receive a greater reward for doing them]. But now that I have heard what Rabbi Hanina taught [I changed my mind]. For Rabbi Hanina said: Greater is the one who is commanded and performs [a mitzvah] than one who is not commanded and performs [a mitzvah]. [Now] whoever would say to me that the law is *not* according to Rabbi Yehudah, I would make a feast day for the sages [in honor of this ruling]. Why? Because, being commanded [and doing the mitzvot] I will receive a greater reward. (B. Baba Kamma 87a)

We begin with Rabbi Yehudah's view that blind persons are exempt from all commandments and judgments. The Bavli provides scriptural justification for his view by citing Deuteronomy 6:1, in which commandments, statutes, and judgments are mentioned together. This can be taken to mean that only those who are subject to the judgments of the Torah are also obligated to perform the commandments therein. So, if a blind person cannot be sued for causing insult, then he cannot be considered obligated for the other judgments and commandments in the Torah.

We next have the opinions of a blind sage, Rav Yosef, who favors the ruling that will allow him the greatest reward. Since it is better (according to Rabbi Hanina) to perform the mitzvot when obligated than when not obligated, he expresses his dissatisfaction with Rabbi Yehudah's view.

That view, which discredits a blind person, is held only by an individual, while the majority is in agreement with Rav Yosef: a blind person's performance of mitzvot, in general, is considered valid and is not discredited, that is, stigmatized. Rav Yosef's statement becomes literally the final word on this topic—and in the Bavli, the opinion expressed last in a passage is usually deemed authoritative. The conscious composition of this passage, then, gives Rav Yosef's words greater authority. The Bavli here allows a blind person to speak for himself and express his desires, instead of simply being the subject of legislation.

When we contrast the situation of the blind person suffering indignity with that of the *cheresh, shoteh v'katan*, we see clearly that the blind person is a full participant in the sages' system, even though more vulnerable than a sighted one. The blind person experiences cultural norms and knows when he has been insulted, unlike the *cheresh, shoteh v'katan*, who are thought to have no such awareness.

Who's In? Who's Out?

Having explored the sages' system of categorizing persons with disabilities, we may ask, "Why did they construct their categories in this way? What did it accomplish?" First of all, it did not supplant the basic priestly system of lineage. It merely creates finer distinctions within that system, focusing on the category "Israelite." Second, within that category, the sages recreated the classifications that had functioned in the Temple:

TEMPLE HIERARCHY	SAGES' HIERARCHY
high priests (ideal participants)	sages
priests (full participants)	grown, free, Jewish men with *da'at*
Levites (liminal)	women, slaves, and minors
impure (stigmatized)	*cheresh, shoteh v'katan*

As ritual impurity disqualifies anyone from participating in the cult, so a lack of *da'at* and communicative abilities disqualifies anyone from participating in the sages' system of intention-motivated action.

CHAPTER

7

The River Flows On

WHILE OUR analysis of Jewish attitudes toward disabilities and persons with them stops at this point, Jewish tradition continued to develop and change. It therefore may profit us to close with a question that falls outside the limits of this study: What do all the texts we have studied, and the attitudes expressed in them, mean today? Let us consider how some of the topics we have examined were treated in later Jewish writings.

A Cursory "Map" and Survey of the Rest of the River

As Judaism developed, and as Jews spread throughout the world, the production of Jewish literature flourished. Jewish legal and mystical sources could well take another entire book to be properly examined, but we will consider very briefly the attitudes expressed in some of the best-known works toward persons with disabilities. In addition, we will take a cursory look at what contemporary authorities have to say about our topic.

DOCUMENT	AUTHOR
Mishneh Torah	Moses Maimonides (Rambam), 1135 (Spain)–1204 (Egypt)
Zohar	Moses de Leon, 1250–1305 (Spain)
Arba'ah Turim	Jacob ben Asher (Ba'al HaTurim), 1270 (?) (Germany)–1340 (Spain)
Shulhan Aruch	Joseph Caro, 1488 (Spain)–1575 (Land of Israel)

While most of the sources we consider in this chapter will concern Jewish law, this is not the only sort of work produced after the era of rabbinic literature ended; nor, as we saw, did the sages consider only the legal consequences of disabilities. Rather, just as the Tanach and rabbinic literature considered legal, religious, and symbolic aspects of disabilities, so these factors were important in later Jewish sources as well.

Moses Maimonides, also called Rambam and Moses ben Maimon, systematized Jewish law in his fourteen-volume work, the Mishneh Torah (The Second Torah). It covers every aspect of Jewish law, including areas that were no longer practiced. The rules governing the Temple and the complicated laws of ritual purity, as well as Jewish laws that were observed in Rambam's day, such as how to pray, observe dietary laws, transact a valid wedding and divorce, and so forth, are all outlined in this comprehensive work.

By way of contrast, Jacob ben Asher, also known as Ba'al Ha-Turim, sifted through the law and created a four-volume work, titled Arba'ah Turim (The Four Pillars), that outlines only laws used by Jews of his day. The four areas of law examined in this work are (1) Orach Hayyim, "The Way of Life": laws about prayers, Shabbat, and festivals; (2) Yoreh Dei'ah, "Teaching Knowledge": dietary laws, family purity, and mourning laws; (3) Even HaEzer; "Stone of Help": laws of marriage and divorce; and (4) Hoshen Mishpat, "Breastplate of Judgment": civil laws, including contracts, wages, damages, and so forth. So important was this work that in 1475, it was the second Hebrew book to be published using the newly invented printing press.

Joseph ben Efrayim Caro, a well-respected authority of his day, was able to unify Jewish law. Using as his sources the codes of Alfasi (a native of Algeria who wrote the greatest pre-Maimonedian Jewish legal code), Rambam, and Ba'al HaTurim, he created the Shulhan Aruch (The Set Table), which eventually came to be accepted as the standard book of Jewish law. The Shulhan Aruch is based on the Arba'ah Turim, using the four rubrics listed above, referred to by the same names, to organize its summary of Jewish law.

While these are some of the outstanding Jewish legal works of the last 1,500 years, the greatest mystical work of this time cannot be overlooked. The Zohar (Book of Splendor) by Moses de Leon is a collection of several mystical works, loosely organized as a commentary to the Torah.

Among the great contemporary writers of halakhic literature are Moshe Feinstein (1895–1985), Eliezer Judah ben Jacob Gedaliah Waldenberg (1917–), and Abraham S. Abraham. Feinstein was born in Belorussia and received his education from his father, a rabbi. He immigrated to the United States in 1937 and served as the Rosh Yeshivah of New York's Metivta Tiferet Jerusalem. His responsa (answers to Jewish legal questions) are titled *Iggrot Moshe* and are organized according to the four basic divisions of the Shulhan Aruch. Waldenberg's collection of responsa is called *Tsits Eliezer* and he is known more commonly by that name than by his given one. He serves as a rabbi and *dayyan* (judge) in Jerusalem. Abraham's three-volume collection of responsa is titled *Nishmat Avraham* and has been summarized and translated into English (1990). Other well-known contemporary authorities on Jewish medical and legal issues are Immanuel Jakobovits, J. David Bleich, and Fred Rosner; and there are many, many others.

Priestly Perfection and Its Extension

Priestly physical perfection was of paramount importance in the Temple and continued to be valued when the priestly blessing, originally performed in the Temple, was offered in the synagogue. Later sources continue to uphold the importance of the priest's perfection at this moment. Yet they also demonstrate some flexibility when the priest is well-known to the congregation, following the dynamic tension already seen in chapter 2 between the Mishnah (M. Megillah 4:7) and Tosefta (T. Megillah 3:29).

Rambam begins by categorically stigmatizing any blemished priest: "Six things prevent [a priest from] raising [his] hands [in the priestly benediction]: tongue [i.e., defective speech] and blemishes and sin and years [i.e., extreme old age] and wine and impure hands" (Rambam, Mishneh Torah, Sefer Ahavah 15:1). This statement is augmented by the reiteration of rabbinic concepts: a priest with deformed hands shouldn't offer the blessing. However, Rambam opines, a priest blind in one eye may, in some circumstances, offer the blessing.

> "And blemishes." How [do they disqualify a priest from saying the blessing]? A priest who has blemishes on his hands or on his face or on his legs, such as [a priest with] curved or twisted fingers ... [should] not raise his hands [in the priestly blessing] because the people will stare at him. . . . A person blind in one eye should not raise his hands [in the benediction] but if he was well-known in his town and everyone was used to this [i.e., his condition] the [priest] blind in one eye ... may [offer the blessing] because the people [of the congregation] will not stare at him. (Rambam, Mishneh Torah, Sefer Ahavah, Hilkhot Tefillah and Birkat HaKohanim 15:2)

Rambam upholds the priestly standards of physical perfection quite rigorously. A man blind in one eye is, after all, sighted, whereas a man with deformed hands could not offer the blessing according to this ruling. Such a partially sighted man would be able to move without stumbling (as a blind man might) and so would not draw the gaze of the congregation and thus constitute a danger to them, for God's presence, as we have seen, was thought to descend during the priestly blessing.

The Shulhan Aruch, however, offers a more flexible description of Jewish law and allows a priest with any sort of blemish to offer the blessing if he is well-known to the congregation: "A priest that has a blemish on his face or his hands shouldn't raise his hands [in the priestly blessing] because the people [of the congregation might] gaze at him . . . but *for all blemishes* [emphasis added], if he was well-known in his town, and everyone was used to his blemish and they would not stare at him [while he offered the blessing], he may lift his hands [in the priestly blessing]" (Shulhan Aruch, Orach Chayyim 128:30). This tension in the treatment of priestly perfection remains. It is a desideratum, but other values, such as inclusiveness, have come to outweigh it when such decisions are made.

In those circumstances in which the requirement for priestly blemishlessness was extended to lay Israelites in the Temple, but not outside it, the Mishnah's restrictions are upheld by Rambam in all their original stringency: "Women and slaves are exempt from [the obligation] of appearing. And every male is obligated [to perform the mitzvah of] appearing except a *cheresh* and a mute person, a *shoteh* and a *katan* and a blind [man] and a lame [man] and an impure [man] and an uncircumcised [man]. And also the elderly and the sick [men] and the tenderfooted man that aren't able to go up [to Jerusalem] on their [own two] feet" (Rambam, Sefer Korbanot Hilkhot Hagigah 2:1). As there is no practical motivation for Rambam to mitigate against the exclusionary tendency of the Mishnah—this mitzvah can only be performed in the Temple—he does not do so.

Persons with Disabilities, Symbolism, and Atonement

One of the best-known Jewish personalities of this century, closely identified with the fate of the Jewish people, is Moshe Dayan, the Israeli general who led his country's army to victory in 1967. He wore an eye patch, but this did not make him seem disabled. Indeed, it contributed to his indomitable image and was in keeping with the twentieth-century Jewish community's image of itself: wounded but still capable of fighting and prevailing. The symbolic value of the body (as seen in the story of Isaiah's suffering servant) persists in every era of Jewish history.

The Zohar, for example, identified the system of Torah and mitzvot with a human body:

> The Torah has a body. The commandments of the Torah are the bodies of the Torah. This body is clothed in garments, which are the narratives of the world. The fools in the world look only upon the clothes, which are the narratives of the Torah; they know no more,

and do not see what is beneath the clothes. Those who know more do not look upon the clothes, but upon the body beneath the clothes. The wise, the servants of the supreme King, those who stood at Mount Sinai, look only upon the soul, which is the foundation of all, the real Torah. (Zohar III, 152a, Tishby 1989, 3:1127)

The physical aspect of the "person" is significant here but it is not of paramount importance. The Zohar in this passage echoes the sages' system of values, placing intellectual and spiritual abilities over physical wholeness.

But the Zohar also expresses the way the body can become a vehicle for punishment and atonement for sin: "Rabbi Abba was once traveling to Cappadocia with Rabbi Yose. During their journey they met a man who had a scar on his face. Rabbi Abba said: Let us pause here, for this man's face testifies that he has transgressed the sexual prohibitions in the Torah. That is why he has a mark on his face" (Zohar III 75b–76a, Tishby 1989, 3:1478). This man's suffering ultimately leads to his complete atonement, but there is no doubt that his physical disability was, and was known to be, caused by his sin.

Stigmatization of persons with disabilities, which may stem in part from this long association of disability with sin, continues to this day. In his study of blind Israeli society, Shlomo Deshen (1992, 25) noted, "When physical disability is culturally constructed through concepts of stigma the physically impaired individual is prone to various forms of discredit. . . . Discredit does not pertain only to individuals, but also to material objects and, paradoxically, even to the implements of aid that disabled people use to assist themselves." Thus, the presence of disabled persons within society and the material items they create in response to their disabilities continue to be powerful symbols of frailty, negativity, and, perhaps, the wages of sin.

Valuation and Categorization of Persons

While the belief that some disabilities develop as a result of sin persists, it is becoming a less acceptable notion in most of the Jewish community.[1] And while stigmatization of disabled persons similarly continues, it, too, is becoming less and less acceptable. Indeed, modern and contemporary authorities seem intent on being as inclusive as possible so far as persons with disabilities are concerned. Rabbi Isaac Herzog, chief rabbi of Israel until 1959, mandated a creative, inclusive stance toward persons with hearing disabilities: "Those [rabbis] who remain in the ivory tower and say the schools [for the deaf] are not good enough do not realize the techniques that have been developed in the schools. . . . You have got to do so and then remove all limitations that still exist surrounding the technically deaf-mute" (quoted in Feldman 1986, 17). In fact, Bleich (1977, 80) points out that changes in the behaviors of the deaf and "mute" have made the category of the *cheresh* all but irrelevant: "The ability to speak, no matter how acquired and even if the speech acquired is imperfect, is yet sufficient to establish full competence in all areas of Halakhah."

Inclusiveness toward persons with visual disabilities is also part of contemporary Jewish ethics, even when no explicit textual basis can be found to support it. For example, while blind persons are still not allowed to ritually read from Torah, they may participate in the central rite of the bar or bat mitzvah ceremony: the recitation of the haftarah (a selection from the Prophets): "A blind child [is permitted] to read the haftarah from memory or from a Braille text. . . . Reading from a printed text [the practice almost all contemporary congregations follow] is in any event tantamount to reading without any text at all but, nevertheless, is permissible in the case of the haftarah because of the reason cited in Gittin 60a: 'At a time when it is necessary to work for the Lord, make void Thy law'" (Bleich 1983, 32–33). Almost all children today are allowed to participate in this ceremony, regardless of their mental, visual, or auditory disabilities.

A conscious effort has been made in all the movements of Judaism to include persons with disabilities. This is deemed by contemporary thinkers such as Carl Astor to be every bit as much in keeping with the ethics and values of previous generations as keeping to the letter of the law might be: "Ultimately we must come to see that making room in our society and in our synagogues for those with disabilities is in our own best interest. . . . We are more enriched to the degree that we open our doors to the disabled. . . . Out of a sense of fairness and justice, we should not exclude members of our community from participating with us" (Astor 1985, 153). Perhaps Daniel Boyarin puts it best. Though he speaks of attitudes toward sexuality, his words are easily extended to refer to disabilities and disabled persons: "My assumption is that we cannot change the actual past. We can only change the present and future, in part by changing our understanding of the past. Unless the past is experienced merely as a burden to be thrown off . . . then constructing a monolithically negative perception of the past and cultivating anger at it seem to be counter-productive and disempowering for change" (Boyarin 1993, 227).

Our sources often portray persons with disabilities in ways that many persons find unacceptable today. The idea that suffering can serve to atone for sin, or that disabilities are related to sin in any way, is not a notion to which most individuals now lend any credence. However, we cannot relate to our past until we understand it. And we cannot change our present until we understand our past. Only when we engage in that work can we come to a more complete understanding of the breadth and depth of the river that determines our journey.

NOTES

1. Introduction

1. An entire book, Morgan (1990), has been written on the issue of Writings' diverse viewpoints and their place in the canon.

2. Strack and Stemberger (1991, 145) note that "The attempt to illustrate a long prehistory of M[ishnah] by way of an early stage of halakhic presentation, based on Scripture and deriving from exegesis, can be considered a failure."

3. But cf. Jaffee (1992) on the role of the written word in the transmission and redaction of the Mishnah, as well as Strack and Stemberger (1991, 155).

4. Halivni (1981, 207), suggests that Tosefta was created due to dissatisfaction with Rabbi Yehudah HaNasi's Mishnah.

5. Kraemer (1995, 115–16), sees this interpretation as basically true but oversimplified.

6. One need only think of the difference between an order to do something and a commercial urging that one take the same action to grasp this concept. Kraemer (1990, 101), points out, "The Bavli is a rhetorical text in the sense that it wishes to convince. It attempts throughout to increase our minds' adherence to its theses. Second, in part the way the Bavli seeks to achieve this goal is by creating argumentational dialogues that ask us to take the position of each respective advocate in turn."

2. Priestly Perfection

1. See Sarna (1991, 158): "[The *mishkan*] functions to make perceptible and tangible the conception of God's immanence, that is, of the indwelling of the Divine Presence in the camp of Israel, to which the people may orient their hearts and minds. A postbiblical extension of this usage of the verb *sh-kh-n* is the Hebrew term *shekhinah* for the Divine Presence."

2. This gives new meaning to the identification of Jerusalem with the world's navel. See B. Sanhedrin 37a; see also Josephus, *The Jewish War* 3.335, and Jubilees 8:19. The Temple and/or the Sanhedrin (the court of seventy-one judges that met in the Chamber of Hewn Stone in the Temple Courtyard) are

the terminus for the umbilical cord that links the world to the divine spheres, which are portrayed as placental.

3. M. Keilim 1:6–9 outlines the ten increasing levels of holiness that begin with the holiness of the land of Israel and move upward to the Holy of Holies in the Temple.

4. See Haran 1985, 187–88. The story of Nadav and Avihu is the prime example of this phenomenon (Leviticus 10:1–2). Interestingly, Philo's interpretation of the priest's outer perfection—as reflecting his inner spiritual elevation (*The Special Laws* 1.16.80–81)—is not found in the sources we consider here.

5. M. Bekhorot 6 outlines the blemishes that disqualify animals from sacrifice and M. Bekhorot 7 does the same for priests.

6. All these descriptions of head shape suggest different premature fusion of the skull's sutures.

7. We should note, however, that the priest is not in the dangerously holy atmosphere of the Temple when offering this blessing, so blemishes pose less of a threat to the priest and no threat to the cult; this may also explain the sages' leniency.

8. The Jewish community of Nehardea was an ancient one, first settled, according to tradition, in the sixth century B.C.E. The synagogue there, built by the exiles from the First Temple's destruction in 586 B.C.E. out of stone and earth brought from the site of the Temple, was where the *Shekhinah* moved and settled. See Krauss (1922, 20–23, 218–21).

9. The Munich manuscript uses the word *yakhol*, "able," rather than *'aluv*, afflicted.

10. As this mishnah itself makes clear, color here does not refer to race but to a stain, usually caused by the priest's profession.

11. R. Haggai's view is not accepted in subsequent Jewish practice. Maimonides (Mishneh Torah, Sefer Ahavah 14:7) not only forbids the congregation to gaze at the priests but prohibits the priests to gaze at the congregation, lest they become distracted.

12. The Bavli appears to be unaware of the case of R. Naftali, who was permitted to offer the blessing despite his crooked hands (Y. Megillah 4:8).

13. Apparently R. Hiyya could not pronounce the letter *chet* except as *hey*. With such a pronunciation, the verse would then mean, "And I shall smite the Lord."

14. This mishnah (M. Megillah 4:7) appears in chapter 3 of the Bavli, chapters 3 and 4 of the Mishnah having been transposed.

15. The Levites, it will be recalled, do not enter the sanctuary itself but only sing from the periphery of the sanctuary level in the Temple.

16. This is consistent with the laws of purity, which serve as a symbolic reminder to Israel to "reject death and choose life" (Milgrom 1991, 47).

17. "Pilgrimages" in Hebrew is *regalim*, which also means "legs." The School of Hillel takes this to mean that a man must appear on his own two legs, since the word *regalim* is plural.

18. Alternatively, the underlying goal of this mishnah may have been to relieve as many persons as possible from the obligation to perform *r'ayon*. The journey to the Temple was surely onerous, and it may have been deemed a boon to many persons not to be obligated to make it. Thus all categories of persons who did not correspond to the priestly image of perfection were here enumerated: *cheresh, shoteh v'katan*, women and slaves, and hermaphrodites and androgynes, as well as persons with other disabilities.

19. According to Lieberman (1992, ad loc.), this passage refers to a person blind in both eyes who is exempt on two counts from the obligation to appear: he cannot see and "he is not able to go up [to Jerusalem] by foot."

20. T. Terumot 1:1, discussed in chapter 6, tells more about these relatives of Rabbi Yohanan ben Gudgada.

21. Relevant words are italicized. Mechilta, Tractate Bachodesh 3, on Exodus 19:11 offers a parallel explanation for the presence of only sighted persons at the revelation.

22. The sages suggest that the passage must not be taken literally. T. Sanhedrin 11:6 states, "There [never] was nor will there [ever] be a stubborn and rebellious son. So why was [the passage about the stubborn and rebellious son] written? To say [to you], 'Expound [this passage] and receive a reward.'"

23. See B. Hagigah 14b, which tells how fire descends from heaven when certain sages study Torah's mysticism and even the angels gather to learn. The story is told (B. Hagigah 13a) that a child was swallowed by heavenly fire because he studied about it in the book of Ezekiel, showing how the lethal force of holiness remained in the sages' conceptual framework. One sage's study made such a powerful connection with heaven that if a bird flew overhead while he was studying, it would immediately be burned (B. Sukkah 28a).

3. Persons with Disabilities, Symbolism, and Collective Israel

1. Similarly, Lakoff (1987, xiv) notes, "Thought is *embodied*, that is, the structures used to put together our conceptual systems grow out of bodily experience and make sense in terms of it; moreover, the core of our conceptual system is directly grounded in perception, body movement, and experience of a physical and social nature." Also see Johnson (1987, xiv–xvi), who demonstrates how our physical interactions with our environment shape our understanding and guide our reasoning.

2. For example, we have had a Miss America with a hearing disability. Be-

cause physical beauty is the main criterion for wholeness in that particular venue, her disability did not carry the value it might have otherwise. Such special definitions of the body and its abilities exist in Jewish subcultures. Thus for priests, like Miss America contestants, physical perfection is essential and communicative abilities are secondary. Indeed, the priests' acts in the cult took place in silence (Levine 1995, 54).

3. A pun is being made on the word *v'naharu* from Isaiah 2:2. This verse is generally translated, "all the nations shall flow unto it [the Temple]." However, the word *n'har* in Aramaic means "to light, to shine, to illumine," and this is the meaning being played on here.

4. Again, the Gemara text puns on the Torah text. Numbers 15:24 describes a ritual for expiating secret sin. The phrase *mei'einei ha'eidah* means "committed in ignorance." Here, the Gemara takes the words in their literal meaning, "from the eyes of the congregation."

5. Shir HaShirim Rabbah, 7:5 ¶ 2, states that the Sanhedrin is the vision, the eyes, of the congregation and that the Sanctuary of the Temple is the forehead from which ornaments (such as *tefillin*) are suspended.

6. For the problems generated by the frequent characterization of Israel as female and God as male, see Eilberg-Schwartz 1994.

7. Miriam died close to the time of the incident at the rock and she died in the same place where the rock was located, i.e., the Wilderness of Tsin (Numbers 20:1). Aaron's death is explicitly linked to his behavior at the waters of Merivat-Kadesh (Numbers 27:13–14).

8. Stern (1991, 146–48, 314 n. 98) notes how difficult it is to ascertain any historical basis for this parable.

9. Commentators suggest that this was accomplished by the sages' enacting laws of modesty that would keep temptation from the *sight* of those prone to stray.

10. Cogan and Tadmor (1988, 318) note, "Blinding was a common punishment of the rebellious slaves in the ancient Near East. . . . References to blinding of large numbers of captives probably relate to gouging out only one eye; this method left the mutilated as a usable slave force."

11. On the sexuality of Talmud study, see Boyarin's (1993, 134–66) description of Torah as "the other woman." He also comments on B. Yoma 69b (61–76).

4. Disabilities, Atonement, and Individuals

1. The Torah text relates that in memory of this moment, Jews do not eat the thigh muscle that the angel wounded (Genesis 32:33). Frazer (1988, 257) provides an interesting explanation of this story, based on ideas of sympathetic magic and certain parallels to Cherokee Indian customs that forbid the eating

of hamstrings from deer: "The Cherokee assign two reasons for the practice [of not eating the thigh sinew in animals]. One is that this tendon, when severed, draws up into the flesh; ergo, any one who should unfortunately partake of the hamstring would find his limbs drawn up in the same manner. The other reason is that if, instead of cutting out the hamstring and throwing it away the hunter were to eat it, he would thereafter easily grow tired in traveling."

2. See Milgrom's (1990, 348–54) commentaries on this passage, "Excursus 9: Adultery in the Bible and the Ancient Near East" and "Excursus 10: The Case of the Suspected Adulteress: Redaction and Meaning." There, he both brings out the symmetry in the literary composition of the text and shows how the biblical text exemplifies the concept of *midah k'neged midah*.

3. We should note that this practice was abolished by Rabbi Yohanan ben Zakkai shortly after the destruction of the Second Temple (M. Sotah 9:9).

4. Neusner (1986a, 64–65) characterizes these chapters as discussing "the sin of the leper, gossip," and "sins that bring disease," respectively.

5. In the Munich manuscript, it is Rabbi Akiba who asks the question to which Nahum Ish Gamzu replies, "You should be happy you see me this way."

A fascinating parallel to this passage is found in Leviticus Rabbah 34:10, Be-har. Rabbi Yohanan and Reish Lakish delay when asked for alms, and the beggar, in the meantime, dies. However, these two sages discover, in the process of preparing him for burial, that he was an impostor and had a great deal of money. There, the point is that we should be grateful that such impostors exist, since otherwise not giving alms to the poor would be a capital crime.

5. Body, Soul, and Society

1. Nickelsburg (1981, 64) also gives a more definite date for the work's composition: between 198 and 175 B.C.E.

2. Skehan (1987, 295), translates this phrase "He bows his head and feigns not to hear, but when not observed, he will take advantage of you."

3. Some translations of Ecclesiasticus are from Charles (1913).

4. One suspects that firm control of the body and its processes may be a desideratum among virtually all religious groups.

5. Neusner, who outlines what he believes to be the themes of these essays (1986a, 59–72), sees this chapter as demonstrating "Sin done by the soul is what causes Israel's condition. Collective responsibility" (60).

6. In an intriguing parallel, Turner (1967, 107) describes an Ndembu ritual, linked to the theme of the human body as "a microcosm of the universe" that uses white, black, and red waters: "They seem to be regarded as powers which, in varying combination, underlie or even constitute what Ndembu conceive to be reality. In no other context is the interpretation of whiteness,

redness, and blackness so full; and nowhere else is such a close analogy drawn, even identity made, between these rivers and bodily fluids and emissions: whiteness = semen, milk; redness = menstrual blood, the blood of birth, blood shed by a weapon, etc.; blackness = feces, certain products of bodily decay, etc."

7. God determines the destiny not only of parts of the body but also for the entire person: "Rabbi Hanina bar Pappa made the following exposition: That angel who is in charge of conception is named 'Night,' and he takes a drop [of semen] and places it before the Holy One, blessed be He, and says, 'Master of the universe, What shall this drop's destiny become? [Shall it be] strong or weak, wise (*hakham*) or ignorant (*tipeish*), rich or poor?'" (B. Niddah 16b).

8. Note the metaphors: women are both flesh, with its obvious association with blood, and furniture, i.e., inanimate objects to be consumed and used.

6. Categorization, Disabilities, and Persons with Disabilities

1. The sages do not make the same distinctions we do between a person with mental disabilities, e.g., retardation, and a person with a mental illness, e.g., schizophrenia. Moreover, they extend the category *shoteh* to include people who have functioning intellects but are merely foolish or morally misguided.

2. Isaiah 7:15–16 also describes a boy who reaches maturity as knowing good from evil.

3. The first three blessings of the Amidah remain constant and consist of God's praise. On weekdays, one may petition God; this fourth blessing is the first of these weekday petitions.

4. Other examples of this meaning of the term *da'at* may be found in M. Eruvin 7:11, M. Nedarim 4:3, M. Yebamot 13:2, M. Makkot 2:3, M. Baba Metsia 5:6, and M. Baba Batra 6:6 and 10:4.

5. The next mishnah, M. Toharot 3:7, compares the actions of a *tinok*, a baby, with those of domesticated animals such as hens, cows, and dogs with regard to issues of ritual impurity. All these entities may affect the ritual purity of an item but no *da'at* is ascribed to any of them.

6. This meaning continues to be important; e.g., in B. Yebamot 56a, 112b, 114b and B. Baba Batra 8a, *pikeiach* is contrasted with the *cheresh*. In B. Gittin 5a, 23a; B. Baba Metsia 9a; and B. Baba Batra 128a, as well as B. Kiddushin 54b, it is contrasted with the *cheresh* and *shoteh*. In B. Kiddushin 42b; B. Baba Kamma 35a, 36a, 39a; and B. Meilah 21a, it is contrasted with the category *cheresh, shoteh v'katan*. In B. Baba Kamma 52b and 54b, it is contrasted with a deaf animal. In B. Arachin 17b–18a, the term is contrasted with the categories *cheresh* and blind.

7. This use of *pikeiach* is also attested to in M. Shabbat 16:3, M. Ketubot 13:8, and M. Nazir 2:5.

8. The text quoted here is Lauterbach's (1961, 1:166–67). The text as it appears in Horovitz (1970, 73) follows the seder text: *tam* is used instead of *tipeish* and the *tam* comes after the *rasha*. In the Yerushalmi, the word *tipeish* is used but following the *rasha*. *Tam*, which designates simplicity in a way connoting perfection, has many more positive connotations than *tipeish*.

9. Neusner (1986a, 65) characterizes the essay's theme as "A Woman's Discharge." While material related to this theme is certainly present, I cannot agree that it is the chapter's true metaphoric focus.

10. The term *tipeish*, not *shoteh*, is used in Tanhuma.

11. For example, see the discussion on page 166 in chapter 2 of M. Sanhedrin 8:4, which disqualifies physically disabled parents from testifying against their rebellious son because the sages wanted to minimize such accusations. However, there is nothing inherent in lameness that bars a lame person from giving testimony in any other case.

12. This would seem to be a corollary to the *sotah* ritual for women (Numbers 5:11–1) in some ways. Both are performed publicly and involve improper, or possibly improper, sexual behavior.

13. Following Lieberman's commentary (1992, ad loc.).

14. The stools of a child who is exclusively breast-fed have a relatively inoffensive odor. Once the child begins to eat solid foods, his stools take on an offensive odor and have to be treated as those of any adult. One is not supposed to pray within four cubits of excrement (M. Berachot 3:5).

15. It is almost as if Tosefta is going through the orders of the Mishnah and determining at which point one obligates a *katan* to do mitzvot in each realm of interest. For holidays (Moed), most prayer (Zeraim), purities (Tohorot), and slaughtering (Kodoshim) a *katan* can function as an adult as soon as he has the requisite *da'at*. Only with regard to women's status (Nashim), civil and criminal penalties (Nezikin), and certain ritual functions (e.g., raising his hands in the priestly benediction) must the *katan* wait for signs of physical maturity before achieving adult status.

16. Compare this with M. Toharot 3:6, discussed above, in which the minor who is grouped with the *cheresh* and *shoteh* is, like them, is considered ritually pure.

17. M. Tamid 4:3 and 5:1 records that in the Temple ritual the Ten Commandments, the Shema, and the priestly benediction were recited after the ritual slaughter of the sacrificial animal and subsequent procession.

18. Even today, in Jewish worship services children are often invited up onto the platform (*bimah*) after almost all of the service is completed in order to sing one of the concluding songs.

19. *Aval pikeiach v'nitchareish, hu koteiv* (MS: *toreim*) *v'hein m'kayyemin al yado.* The manuscript variant indicates not that he would write down his intention but that he would perform the separation and, as in the case of the *cheresh* from birth, the administrators would validate his actions. The difference is significant, as writing replaces the faculties of hearing and speech and serves as valid communication of intention by the *cheresh*.

20. In this case, it is the action which is crucial, not the agency of that action. We find another example of this attitude in M. Yadayim 1:5: "All are eligible to pour [cleansing water] over the hands, even a *cheresh, shoteh v'katan*. One may put a cask between his knees and thus pour out [the cleansing water onto his hands]; one may turn a cask on its side and so let the water fall [on his hands]; and an ape may pour out [the cleansing water] on [one's] hands; [but] R. Yose pronounces [the water] invalid in these two [last cases]."

21. The *Diagnostic and Statistical Manual of Mental Disorders* (3rd ed.) (American Psychiatric Association 1987, 193), notes how difficult it may be to make the distinction between the two conditions. It states, "In Mental Retardation, low level of social functioning, oddities of behavior and impoverished affect and cognition all may suggest Schizophrenia. Both diagnoses should be made in the same person only when there is certainty that the symptoms suggesting Schizophrenia, such as delusions or hallucinations, are definitely present and are not the result of difficulties in communication."

22. The treatment of the *cheresh, shoteh v'katan* recalls both the insanity defense and the leniency that traditionally has been granted minors in American law.

23. This form of presenting a problem, ending with *teiku*, is a late literary form found only in the Bavli. See Jacobs (1981), particularly his conclusions (290–95).

24. Avery-Peck (1988, 535 n. 55) convincingly argues that the addition of the *shoteh* here is a scribal error.

25. As, for example, in M. Makkot 2:3, where R. Judah exempts the blind slayer from the necessity of fleeing into exile; or M. Megillah 4:6, where he holds that a blind person may not recite the Shema and its blessings for the congregation.

7. The River Flows On

1. We should note, however, that observant Jews who suffer tragedy or infirmity often have the mezuzot (the scrolls of Torah passages affixed to their doors) checked to see if they are defective, thus making the owner of the home a sinner.

GLOSSARY

aggadah/aggadot/aggadic Stories in rabbinic literature, as distinct from material pertaining directly to Jewish law. Aggadot differ from midrashim (see below) in that these stories are not necessarily related to a scriptural text.

Amidah/Amidot; shemonah esrei Literally, "standing" and "eighteen": the prayer par excellence in Judaism. It contains nineteen benedictions on regular days and eighteen or fewer benedictions on Shabbats and holidays, and it is said standing three times each day.

B.C.E. Before the common era (equivalent to B.C.).

baraita/baraitot Literally, "external": a source from the mishnaic era that is not included in the Mishnah of Rabbi Judah HaNasi but is cited in the Gemara.

Bavli See **Gemara**.

C.E. The common era (equivalent to A.D.).

cheresh/chereshet/chershim/chershot Most often, persons with speaking and hearing disabilities, typically since birth; less often, persons with hearing disabilities only.

bimah Literally, a "stage" or "platform": the raised dais from which Torah is read in the synagogue.

eruv Literally, "joining." A person is not permitted to walk more than 2,000 cubits from one's place of residence on the Sabbath. By placing a meal within this 2,000 cubit limit one may extend the limit another 2,000 cubits, as the place where the meal rests is considered the person's place of residence.

festivals The festivals ordained in the Torah—Passover, Sukkot, and Shavuot, as well as Rosh Hashanah and Yom Kippur—share many of the same restrictions that apply to Shabbat, such as the prohibitions against carrying items from one domain to another.

Gemara Commentary on the Mishnah. The Babylonian Gemara, called the Bavli, was formulated between 200 and 500 C.E. The Talmud of the land of Israel, called the Yerushalmi, was probably formulated some 50 to 75 years earlier.

get/gittin A Jewish bill of divorce.

Haftarah A selection from the Prophets read during Shabbat and holiday worship services.

halakhah/halakhic Literally, "a way": Jewish law.

halitsah Literally, "removal": the ceremony that frees the widow of a man who dies without children from the obligation to marry one of her deceased husband's brothers and allows her to remarry as she wishes (see Deuteronomy 25:7–10).

katan/k'tanah/k'tanim A boy or girl who has not produced two pubic hairs, i.e., reached maturity, and is therefore not considered legally competent.

levirate marriage The obligatory marriage between a man whose brother died without leaving children and his brother's widow. Alternatively, he may perform the ceremony of *halitsah* with her (Deuteronomy 25:5–10).

maftir The short section at the end of a weekly or festival Torah portion that is reread once it has been included in the regular Torah reading (the term is related to the word "Haftarah"). The person who says the blessing over this short portion then proceeds to read the Haftarah.

Mishnah/mishnayot Literally, "teaching." It refers both to the collection of tannaitic learning compiled by Rabbi Judah HaNasi in 200 C.E. and to individual segments within that compilation.

megillah/megillot Literally, "a scroll," and, informally, "a story." It usually refers specifically to the Book of Esther or to one of five megillot in the Tanach: Song of Songs, Eicha (Lamentations), Kohelet (Ecclesiastes), Esther, and Ruth.

midrash/midrashim Rabbinic expositions of biblical texts.

mitzvah Literally, "commandment": a deed that one must perform or an action one must refrain from doing that is derived from the Torah or from a dictate of the sages.

Noachide commandments The laws given to humanity before there were any Jews or laws for Jews. These laws, which apply to everyone, prohibit idolatry, blasphemy, bloodshed, sexual sins (e.g., incest), theft, and eating from a living animal. In addition, these laws required that legal systems must be established (T. Avodah Zarah 8:4).

peah Literally, "corner": the portion of a crop left unharvested in the corners of a field so that the poor might glean there (Leviticus 19:9). It is at least one-sixtieth of the crop.

Pentateuch The first five books of the Bible, i.e., Genesis, Exodus, Leviticus, Numbers, and Deuteronomy.

Pesach Literally, "to pass over": the festival in the spring that celebrates the exodus from Egypt. This holiday marks the end of winter.

pikeiach/pikachat/pikchim A person with functioning hearing, sight, speech, and cognition; also, a sharp-witted person.

Purim Literally, "Lots": the holiday that celebrates the Persian Jews' deliverance from their enemy, Haman. On this day, the Book of Esther is read.

Rosh Hashanah Literally, "The Head of the Year": the Jewish new year, which occurs in the fall. The shofar (ram's horn) is sounded on this day.

The School of Hillel The school that developed to expound the ideas of Hillel. The laws of this school are almost always adopted over those of the School of Shammai. These two houses existed during the first generation of tannaim, i.e., 10–80 C.E.

The School of Shammai The school that developed to expound the ideas of Shammai.

seder: Literally, "order": the ritual performed at home for the beginning of the holiday of Pesach. When the Temple stood, a lamb was sacrificed and eaten as part of this ritual.

Shabbat/Shabbatot The Sabbath, which is the seventh day of the week, a day of rest. This is the most holy day in the Jewish week.

Shavuot Literally, "Weeks": the spring holiday that celebrates the offering of the first fruits in Jerusalem and the giving of the Ten Commandments. The Book of Ruth is read on this day.

Shekhinah God's indwelling presence.

shofar A ram's horn, blown on the Jewish new year.

sotah The ritual whereby a woman suspected of adultery by her husband is cleared or proven guilty (Numbers 5:11–31).

stamma/stammaitic Literally, "anonymous": the later layer of the Bavli, composed between 427 and 501 or 520 (Halivni 1986, 76).

Talmud The Mishnah and Gemara (s.vv.) together form the Talmud.

Tanach: The Hebrew acronym for the Scriptures: **T**orah, **N**eviim (Prophets), and **K**etuvim (Writings).

tanna/tannaim: A teacher of the Oral Law; one who recites mishnayot. The tannaim are the sages of the mishnaic period, 10–220 C.E.

tefillah/tefillot Literally, "prayer."

tefillin Phylacteries: that is, cube-shaped leather boxes that are tied to the hand and head during prayer. They contain parchment on which the following passages are written: Deuteronomy 6:4–9, Deuteronomy 11:13–21, Exodus 13:1–10, and Exodus 13:11–16.

Torah The first five books of the Bible, i.e., Genesis, Exodus, Leviticus, Numbers, and Deuteronomy. This term can also denote Jewish learning in general and the actual scroll of the Torah, which is ritually read.

Tosefta/toseftot Literally, "addition" or "supplement": tannaitic material collected into a compendium as an addition to the Mishnah. Toseftot do not have the authoritative stature of mishnayot.

Yerushalmi See **Gemara**.

Yom Kippur Literally, "Day of Atonement": a day of fasting, purification, prayer, and forgiveness that comes ten days after the Jewish new year.

BIBLIOGRAPHY

Abraham, Abraham S. 1990. *The Comprehensive Guide to Medical Halachah*. New York: Feldheim.

Albeck, Hanoch. 1952. *The Mishnah*. Jerusalem: Mosad Bialik.

American Psychiatric Association. 1987. *Diagnostic and Statistical Manual of Mental Disorders [DSM-III-R]*. 3rd ed., rev. Washington, D.C.: American Psychiatric Association.

Aries, Phillipe, and Georges Duby, eds. 1987. *A History of Private Life*. Vol. 1, *From Pagan Rome to Byzantium*, edited by Paul Veyne. Cambridge, Mass.: Belknap Press of Harvard University Press.

Astor, Carl. 1985. . . . *Who Makes People Different: Jewish Perspectives on the Disabled*. New York: United Synagogue of America, Department of Youth Activities.

Avery-Peck, Alan. 1988. *The Talmud of the Land of Israel*. Vol. 6. Chicago: University of Chicago Press.

Baumgarten, Joseph M. 1977. *Studies in Qumran Law*. Leiden: E. J. Brill.

Blackman, Philip. 1977. *Mishnayoth*. Gateshead [England]: Judaica Press.

Bleich, J. David. 1977. "Survey of Recent Halakhic Periodical Literature: Status of the Deaf-Mute in Jewish Law." *Tradition* 16 (5): 79–84.

———. 1983. *Contemporary Halakhic Problems*. Vol. 2. New York: Ktav.

Boyarin, Daniel. 1993. *Carnal Israel: Reading Sex in Talmudic Culture*. Berkeley: University of California Press.

Brown, Francis, S. R. Driver, and Charles A. Briggs. 1975. *Hebrew and English Lexicon of the Old Testament*. Oxford: Clarendon Press.

Brown, Peter. 1987. "Late Antiquity." In *A History of Private Life*, edited by Phillipe Aries and Georges Duby. Vol. 1, *From Pagan Rome to Byzantium*, edited by Paul Veyne, 235–312. Cambridge, Mass.: Belknap Press of Harvard University Press.

———. 1988. *The Body and Society: Men, Women, and Sexual Renunciation in Early Christianity*. New York: Columbia University Press.

Charles, R. H., ed. 1913. *The Apocrypha and Pseudepigrapha of the Old Testament in English*. Oxford: Clarendon Press.

Cogan, Mordechai, and Hayim Tadmor. 1988. *II Kings, The Anchor Bible*. New York: Doubleday.

Cohen, Stuart A. 1990. *The Three Crowns: Structures of Communal Politics in Early Rabbinic Judaism*. Cambridge: Cambridge University Press.

Davies, Douglas. 1985. "An Interpretation of Sacrifice in Leviticus." In *Anthropological Approaches to the Old Testament*, edited by Bernhard Lang, 151–63. Philadelphia: Fortress Press.

Deshen, Shlomo. 1992. *Blind People: The Private and Public Lives of Sightless Israelis*. Albany: SUNY Press.

Dimant, D. 1984. "Qumran Sectarian Literature." In *Jewish Writings of the Second Temple Period*, edited by Michael Stone, 483–550. Philadelphia: Fortress Press.

Douglas, Mary. 1966. *Purity and Danger: An Analysis of Concepts of Pollution and Taboo*. New York: Praeger.

Eilberg-Schwartz, Howard. 1986. *The Human Will in Judaism: The Mishnah's Philosophy of Intention*. Atlanta: Scholars Press.

———. 1990. *The Savage in Judaism: An Anthropology of Israelite Religion and Ancient Judaism*. Bloomington: Indiana University Press.

———. 1994. *God's Phallus and Other Problems for Men and Monotheism*. Boston: Beacon.

Fallon, April. 1990. "Culture in the Mirror: Sociocultural Determinants of Body Image." In *Body Image: Development, Deviance, and Change*, edited by Thomas Cash and Thomas Truzinsky, 80–109. New York: Guilford Press.

Feldman, David. 1986. "Deafness and Jewish Law and Tradition." In *The Deaf Jew in the Modern World*, edited by Jerome D. Schein and Lester J. Waldman, 12–23. New York: Ktav.

Finkelstein, Louis, ed. 1969. *Sifre on Deuteronomy*. New York: Jewish Theological Seminary.

Fisch, Harold. 1980. *The Jerusalem Bible*. Jerusalem: Koren.

Flesher, Paul Virgil McCracken. 1988. *Oxen, Women, or Citizens? Slaves in the System of the Mishnah*. Atlanta: Scholars Press.

Flusser, David. 1989. *The Spiritual History of the Dead Sea Sect*, translated by Carol Glucker. Tel Aviv: MOD Books.

Foucault, Michel. 1986. *The Care of the Self*. Vol. 3 of *The History of Sexuality*, translated by Robert Hurley. New York: Pantheon Books.

Fraade, Steven D. 1983. "Sifre Deuteronomy 26 (ad Deut. 3:23): How Conscious the Composition?" *Hebrew Union College Annual* 54: 245–301.

———. 1991. *From Tradition to Commentary: Torah and Its Interpretation in the Midrash Sifre to Deuteronomy*. Albany: SUNY Press.

Frank, Gelya. 1986. "On Embodiment: A Case Study of Congenital Limb

Deficiency in American Culture." *Culture, Medicine, and Psychiatry* 10: 189–219.

Frazer, James G. 1988. *Folklore in the Old Testament: Studies in Comparative Religion, Legend, and Law.* Abridged ed. New York: Avenel Books.

Gilbert, M. 1984. "Wisdom Literature." In *Jewish Writings of the Second Temple Period*, edited by Michael E. Stone, 283–324. Philadelphia: Fortress Press.

Goffman, Erving. 1963. *Stigma: Notes on the Management of Spoiled Identity.* New York: Simon and Schuster.

Goldberg, Abraham. 1987. "The Tosefta—Companion to the Mishnah, the Palestinian Talmud, the Babylonian Talmud." In *The Literature of the Sages*, edited by Shmuel Safrai, 283–350. Philadelphia: Fortress Press.

Goodblatt, David. 1975. *Rabbinic Instruction in Sasanian Babylonia.* Leiden: E. J. Brill.

Gruber, Les. 1986. "Moses: His Speech Impediment and Behavior Therapy." *Journal of Psychology and Judaism* 10: 5–13.

Halbertal, Moshe, and Avishai Margalit. 1992. *Idolatry*, translated by Naomi Goldblum. Cambridge, Mass.: Harvard University Press.

Halivni, David Weiss. 1981. "The Reception Accorded to Rabbi Yehudah's Mishnah." In *Jewish and Christian Self-Definition*. Vol. 2, *Aspects of Judaism in the Graeco-Roman Period*, edited by E. P. Sanders et al., 204–12. Philadelphia: Fortress Press.

———. 1986. *Midrash, Mishnah, and Gemara: The Jewish Predilection for Justified Law.* Cambridge, Mass.: Harvard University Press.

Hammer, Reuven. 1986. *Sifre: A Tannaitic Commentary on the Book of Deuteronomy.* New Haven: Yale University Press.

Haran, Menahem. 1985. *Temples and Temple Service in Ancient Israel.* Winona Lake, Ind.: Eisenbrauns.

Hauptman, Judith. 1988. *Development of the Talmudic Sugya.* Lanham, Md.: University Press of America.

Herr, M. D. 1972a. "Mekhilta of R. Ishmael." In *Encyclopedia Judaica*. Jerusalem: Keter.

———. 1972b. "Tosefta." In *Encyclopedia Judaica*. Jerusalem: Keter.

Higgins, Paul C. 1980. *Outsiders in a Hearing World: A Sociology of Deafness.* Beverly Hills, Calif.: Sage Publications.

Horovitz, H. S. 1970. *Mechilta D'Rabbi Ishmael.* Jerusalem: Wahrmann Books.

Jacobs, Louis. 1981. *Teyku: The Unsolved Problem in the Babylonian Talmud.* East Brunswick, N.J.: Cornwall Books.

Jacobsen, Thorkild. 1976. *The Treasures of Darkness: A History of Mesopotamian Religion.* New Haven: Yale University Press.

Jaffee, Martin S. 1992. "How Much 'Orality' in Oral Torah? New Perspectives on the Composition and Transmission of Early Rabbinic Tradition." *Shofar* 10 (2): 53–72.

Jastrow, Marcus. 1903. *A Dictionary of the Targumim, the Talmud Babli and Yerushalmi, and the Midrashic Literature*. 2 vols. London: Luzac; New York: G. P. Putnam's Sons.

Jewish Publication Society. 1917. *The Holy Scriptures*. Philadelphia: Jewish Publication Society.

Johnson, Mark. 1987. *The Body in the Mind: The Bodily Basis of Meaning, Imagination, and Reason*. Chicago: University of Chicago Press.

Kaufmann, Yehezkel. 1977. *History of the Religion of Israel*. Vol. 4. New York: Doubleday.

Kleinman, Arthur. 1980. *Patients and Healers in the Context of Culture*. Berkeley: University of California Press.

Knohl, Israel. 1987. "The Priestly Torah Versus the Holiness School: Sabbath and the Festivals." *Hebrew Union College Annual* 58: 65–118.

Kraemer, David. 1988. "Composition and Meaning in the Bavli." *Prooftexts* 8 (3): 271–91.

———. 1990. *The Mind of the Talmud: An Intellectual History of the Bavli*. New York: Oxford University Press.

———. 1995. *Responses to Suffering in Classical Rabbinic Literature*. Oxford: Oxford University Press.

Krauss, Samuel. 1922. *Synaogogale Altertumer*. Berlin: Benjamin Harz.

Lakoff, George. 1987. *Women, Fire, and Dangerous Things: What Categories Reveal about the Mind*. Chicago: University of Chicago Press.

Lakoff, George, and Mark Johnson. 1980. *Metaphors We Live By*. Chicago: University of Chicago Press.

Lauterbach, Jacob Z. 1961. *Mekilta de-Rabbi Ishmael*. 3 vols. Philadelphia: Jewish Publication Society.

Leach, Edmund. 1976. *Culture and Communication*. New York: Cambridge University Press.

Levine, Herbert J. 1995. *Sing unto God a New Song: A Contemporary Reading of the Psalms*. Bloomington: Indiana University Press.

Lieberman, Saul. 1962. *Tosefta*. New York: Jewish Theological Society.

———. 1992. *Tosefta K'Fshuta*. 2nd aug. ed. Jerusalem: Jewish Theological Society.

Lucretius. 1988. *On the Nature of the Universe*, translated by Ronald Latham. London: Penguin.

MacDowell, Douglas M. 1986. *Spartan Law*. Edinburgh: Scottish Academic Press.

MacMullen, Ramsey. 1981. *Paganism in the Roman Empire*. New Haven: Yale University Press.

Marx, Tzvi. 1993. *Halakha and Handicap: Jewish Law and Ethics on Disability*. Amsterdam: Tzvi Marx.

McCarter, P. Kyle, Jr. 1980. *I Samuel, The Anchor Bible*. New York: Doubleday.

———. 1984. *II Samuel, The Anchor Bible*. New York: Doubleday.

McKenzie, John L. 1968. *Second Isaiah, The Anchor Bible*. New York: Doubleday.

McKenzie, Steve L., and Stephen R. Haynes, eds. 1993. *To Each Its Own Meaning: An Introduction to Biblical Criticisms and Their Application*. Louisville, Ky.: Westminster/John Knox Press.

Milgrom, Jacob. 1990. *The JPS Torah Commentary: Numbers*. Philadelphia: Jewish Publication Society.

———. 1991. *Leviticus 1–16, The Anchor Bible*. New York: Doubleday.

Mirkin, Moshe Aryeh. 1977. *Midrash Rabbah*. Tel Aviv: Yavneh.

Morgan, Donn F. 1990. *Between Text and Community: The "Writings" in Canonical Interpretation*. Minneapolis: Fortress Press.

Muffs, Yochanan. 1992. *Love and Joy: Law, Language, and Religion in Ancient Israel*. New York: Jewish Theological Society.

Neusner, Jacob. 1986a. *Judaism and Scripture*. Chicago: University of Chicago Press.

———. 1986b. *The Tosefta: Its Structure and Its Sources*. Atlanta: Scholars Press.

———. 1990. *The Midrash: An Introduction*. Northvale, N.J.: Jason Aronson.

Nickelsburg, George W. E. 1981. *Jewish Literature between the Bible and the Mishnah*. Philadelphia: Fortress Press.

———. 1984a. "The Bible Rewritten and Expanded." In *Jewish Writings of the Second Temple Period*, edited by Michael E. Stone, 89–156. Philadelphia: Fortress Press.

———. 1984b. "Stories of Biblical and Early Post-Biblical Times." In *Jewish Writings of the Second Temple Period*, edited by Michael E. Stone, 33–87. Philadelphia: Fortress Press.

Philo. 1929–62. *Philo*, with translation by F. H. Colson and G. H. Whitaker. 12 vols. Cambridge, Mass.: Harvard University Press; London: Heinemann.

Plato. 1987. *Republic*, translated by Desmond Lee. London: Penguin Books.

Pope, Marvin H. 1973. *Job, The Anchor Bible*. New York: Doubleday.

Rouche, Michel. 1987. "The Early Middle Ages in the West." In *A History of Private Life*, edited by Phillipe Aries and Georges Duby. Vol. 1, *From Pagan Rome to Byzantium*, edited by Paul Veyne, 411–550. Cambridge, Mass.: Belknap Press of Harvard University Press.

Sarna, Nahum M. 1966. *Understanding Genesis*. New York: Schocken.

———. 1989. *The JPS Torah Commentary: Genesis*. Philadelphia: Jewish Publication Society.

———. 1991. *The JPS Torah Commentary: Exodus*. Philadelphia: Jewish Publication Society.

Schein, Jerome D., and Lester J. Waldman, eds. 1986. *The Deaf Jew in the Modern World*. New York: Ktav.

Scott, R. B. Y. 1965. *Proverbs and Ecclesiastes, The Anchor Bible*. New York: Doubleday.

Skehan, Patrick W. 1987. *The Wisdom of Ben Sira, The Anchor Bible*. New York: Doubleday.

Soranus of Ephesus. 1956. *Soranus' Gynecology*, translated by Owsei Temkin, Ludwig Edelstein, and Alan F. Guttmacher. Baltimore: Johns Hopkins Press.

Steinsaltz, Adin. 1983. *Talmud Bavli*. Jerusalem: Israel Institute for Talmudic Publication.

Stern, David. 1991. *Parables in Midrash: Narrative and Exegesis in Rabbinic Literature*. Cambridge, Mass.: Harvard University Press.

Stone, Michael E., ed. 1984. *Jewish Writings of the Second Temple Period*. Philadelphia: Fortress Press.

Strack, H. L., and G. Stemberger. 1991. *Introduction to the Talmud and Midrash*, translated by Markus Bockmuehl. Edinburgh: T. and T. Clark.

Temkin, Owsei. 1956. Introduction to *Soranus' Gynecology*, translated by Owsei Temkin, Ludwig Edelstein, and Alan F. Guttmacher, xxv. Baltimore: Johns Hopkins Press.

Tishby, Isaiah. 1989. *The Wisdom of the Zohar*. 3 vols. London: Littman Library.

Turner, Victor. 1967. *The Forest of Symbols*. Ithaca: Cornell University Press.

———. 1969. *The Ritual Process: Structure and Anti-Structure*. Ithaca: Cornell University Press.

Van Cleve, John V., ed. 1987. *Gallaudet Encyclopedia of Deaf People and Deafness*. 3 vols. New York: McGraw-Hill.

Veyne, Paul. 1987. "The Roman Empire." In *A History of Private Life*, edited by Phillipe Aries and Georges Duby. Vol. 1, *From Pagan Rome to Byzantium*, edited by Paul Veyne, 5–234. Cambridge, Mass.: Belknap Press of Harvard University Press.

Vermes, Geza. 1987. *The Dead Sea Scrolls in English*. New York: Penguin Books.

Wegner, Judith R. 1988. *Chattel or Person? The Status of Women in the Mishnah*. New York: Oxford University Press.

Weinfeld, Moshe. 1991. *Deuteronomy 1–11, The Anchor Bible*. New York: Doubleday.

Zukermandel, Moshe. 1970. *Tosefta*. Jerusalem: Sifrei Vahrman.

INDEX

Entries with page numbers followed by an italicized *t* refer to tables.